WILDE'S LOUGH CORRIB

Lough Corrib:
Its Shores and Islands

William Wilde

Kevin Duffy
Headford, County Galway
2002

First published in 1867
by McGlashan & Gill, Dublin.

Reprinted 2002 by Kevin Duffy,
Headford, County Galway.

Second reprint Sept 2002
Reprinted March 2007

Printed in Dublin by Betaprint

A catalogue record for the book is available
from the British Library.

ISBN 0-9540034-1-1

INTRODUCTION

In a way, it seems I was destined to reprint Sir William Wilde's Book *Lough Corrib, Its Shores & Islands* originally published in 1867. Wilde spent his early years at his ancestral home at Moytura, Cong, County Mayo and also the latter part of his life where he wrote the Book. His house overlooked the Corrib — presently owned by a member of the band U2. I, too, live on the Shores of Lough Corrib only two miles away and I am also a native of Cong. We both fished the same waters of the Lake. Alongside my ancestors' grave in Cong there is a plaque erected by the Wilde Family in remembrance of their housekeeper who served them faithfully for forty years. Copies of his first edition are now a collectors item and fetch huge prices. Over the years, I've managed to collect three such copies. This edition is a facsimile of the original.

Wilde's *Lough Corrib* is, without shadow of doubt, the acknowledged documentary on this region — 'The Jewel in the Crown' of Lough Corrib's glorious past. In it, he lists the Ruined de Burgo and O'Flaherty Castles, its Monastic Settlements, Caves, Cairns, Abbeys and Friaries. A renowned Physician — who set up his own eye and ear Hospital in Dublin, Archaeologist, Antiquarian, member of the Royal Irish Academy. He managed to cram a lot into his short life. He died at the age of sixty one. Those interested in the history of this lovely region, will, no doubt, welcome this edition, I hope you will enjoy it. It should have wide appeal throughout Ireland and abroad.

Kevin Duffy
Headford, County Galway

FOREWORD
to the reprint
by
Doctor Peter Harbison
Royal Irish Academy

The polymath Sir William Wilde (1815-1876) is one of my great heroes, well deserving of the compliment paid to him by Sir Peter Froggatt in a centenary article in the *Proceedings of the Royal Irish Academy* in 1977 to the effect that Wilde was 'one of the most remarkable *savants*' of the nineteenth century — 'and one of the greatest Irishmen of his time'. Fortunately he was possessed of a boundless energy to match his wide-ranging talents, which are listed as follows on the plaque between the two front windows of his former home at No. 1 Merrion Square in Dublin:

> Aural and opthalmic surgeon, archaeologist, ethnologist, antiquarian, biographer, statistician, naturalist, topographer, historian and folklorist.

Few of us could ever claim to be anything more than two of those things in a lifetime, yet they proclaim the great width of Wilde's interests — far greater than those of his also brilliant, but better-known, son, Oscar.

Born in Castlerea, Co. Roscommon, Wilde used often accompany his medical father on his rounds as a schoolboy, and became a qualified doctor himself at the age of twenty-two, only to be admitted two years later as surely one of the youngest members ever of the Royal Irish Academy. For the next two decades, he devoted himself wholeheartedly to his medical profession, specialising in eyes and ears, and writing in 1853 a classic text-book on aural surgery and diseases of the ear which, however, did not escape controversy — like some of his other activities.

But for the final twenty years of his life, Wilde was able to devote much of his time to his two great interests: the statistics of Census returns — and archaeology. The Statistical Society would regard him as their founder and, when conferring a knighthood on him in 1864, the Lord Lieutenant stressed that it was not for on him in 1864, the Lord Lieutenant stressed that it was not for his European-wide reputation as a man of medicine that he was being honoured, but for the service he had rendered to Statistical Science.

Seven years earlier, he had worked day and night to re-organise the Royal Irish Academy's Museum collection (now in the National Museum) and produce for it the first volume of a Catalogue in which he ingeniously organised the objects not according to age or period, but according to materials and usage — a novel concept which made his Catalogue a leader in the Europe of his day. The work was undertaken, and completed just in time, for a meeting of the British Association in Dublin in 1857, for which Wilde also organised a now-legendary outing to Dun Aengus on the Aran Islands.

In the pages of *The Journal of the Royal Historical and Archaeological Association of Ireland* of the early 1870s. Wilde wisely dragged out from oblivion the reputation of the eighteenth-century Huguenot topographical watercolourist Gabriel Beranger (1730-1817), giving details from the artist's diary which Wilde had, but which has since disappeared. I would be grateful to hear from anyone who may know of its present whereabouts, but even the extracts which Wilde published from the diary have been invaluable to me in the preparation of a book on Beranger's tour of Connacht in 1779, which is due to appear this year.

Even from his early medical days, Wilde was an adept at writing perceptive travel books, his first one — dating from 1840 — being about a voyage he undertook to Madeira and Tenerife for the good of his health. Nine years later he followed this with his *Boyne and the Blackwate*, illustrated with a series of attractive woodcuts which were used in the 1949 reprint by Colm O Lochlainn, who described Wilde as 'the first, and still the greatest, of our scientific archaeologists'. Praise indeed! It must have been this volume which acted as his model when he turned for further inspiration to his beloved Lough Corrib after he had built his house at Moytura, above the Lake, in 1865. He uses the same recipe, cleverly mixing accurate description with well-researched history and a varied selection of woodcuts in what I would describe as:

one of the first and best
of the Guidebooks to the West

The book was to be an educational Vademecum rather than a vulgarly entertaining potpourri of tourist jokes and stories — designed, it would appear, for those who wanted to explore Lough Corrib and its hinterland (including Lough Mask) from the safety of the Galway-based steamer 'Eglinton', of which he gives a beautifully atmospheric illustration beneath the grandeur of Ashford Castle. Even without the advantage of such leisurely paddle-steaming (God be with the days), Wilde's text is still valid for today's more land-based traveller, his purple-passaged prose being as enticing as fresh as the day he wrote it, and his descriptions as lively and eye-opening as anyone could wish for. His continuous narration covering varied themes and topics makes *Lough Corrib* an enjoying and entrancing read, and a book which continues to fascinate, one hundred and thirty years after its first appearance.

Colm Ó Lochlainn's abbreviated reprint, also using the old wood-blocks, placed parts of it again on the market half a century ago, but now both original and reprint are long out of stock, the former, in particular, only obtainable by the few lucky enough to be able to pay the high price required for the rare first and second editions of 1867 and 1872 respectively. For one of Connacht's greatest sons of the last two centuries who has no memorial I know of in his native province, Kevin Duffy's reprint is a worthy and well-deserved testimonial to Wilde's love of the western lakes where he chose to build a home and linger when his duties did not recall him to the capital. This full-length reprint will do honour to Wilde's style, enthusiasm and knowledge — even without the advantage of the 'Eglinton' — and will hopefully introduce more people of our generation to the delights that await the observant antiquarian traveller on and around the shores of Corrib and Mask. In addition, it will make this long-out-of-print classic available again to people from Connacht and elsewhere, and at a price so much more affordable than any second-hand copy of the original edition. For this noble initiative in honouring a great fellow-Connachtman by reprinting his masterwork on two major lakes of the province, Kevin Duffy deserves our thanks — and our good wishes for the success of his enterprise.

LOUGH CORRIB,

ITS SHORES AND ISLANDS:

WITH NOTICES OF

LOUGH MASK.

BY

SIR WILLIAM R. WILDE, M.D.,

VICE-PRESIDENT OF THE ROYAL IRISH ACADEMY;
CHEVALIER OF THE SWEDISH ORDER OF THE NORTH STAR;
AUTHOR OF "NARRATIVE OF A VOYAGE TO MADEIRA AND THE MEDITERRANEAN,"
"THE BEAUTIES OF THE BOYNE,"
"CATALOGUE OF THE MUSEUM OF THE ROYAL IRISH ACADEMY;"
ETC. ETC.

Illustrated with numerous Wood Engravings.

DUBLIN:
McGLASHAN & GILL, 50, UPPER SACKVILLE-STREET.
LONDON: LONGMANS, GREEN, AND CO.
1867.

PREFACE.

THE Preface—usually an *ex post facto* excuse for writing—shall be short. Well acquainted in days gone by with the Shores and Islands of Lough Corrib, and not insensible to the beauties of Lough Mask, I was not a little surprised, when returning to the old nest there a few years ago, to find that, notwithstanding its perfect accessibility, this interesting district was comparatively unknown to tourists, and the true character and history of its monuments were neither appreciated nor understood by its inhabitants.

In the hope of removing, in part at least, some of those deficiencies, and as a pleasing occupation during leisure hours, I have written this book, for many of the illustrations of which my readers are indebted to the liberality of Sir B. L. Guinness to whom, and to Mr. Lynch Staunton, and to the various other friends in the West, of all classes and denominations, who have promptly afforded whatever information I required, I beg to return my best thanks.

I had intended appending some notes on the zoology and legends, &c., of the district; but subjects of so much more general and popular interest crowded upon me towards the conclusion of the work, that, together with my anxiety to produce the book during the present season, I am compelled to apologize for the Appendix, the subject matter of which I hope to bring out on a future occasion.

The Map contains only those roads which appertain to the tourist's route.

1, Merrion-square, Dublin,
August 24, 1867.

CONTENTS.

CHAPTER I.—Introductory.

Page.

Character of the Scenery of the West. Objects of the Tour, and special Subjects of Interest. Route from Dublin to Galway. An Hour's Ramble through "The City of the Tribes." Its Celebrities, Name, and History. The River Gallieve, and Lady Gallvea. Plan of the Excursion. Hotels and Conveyances, ... 1

CHAPTER II.—Description of Lough Corrib.

Lough Corrib: its Direction, Name, Extent; Ancient Territories adjoining; Sources, Rivers, Turloughs; Division; Knochmagh; Scenery and Mountains surrounding Lake; Geology, Mines, Natural Woods; Drainage; Navigation, the Eglinton Canal; Outlets, the Friars' Cut, . . . 18

CHAPTER III.—Galway to Annaghdown.

Parish of St. Nicholas. Terrilan Castle. Annals of Galway. The De Burgos. Menlough. Parish of Oranmore. The Lower Lake. Clare-Galway Parish, Castle, and Convent Church. Ancient Ploughs. Knocknatuath; the Battle of the Chieftains; the Irish against the Irish; the Book of Howth; the Engagement, and the Rout. Cregg Castle; Athcloiggeen; the Hag's Castle, ... 39

CHAPTER IV.—Annaghdown to Kylebeg.

Annaghdown Parish, and Ancient Bishopric; St. Brendan. The Desmond and O'Donnell Costume. The Monastery and Abbey. Ancient Tombs. The Nunnery. Window of Modern Church. The Cloichtheach of

Page.

Annaghdown. The Castle and Holy Wells. Castle Creevy. Kilcoona Parish ; Church, and Round Tower. History and Writings of St. Coona. Parish of Killeany. Cloch-an-Uaibher Castle. Lee's Island. Knock Ferry and Kylebeg, ... 63

CHAPTER V.—Kylebeg to Inchiquin.

Cargin Parish, Church and Castle. Killeens. Iniscreawa. Annals of Lough Corrib. Irish Pagan and Christian Architecture. Cahergal. Clydagh. Killursa Parish. History of St. Fursa. Inchiquin. Castle of Annakeen. Cairns. Giants' Graves. Church of St. Fursa. Early Irish Church Architecture. Ross-Errilly. The Locust Plague. Moyne Castle. The Black River, ... 87

CHAPTER VI.—Inchiquin to Inchangoill and Cong.

County of Mayo. The Islands of Lough Corrib. Inishanboe. Parish of Shrule. Ballycurrin, Ballisahiney, and Moceara Castles. Forts. Parish of Cong. Inchangoill. St. Patrick's and the Saint's Churches. Stone of Lugnaedon. South-east border of Cong Parish. Castletown. Inchmicatreer. Cross. Ancient Churches of Kilfraughaun and Killarsagh. Moytura. Lackafinna. Lisloughry. Cong Islands. Kinlough. Ashford. Strand Hill. Cong, ... 128

CHAPTER VII.—Cong.

Cong Village. Rivers. Annals. St. Fechin. The Abbey, and its History. The O'Duffys. Ireland's last Monarch. Ashford. The Street Cross. The Irish Language. Reliques ; the True Cross ; the Tooth of St. Patrick. The Black Bell. Wayside Monuments. The Castle of Aughalard. Caves. The Pigeon Hole, ... 161

CHAPTER VIII.—The Battle and Battle-field of Moytura.

The Primitive Irishman. Fomorians. Partholan. Nemeth. The Firbolgs. Tuatha de Danaan. The Plain of Moytura. Knockma. Ceasair. Kings Eochy and Nuadh. The Battle-field. The Warriors, Druids, and Physicians. Existing Monuments; Cairns, Caves, Cahers, Stone Circles, and

Page.

Pillars. The Four Days' Fight. The Meane Uisge. Sepulchral Urn. Standing Stones at Inishowen. The Dagda and the Fathach. Nymphsfield Monuments. Caher Mac Turc. Belor of the Magic Eye. The Neale Monuments. The Hill of Carn. Caher Robert. History of the Moytura Manuscript, ... 210

CHAPTER IX.—Lough Mask.

Parish of Ballinchalla. Lough Mask Castle. Edmond de Burgo. Inishmain. Eogan-Beil and St. Cormac. Inishmain Abbey. Ancient Fort. The Penitentiary. Inishowen. The Hag's Castle. Ross Hill. St. Patrick's Church. Upper Lough Corrib. Doon and Castle Kirk. St. Fechen's and St. Enna's Wells. Caislean na Kirka. Maam, ... 249

CHAPTER X.—Maam to Galway.

Parish of Kilcummin. Oughterard. Lemonfield. Gnomore and Gnobeg. Killeroon Church. Aughnanure Castle. Killannin Parish. Lough Naneevin. Kilbrecan. Ross Lake, Castle, and Churches. The Fossil Wood. Teampul-beg-na-Neave. Moycullen Parish and its Churches. The Battle Stone. Danesfield. Rahoon Parish. Conclusion, . . . 278

LIST OF ILLUSTRATIONS.

No.	Name.	Drawn by.	Engraved by.	Page.
1.	Terrilan Castle, ...	Wakeman, ...	Oldham, ...	40
2.	Menlough Castle, ...	„	„	45
3.	Clare-Galway Abbey, ...	„	„	52
4.	„ „ Ploughs, ...	Rogers, ...	Shepherd, . . .	53
5.	Tollokyan Castle, ...	Wakeman, ...	„	62
6.	Annaghdown Ruins, ...	„	Oldham, ...	67
7.	„ Tomb, ...	„	„	69
8.	„ Church Window, .	Photograph, . . .	„	72
9.	„ Window Ornament,	Wakeman, ...	„	73
10.	„ Castle, ...	„	„	75
11.	Kilcoona Round Tower, ...	Photograph, . . .	„	79
12.	Cargin Castle, ...	Miss E. L. Staunton,	„	88
13.	Inniscreawa, ...	„	„	89
14.	Cahergal Fort, ...	Wakeman, ...	„	95
15.	„ Steps, ...	„	„	96
16.	Clydagh, ...	Photograph, . . .	„	97
17.	Annakeen Castle, ...	„	„	100
18.	Ross-Errilly, ...	Wakeman, ...	„	112
19.	D'Arcy's Cottage, ...	Photograph, . . .	„	130
20.	Ballycurrin Castle, ...	Wakeman, ...	„	131
21.	Inchangoill, Lugnaedon's Stone, .	„	Shepherd, . . .	136
22.	„ Inscription, ...	„	Oldham, ...	136

No.	Name.	Drawn by.	Engraved by.	Page.
23.	Inchangoill, St. Patrick's Church,	Photograph,	Oldham,	142
24.	,, Saints' Church,	Wakeman,	,,	143
25.	,, Bearded Capitals,	,,	,,	145
26.	,, Choir Arch,	Photograph,	,,	146
27.	,, Greek Cross,	Wakeman,	,,	147
28.	Cross Castle and Church,	,,	,,	153
29.	East Window of do.,	,,	,,	154
30.	Kilfraughaun Doorway,	,,	,,	155
31.	Killarsagh Window,	,,	,,	157
32.	Moytura House,	,,	,,	158
33.	Cong River, and Ashford,	,,	,,	160
34.	,, The Bullaun Stone,	,,	,,	164
35.	,, Abbey,	S. Lover,	,,	170
36.	,, Terminal Cross,	Wakeman,	,,	175
37.	,, O'Duffy's Cross,	,,	Shepherd,	176
38.	,, Inscription on do.,	,,	,,	176
39.	Moytura Cross,	,,	,,	178
40.	Façade of Cong Abbey,	,,	Oldham,	179
41.	Ashford House,	,,	,,	182
42.	Market Cross of Cong,	,,	Shepherd,	185
43.	The True Cross,	Du Noyer,	Hanlon,	193
44.	Inscription on do.,	Wakeman,	Oldham,	194
45.	The Black Bell,	,,	A. Oldham,	197
46.	Wayside Monuments,	Fairholt,	Electrotype,	198
47.	Aughalard Castle,	Wakeman,	Shepherd,	199
48.	Plan of Kildun Cave,	M'Donagh,	A. Oldham,	205
49.	,, Cooslogha Cave,	,,	,,	206
50.	Cooslogha Cave, interior,	Wakeman,	Shepherd,	207
51.	Cairn of the Hurlers,	,,	,,	219
52.	,, of First Day's Battle,	,,	,,	222
53.	The One Man's Cairn,	,,	Oldham,	224

LIST OF ILLUSTRATIONS.

No.	Name.	Drawn by.	Engraved by.	Page.
54.	Sepulchral Urn,	Wakeman,	Mrs. Millard,	225
55.	The Flagstones of Caelchu,	,,	Shepherd,	228
56.	Caher-Speenaun,	,,	Oldham,	230
57.	Nymphsfield Circle,	W. Wilde,	Shepherd,	234
58.	,, ,,	Wakeman,	,,	237
59.	Long Stone of The Neale,	,,	Oldham,	240
60.	Neale Inscription,	Rubbing,	,,	241
61.	Eochy's Cairn,	Wakeman,	,,	243
62.	Lough Mask Castle,	Rubbing,	Shepherd,	250
63.	Inishmain, Doorway in,	Wakeman,	Miss Keely,	254
64.	,, Abbey,	,,	Oldham,	255
65.	,, Capital of Pillar,	,,	Shepherd,	256
66.	King Beil's Fort,	,,	,,	257
67.	The Penitentiary,	,,	,,	258
68.	,, Interior,	Rogers,	Oldham,	259
69.	The Hag's Castle,	W. Wilde,	Shepherd,	261
70.	Dun Aengus,	Cheyne,	Oldham,	265
71.	The Hen's Castle,	Wakeman.	,,	271
72.	Lemonfield,	,,	Shepherd,	282
73.	Aughnanure Castle,	,,	Oldham,	288
74.	,, Window,	,,	Shepherd,	290
75.	St. Annin's Church,	R. Willis,	Oldham,	296
76.	The Fossil Yew,	Kinahan,	,,	299

LOUGH CORRIB.

CHAPTER I.

INTRODUCTORY.

CHARACTER OF THE SCENERY OF THE WEST. OBJECTS OF THE TOUR, AND SPECIAL SUBJECTS OF INTEREST. ROUTE FROM DUBLIN TO GALWAY. AN HOUR'S RAMBLE THROUGH "THE CITY OF THE TRIBES." ITS CELEBRITIES, NAME, AND HISTORY. THE RIVER GALLIEVE, AND LADY GALLVEA. PLAN OF THE EXCURSION. HOTELS AND CONVEYANCES.

WESTWARD, ho! Let us rise with the sun, and be off to the land of the West—to the lakes and streams—the grassy glens and fern-clad gorges—the bluff hills and rugged mountains—now cloud-capped, then revealed in azure, or bronzed by evening's tints, as the light of day sinks into the bold swell of the Atlantic, and leaves his reflection in long level streaks of crimson, green, and orange, among the greyish-purple robe of twilight, when the shadows of the headlands sink deep into the placid waters of the lake. But, whether seen in sunshine or in shade—curtained by the mist, or with the bright light of morning playing upon the brown scores and landslips on the mountain side, or when the streamlets form threads of molten silver as they gleam through the purple heather and the yellow-lichened rocks ere they leap into the lake—the land we invite you to is ever beautiful in outline, and graceful in form; and as the warm breezes, carried on to us with the great Gulf stream, steal in among the West Connaught, Joyce Country, and Connamara ranges—the Jura and the Alps of Ireland—and give fitful atmospheric changes to the colouring of the landscape, from bright early dawn to sombre eve, scenes of beauty and sublimity are presented that leave us nothing to envy, even in the everlasting snowtops with their vine-clad slopes and dark pine-robed sides, the mighty glaciers, the rushing avalanches, nor the deep ultramarine skies of other lands.

Let us then be off to the Far-West, to which (with a choice for a warmer region) the inhabitants of other portions of this island were transplanted some centuries ago;—to the ancient home of the aborigines—the land of the Firbolgs, the Tuatha de Danann, and the Milesians—the last resting-place of the Celt, ere, fulfilling the destiny of his race, and the earliest impulses of mankind, he has followed from the cradle of humanity the declining sun. Here we can view the battlefields and civic vestiges of our Pagan ancestors, crowded with caves and cairns, raths, tumuli, monoliths, and stone circles, memorials of one of the earliest human occupancies in North-western Europe; or investigate the small primitive churches that mark the footprints where the early Christian Missionary replaced the Druid Priest; or linger by the thorn-shaded holy wells, or admire the noble abbeys and extensive monasteries of the learned and artistic Franciscans and Augustinians.

Let us first take a peep at the "City of the Tribes," of the Blakes, Bodkins, and Browns, Ffonts, Martins, Morrisses, Lynches, D'Arcys, Athys, Frenchs, Joyces, Kirwans, and Skerretts, &c., and then launch on the blue, island-studded waters of Lough Corrib, where, traversing its breadth in a trim and commodious steamer, or gliding into its glassy bays in a rowboat, we can enjoy some of the most picturesque scenery in the land, explore the natural curiosities, and speculate upon the influences and actions which, in remote times, produced these fantastic forms and disruptured chasms that present at the western termination of our great limestone formation;—or examine the architecture of the old feudal castles and ecclesiastical buildings along its peaceful shores. Our object is rather to interest the reader and the tourist in the history, antiquities, and scenery of this portion of the West, than amuse him with tales respecting pigs, pipers, praties, or potheen; fools or fiddlers; bailiffs, bullocks, or buckeens; graziers, gaugers, or ganders; wayside waiters, with their dry jokes for the "gintlemen," or wandering dancing masters, and poetasters, once so common in the West. We do not claim your sympathy for facetious car drivers, cunning codgers, or knowing gossoons; nor present to you miserably clad spalpeens, ragged urchins, wretched peat hovels, importunate beggars, lying guides, oppressed tenantry, griping landlords, or tyrannical agents. We have nothing to say about priests or patterns; politics, peelers, or parsons; soldiers, soupers, or sauggarths; Young-Irelanders or old ones; Fenians or Repealers. There is still plenty of fun, frolic, and folk-lore in the West; but, for the present, we have no stories to relate about friars or fairies; and we have no opinion to obtrude upon you respecting tithes or tenant-right; High Church or Low Church; Ultramontanism or Muscular Christianity; we have no official advertisements nor railway puffings, with which to enrich our pages or our publisher; nor can we stop to repeat Syphie Burke's "Costello Shentlemen," or gossip among the "Rakes of Galway" about—

> "The herrings and the haikes,
> And the Bodkins and the Blakes."

We may look at the turnips, and taste the murphies; but we promise not to remind you of the fearful scenes of the famine,* or anticipate the ravages of a Rinderpest. We

* See the Author's "Irish Popular Superstitions," Dublin, 1849; and the Treatise on the Famine of 1847, in the Irish Census Commissioners' Report for 1851, vol. v., part ii.

have no desire to introduce imaginary conversations in broken English, to amuse our Saxon friends at what is styled "the vulgarity of the lower order of Irish." We wish to take you, as intelligent tourists, with eyes to see and hearts to admire the beauties of nature; where the stately ruin or the cultured demesne blends harmoniously with the graceful outline of the surrounding landscape; where your architectural or antiquarian tastes may be gratified; your historic knowledge increased by the legend or the annal; your scientific inquiries into the geological structure and biological productions of the country obtain a wide scope; and the hitherto neglected resources of a portion of our island may be glanced at if not profoundly studied; and we hope to bring you back from your pleasant and cheap excursion on Lough Corrib in good health and spirits, pleased with the scenery and the inhabitants of the West, satisfied with our guidance, and better acquainted with an, as yet, undescribed district than you have been heretofore by flying visits to this portion of the Emerald Isle.

Leaving the Broadstone Terminus of the Midland Great Western Railway by the 8.30 A. M. train for Galway, and running for a great portion of our way along the Royal Canal, through which we were formerly dragged at the rate of four miles an hour to Alma Mater by a pair of gerrauns, we traverse the uninterrupted plain that extends across the island from East to West, for 126 miles, from the Channel to the Atlantic. Glancing at O'Connell's round-tower monument as we start; getting glimpses of ancient raths, barrows, churches, and some of the ruined castles of the Pale, as we proceed, we obtain views of the Dublin and Wicklow Mountains on our left; and, passing rapidly over the valley of the Rye-water, where, leaving Carton Demesne, it courses to the Liffey, we proceed onwards to Maynooth, where the noble keep of the ancient castle of the Fitzgeralds contrasts with the formal modern buildings of the College of St. Patrick, where the parochial Roman Catholic clergy of Ireland are chiefly educated. We rush by the mud hovels of Kilcock, in the county of Kildare; over portions of the great Bog of Allen, with its thousands of unreclaimed acres, tenanted by grouse and hares; and pass within view of Clonard, the ancient seminary, whither, even in the time of Alfred, our Saxon neighbours came in hundreds to be instructed. On with us over the Boyne Water, with greater speed and safety than it was crossed in 1690; through the fat lands of Westmeath, over the Brusna, into Mullingar; beside the clear trout-full waters of Lough Ennel (now styled Belvidere), and beyond it catch a distant view of the famed Hill of Ushnach, second only to Tara and Emania in importance in early Irish history; margining the site of the rath and crannoge of Moate—glancing at sections of the great esker that stretches from east to west, and formed the ancient boundary between the north and south portions of the kingdom—we speed onwards to the noble Shannon, the fords and *toghers* of which were so often invaded and defended by the Lagenians and Connacians; and here, over the splendid iron railway bridge, enter Connaught. Onwards still we pass, under the batteries of Athlone (*Ath Luin*, "the Ford of Luin"), which Ginkell wrested from St. Ruth in 1691;—along the intersecting stone walls and patches of russet bog through the county of Roscommon; across the deep sullen waters of the Suck, winding through the low callows and green inches of Ballinasloe, the seat of the Clancartys, and the site of the greatest stock fair in Europe*—forwards through the county of Galway, by the lovely Abbey of Kilconnell—passing Woodlawn, the residence of Lord Ashtown; then to Athenry, the city of "the ford of the king," crowded with ancient remains, civil, military, ecclesiastical, and domestic. Coursing now along the northern margin of the great plain, once the hunting ground of Queen Meave, that sweeps the lower edge of the Burren hills, and on which stand the towns of Gort and Loughrea, and the round towers of Ardrahan and Kilmacduagh, we

* Ballinasloe—in Irish, *Beal-ath-na-Sluaigead*, "the mouth of the ford of the hosts," which shows that it was a place of meeting, and probably of barter, like that at Telltown, in Meath, in early times. The oldest name of the place was, however, *Dun Leodha*, or Dunlo, from its dun, or fort, which formerly stood over the Suck, but was removed in 1838, when the Roman Catholic chapel was built on its site. The Earl of Clancarty's eldest son takes his title from this name.

rush by Derrydonnell Castle, and soon feel the western breezes playing upon us from Galway Bay, as it indents the shores and laves the walls of the old castle of Oranmore; we cross the great level, studded with the feudal halls of the De Burgos, and get a foretaste of the Petræa, upon which our pilgrimage in search of the picturesque and beautiful is about to commence. But the sterility in the foreground is relieved by a view of the blue hills of Clare, and occasionally in clear weather with glimpses of the distant Isles of Aran, that sentinel the magnificent bay of Galway, and break the swell of the mighty waves of the Atlantic. We must keep a sharp look out to the south-west to see "the round tower of other days," standing by the lone sea shore, and cutting tall and dark against the leaden sky that is now obscuring the outline of Black Head on the distant side of Lough Lurgan,* catching a view of Mutton Island and its light-house, beside which we could recently admire those great leviathans of the deep that brought us in six days to American land—but by which, alas! we lost our cash, the Government its subsidy, and the London directory some of its credit. * * * * Well, while we "mourn the

* Lough Lurgan is the ancient Irish name for the bay of Galway. The Round Tower of Roscam, alluded to above, stands on the Murrough, in the parish of Oranmore, and is about four miles from Galway; and with those of Kilmacduagh, Meelick, Aran, Kilbannon, Inishcaltra, Killcoona, and Ardrahan, forms the eighth of those remarkable structures in that county.

hopes that leave us," we still expect to see that good time come, when, with capital and common prudence, the great natural and geographical advantages of the nearest seaport in the old world at which to launch us for the new will be appreciated. Swiftly we glide over the salt water estuary of Lough Athalia, into the great terminus of Galway, at 1.45 o'clock, and out through it into the enormous limestone hotel, built, "regardless of expense," by the original directors of the railway; and from whence, after a "bit and a sup," we emerge among the beggars into Eyre-square, surrounded by hotels, club-houses, banks, private residences, and coach offices, whence the great "Bian" can forward us to "anywhere," and in which we can choose our newspaper according to our politics or polemics. Down let us pass through William-street, to look at the old mansion of Geoffrey Lynch, the "Spanish Parade," and on by the house where the skull and crossbones commemorate the scene of the "Warden of Galway;" among the turf-kishes, and potatoe baskets, and the carts of sea wrack—along through handsome groups of blue-eyed, black-haired, barefooted colleens, with their graceful carriage, red petticoats, and blue and scarlet cloaks—down to the Fishmarket gate, erected to defend the peaceful burgesses against the "Ferocious O'Flahertys," where we may see the Aran fisherman, in his knee-breeches and *pampootas*, bargaining with the silver-haired Claddagh crone, whose shrimps are jumping out of her apron; where the cockles are smacking their lips with the heat, the johndories are alive, and the lobsters are playing pitch and toss with the crabs; till we reach the bridge, in the bright stream beneath which—

"The trout and salmon
Played backgammon,"

long before Dick Millikin immortalized that feat in song, or the gifted Father Prout heard "The Bells of Shandon," or wandered by the banks of "Sweet Castlehyde."

Give a look at the Queen's College, and the Eglinton Canal; carry your eye along the bright gleam, where the waters of the lake in one unbroken line pour over the weir, and arrange for a few days' fishing with Mr. Miller on your return. Do not stop to see which of the six salmon now hooked will be killed first, but get round to the Wood-quay, for there goes the steamer's first bell at $\frac{1}{4}$ to 3 o'clock.

Now, that we are on the quarter deck, and have made the acquaintance of Ellis, the polite and intelligent Captain of the "Eglinton," and arranged with that most attentive and careful of clerks, Mr. O'Hara, let us, while the steam is getting up, have a short chat about Galway, the Metropolis of the West, a corporate town, a Bishop's see—the last locality of a "Warden" in Ireland—the birthplace, or the early home or school residence of Kirwan the chemist, and Kirwan the orator; of Duald Mac Firbis, the genealogist and antiquary; of Roger O'Flaherty* and James Hardiman, the historians; and of Father Peter, who was for so long a period "the man for Galway." It contained in early days the chief establishments of the Dominican, Franciscan, Capuchin, Augustinian, Jesuit, and Carmelite Orders in Connaught, and was at one period the principal trading and commercial city in this portion of the United Kingdom, and in that respect considered second only to London and Dublin. It was formerly renowned for its foreign trade, and celebrated for the hospitality of its merchants; but, while the latter remains unimpaired, the former is, alas! at a low ebb; and, with immense natural capabilities and vast resources, the Metropolis of Connaught, and the great western seaport of Europe, with a population of 16,967 persons in 1861, although it still manufactures whiskey, flour, and paper; beer, brushes, and boats; besides the ordinary necessaries of daily life, lacks the energy or means of raising

* Roderick O'Flaherty, descended from the Chieftains of the West, and to whom reference is here made as connected with this locality, was one of the most learned Irishmen of the day: his principal works are the "Ogygia or Chronology of Irish Events," written in 1665, and his "Chorographical Description of West or H-Iar Connaught," the MS. of which, written in 1684, was printed by the Irish Archæological Society in 1846, and carefully edited and annotated by the late James Hardiman, the only commentator at the period capable of doing justice to the great historian of the West. O'Flaherty died in indigence at Park, near Galway, at a very advanced age, in 1717.

itself from the applicability of the old adage of "pride, poverty, and devotion."

The name of Galway has given rise to several philological speculations; but it is plainly derived from that of *Gailleamh*, the daughter of Breasil, the prosperous King of the Firbolgs, who, it is said, having—

> "Bathed in the full cool stream,
> The bright branch was drowned;"

and whose monument stood on the river's bank at the time the original of this ancient Irish distich was written in the Dinn Seanchus, a MS. of great antiquity, still in existence. The rock at which she was drowned is marked on the western bank of the river in the celebrated Map of Galway, made in 1651, when the Lord Deputy Clanricarde pledged the City of the Tribes to the Duke of Lorraine; and is thus referred to on the margin of that remarkable document:—"The rock where the woman Galvea is said to have been drowned, from which the city of Galway was named." Hardiman in his notes to O'Flaherty's "West Connaught," says, "Here it is intended by some of the spirited inhabitants of the town to restore that remarkable monument, by erecting a column on the spot, with the above inscription, in order to distinguish the place from which so large a portion of that part of Ireland has been named." And now that the Crimean guns, which were pointed against the Railway Hotel in Eyre-square, have been removed from the grasp of the "Irish Republic virtually established," we really think some of the public spirit alluded to by our deceased friend might find vent for itself in commemoration of the lady who left her name to the locality, and give at least one statue to the Metropolis of Connaught.*

In ancient Irish writings the city of Galway is styled *Dun Gaillve,* the Doon or fortified place at the mouth of the River Gaillve; and in the modern vernacular it is always called *Cahir Gallieve.*

It is related that the river of Galway was dry on several occasions, both in summer and winter; so much so, that articles dropt therein centuries before were then discovered, as in A.D. 1178, in 1190, in 1647, and in 1683, &c.†

* With the exception of the white marble statue of William III., formerly standing on the bridge of Boyle, where in olden days we saw it dressed in "Orange and Blue," even after its head had been cut off, and thrown into the river, and which is now preserved in the public grounds of that famed locality, there is no public statue in the province of Connaught!

† Mr. Kinahan, of the Geological Survey, has very ingeniously endeavoured to account for these droughts, by supposing that the water of the Galway river had suddenly found its way through some of the old subterranean passages, one of which exists at Castlegar, leading across into Lough Athalia. These outlets, previously choked up with sand, became clear at very low tides. See the "Geological Magazine" for November, 1866, for his Paper "On the formation of the Rock Basin of Lough Corrib." "The passage to the Castlegar outlet was closed about fifteen years ago by the Board of Works, to facilitate the navigation of the Lough." It had previously been closed by the Lough Corrib Navigation Company—see note, page 32.

The present arms of Galway are an antique galley, bearing a shield with a lion rampant at the masthead, and having this motto, "*Laudatio ejus manet in seculum seculi.*"

The Wardenship of Galway, last held by the Rev. James Daly, of the Dunsandle family, was done away with in 1840, and the title of city reduced to that of town. It is in the Protestant diocese of Tuam, which includes the whole region of South-west Connaught; but the town and parishes of St. Nicholas and Rahoon form a special Roman Catholic diocese, and the jurisdiction of its present Bishop, Dr. Mac Evilly, has lately been increased by his accession to the administration of the ancient sees of Kilmacduagh and Kilfenora.

Now, that the reader is about to launch on Lough Corrib—whether as a peruser of this work in Belgravia or Merrion-square, or absolutely on board the Eglinton, it matters little—we will develope our plan. Generally speaking, our survey will be littoral and parochial; beginning on the east, traversing the north, and pursuing our route in the most convenient manner round the north and west shores of the lake, but occasionally, when objects of interest connected with the locality present, diverging a short distance inland.

The road from Galway to Cong, through Clare-Galway, by Annaghdown, Headford, and Cross, &c., is a fair day's journey of about thirty miles, and will enable the antiquarian tourist to visit everything of note on that side of the lake, either going or coming. Arrived at Cong by road or lake, and taking up his quarters there for a couple of days, the objects of interest surrounding that locality, as well as the eastern shores of Lough Mask and the plain of Moytura, may be investigated; and the island of Inchingoil can be visited within the space of an hour by a rowboat. Pedestrians will be amply rewarded by a walk over the hills from Cong to Maam, and ladies can have conveyances for the same purpose; or, what is preferable in calm weather, a boat may be obtained at Cong to visit the upper lake, and proceed by Doon and the Hen's Castle to Maam Hotel, a distance of about twelve miles by land, and thirteen or fourteen by water.

During summer, excursions are frequently made by the steamer from Galway to Oughterard, and thence by the south of Inchingoil through the upper lake to Castlekirk, and as far as the Hen's Castle.

From Maam a road four miles long, proceeding nearly due south, and commanding scenes of great beauty, takes us to the highroad leading from Clifden, by Ballinahinch and Oughterard, to Galway, on which public cars ply twice daily. Thus the shores of the lake may be circumambulated with facility.

Tourists pressed for time, or not much interested in archæological investigations, but anxious to obtain a general view of the extreme western limit of the British Isles in the shortest possible space of time, can leave London by the night mail, and at a very trifling expense, and with little wear and tear, reach Galway at 1.45 P.M., next day; and dine at Cong at 6.30; or, if determined on a rush, take a seat on Bianconi's long car, and, passing through some of the wildest portion of Connamara, sleep at Clifden, proceed next day by public or private conveyance, by Kylemore and Leenane, and, leaving the Westport road at the head of the Killeries, pass down through the lovely valley of Maam to Lough Corrib; and there either take boat or car for Cong; and, returning by the steamer next morning, be in Dublin at 5.15 o'clock in the afternoon of the third day, and in Euston-square early the next morning. He will thus have traversed about 1031 miles by railway (first class), and other conveyance, for about £6. See advertisements.

Good accommodation, although not very extensive, may be procured at Headford, Cong, Maam, and Oughterard, each locality possessing a post office; and what may be wanting in hotel appliances will be found to be made up for in civility and moderation of charges.

The tourist may also proceed by Maam, through the valley between Joyce Country and Connamara to the Killeries, by Leenane and Kylemore, to Clifden, where good accommodation can be procured; or from Leenane to Westport, which, however, is the less attractive route. The romantically situated hotel at the Kylemore Lake has been recently refitted, and good fishing and boats may be procured there. There is also good accommodation, and great civility to be had at the Leenane hotel.

Whether by land or water, our descriptive route, proceeding parochially, will describe the lacustrine margins of St. Nicholas, the western extremity of Oranmore, then Clare-Galway, Annaghdown, Kilcoona, Killeany, Cargin, Killursa, and Shrule on the east; Cong upon the north; Ross at the extreme west, Kilcummin on the south-west; and Killannin, Moycullen, and Rahoon on the south and west shores of the lake and its tidal river.

The "Eglinton" steamer, of 40 horse power, and 67 tons, which was built specially for Lough Corrib, is 120 feet long, and 15½ in beam, and is most commodiously fitted up in every respect.

In the following Chapter will be found a description of Lough Corrib, which the tourist can read at his leisure, or during the progress of the voyage; but which, if time presses, or that he has already perused it in the train, he can now skip, and pass on to Chapter III., where our aquatic excursion commences.

CHAPTER II.

DESCRIPTION OF LOUGH CORRIB.

LOUGH CORRIB: ITS DIRECTION, NAME, EXTENT; ANCIENT TERRITORIES ADJOINING; SOURCES, RIVERS, TURLOUGHS; DIVISION; KNOCHMAGH; SCENERY AND MOUNTAINS SURROUNDING LAKE; GEOLOGY, MINES, NATURAL WOODS; DRAINAGE; NAVIGATION, THE EGLINTON CANAL; OUTLETS, THE FRIARS' CUT.

LOUGH CORRIB, which is the second largest sheet of inland fresh water in Ireland, is about thirty-five miles in length from Galway to Maam; and varies in breadth, from eight miles, as between Oughterard and Cong, to one quarter of a mile, as from the Wood of Doon to Curraun Point, where it narrows between the Joyce Country and Iar-Connaught hills. Its general direction is from west-north-west, in a curvature, to south-south-east. In depth it varies considerably, being in many parts full of rocky shoals, left dry in summer; and, even in the navigation course, having but six or seven feet of water in some places; and in other parts descending to 152 feet, as between the island of Inchmicatreer and Cong, and between Doorus Island and Farnaght Point, which portions are styled by the fishermen "The Old Lough." The accompanying map, reduced to a scale of half an inch to the statute mile, taken from the Admiralty Chart made in 1846, and the Ordnance Survey Maps, shows the principal islands, the navigation course, the rivers, and the chief objects of interest along its shores, referred to in this work.

At the commencement of its tortuous course among the Western mountains, it has the county of Galway on both sides, along the baronies of Ross and Moycullen. At the north-east, it divides the counties of Mayo and Galway, along the south margin of the barony of Kilmaine in the former, from the river of Cong to the Black-river of Shrule, about a mile to the north of the ruins of Annakeen Castle, on the east shore. From thence southwards, during the remainder of its course, it has the county of Galway on both sides—the barony of Clare on the east, and that of Moycullen on the west; but the river between the south end of the lake and the sea passes through the Barony, formerly styled "the county of the town" of Galway.

The old Irish name of this sheet of water was Lough Orbsen or Orib, now corrupted into Corrib, and derived from the ancient Danann navigator, Orbsen Mac Alloid, commonly called Mannan Mac Lir, "The Son of the Sea," from whom the Isle of Man is designated. He was slain in conflict by Uillin, grandson of Nuadh of the Silver Hand, the Danann King of Ireland, in a great battle on the western margin of the lake; and from that circumstance this district is called Magh-Uillin, or Moycullen, the plain or field of Uillin; and O'Flaherty says that in his day a great stone thereon, six miles from Galway, marked the scene; it still exists. See Parish of Moycullen.

The ancient territories along it were Iar or West Connaught, comprising Gnomore and Gnobeg—names derived from ancient chieftains—with Conmaicne-Mara, now Connamara,* on the west, and Hy-Brien Seola on the east border, and towards the north-west Ducaid Seoigeach, between it and Lough Mask; and more to the north-east, Conmaicne-Cuile-Tolad, or the plain on which the first great battle of Moytura was fought.

Lough Corrib covers a space of 44,000 acres, and its

* Connamara—Conmaicne-Mara, or Maritima—the Maritime Conmaicne, or territory of Conmac, a descendant of one of the sons of the celebrated Meave, Queen of Connaught, and Fergus, ex-King of Ulster, whose posterity were numerous in the West. Properly speaking, this district is included within the present barony of Ballynahinch, where of old

"Dick Martin ruled the wilds of Connamara;"

but erroneously the name is applied to the region west of Galway town, more especially to that beyond Oughterard. Conmac gave his name to several localities, such as Conmaicne Cuile-Tolad, between Loughs Mask and Corrib; Conmaicne Cinel-Dubheen, near Dunmore; Conmaicne Moy-Rein, in Leitrim, and other places. The O'Cadhlas, the descendants of Conmac, possessed Connamara prior to the O'Flahertys. See O'Donovan's Manuscript "Ordnance Letters;" also the "Annals of the Four Masters," and the Poems of O'Heeran and O'Duigan; and Mac Mahon's "Report on the Drainage of Lough Corrib:" Thom, 1846.

watershed in the counties of Mayo and Galway comprises an area of 780,000 acres. The summer level of the lake is fourteen feet above the medium data of the sea in Galway Bay, and thirty-seven feet below the surface of Lough Mask. This sheet of water formerly extended over a much larger space; but by the drainage operations carried on from 1846 to 1850 it was lowered, much valuable land relieved from flooding, and large tracts rendered capable of cultivation; and I myself remember passing in a boat over places now in good pasturage, and fishing in places at present occupied by flourishing plantations. Its chief western supply is from the great catchment basin of the valley of Maam,* stretching

* Maam—pronounced *Mawm*, a gap or pass, and also applied to the hollow of the hands—is a term of frequent application in Joyce's Country and Connamara. That referred to in the text is, in all probability, the gap upon the hill, where the tourist, passing westwards, first obtains a glimpse of the Hen's Castle; but it has in later days been applied to the passage between the river and the mountain, where the bridge and the hotel now stand, and which divides the Joyce Country and Connamara Mountains. Directly opposite this point, and leading southward to the great Connamara or Ballynahinch road, is *Maamwee*, "the yellow pass;" and farther on up the great glen leading to the sea is *Maameen*, "the little pass," through the mountain tops of the range that borders the great plain that stretches between their southern face and the seaboard margin of Roundstone Bay. From here, it is said, St. Patrick, advancing upon his missionary tour, and viewing the flat, brown, desolate southern region, enlivened only by the blue waters of numbers of inland lakes, took up his abode for the night; but said—according to the phraseology of the guides—"I'll bless you, any way; but sorra foot I'll ever put upon you."

westwards towards the salt water fiord of the Killeries,* and affording the vast supply of water from the sea clouds caught on the Joyce Country and Connamara Mountains, and pouring it down through the River Bealnabreac, the head or "mouth of the [ford of the] trout"—generally interpreted as the river of "the trout's mouth"—(the largest stream in Ireland for its length), and its tributary the Failmore, into the lake at Bunbannon, near Maam, where they coalesce.

On the north-west the principal supply is from the Dowega, which collects the watershed between the west and south-west sides of Benlevy and the south shoulder of the

Here, upon the first Sunday in August—called in Irish "*Donach-Crom-Dubh*," or the Sunday of the great Irish Pagan deity, and in English "Garland," or "Garlic Sunday"—the celebrated "pattern" of Connamara is held, in remembrance of the overthrow of the statue of that Pagan by our patron saint. That day is always regarded as the beginning of harvest, when the new potatoes are first tried; and it is remarkable how few "patterns" are held upon the saint's own festival, and how many on that referring to the Druid deity. In addition, we have *Maam-Turc*, "the pass of the wild boar," a little farther on; also *Maam-Luachra*, "the rushy pass," and several other instances might be named.

* Killeries—in Irish, *Coilshally Ruadh*—*Coil-Saile-Ruadh*, "the narrow red brine," or salt water, which, by one of those extraordinary transmutations, partly in the original, and partly in English, produced in time *Keel-paaly* and eventually *Keel-airy*. See O'Donovan's letters in the Ordnance Books for Galway County, in the Library of the Royal Irish Academy.

hills that run from Lough-na-Foohy* and Lough Mask to Lough Corrib, and which delivers its waters near Curnamona—"the rough field of the bog." The great water source is, however, from Lough Mask, that has, with its tributaries, and the Partry range of mountains, a catchment basin of 225,000 statute acres, and which, filtering subterraneously through the cavernous limestone neck that divides the two lakes between Ross Hill and Cong, rises in an immense body of water at the latter place, and forms the great river of Cong, into which the "Eglinton" steamer enters, and conducts us to the termination of our first day's tour; besides which, the waters of Lough Mask pour into the Corrib lake in numerous places from Cong to Cross, where there is a small stream feeding it with the various springs and turloughs† of that end of the barony of Kil-

* Lough-na-Foughy is a large basin of water, occupying a deep hollow in the mountains behind and to the north-west of Maam, and which empties itself into Lough Mask. At the western extremity of the river which collects the mountain streams for this lake, the water, pouring in an uninterrupted sheet over a smooth convex rock into a basin sheltered by natural wood, forms, at certain seasons, one of the most picturesque cascades in Ireland, although but seldom visited by the tourist. The lake abounds with pike.

† Turloughs are almost peculiar to the West, and consist of basins of rain water, chiefly in limestone districts, covering large tracts of land in winter, but generally completely dry in summer, when their waters are absorbed by *slugga*, or "swallow holes," and underground passages, chiefly through cavernous rocks. Turlough-More and Turlough-Cor are two of the chief sources of winter supply on the eastern side of Lough

maine, and also from the well of St. Frughaun, in the immediate vicinity of the village of Cross.

Still farther to the south-east the rivers of Shrule, Cloughenower, Killroe, Cregg, and Clare-Galway, pour in their tributes: the latter, in particular, which is now partially converted into a canal, and has drained several of the principal turloughs on the eastern border of the lake from Tuam westwards, is, next to the Lough Mask supply, one of the chief water sources of Lough Corrib, and also affords a ready transit and good spawning ground for salmon for many miles inland.

On the west and south sides are a number of small streams, carrying down the surplus waters of the range of hills that stretch from the village of Moycullen by Carn Seefin till they culminate in Leackavrea, which shadows the upper lake opposite the romantic basin in which rest the Island and Castle of Caislean-na-Kirka. On this side also underground passages and now a canal carry in the waters of Ross and Ballyquirk Lakes; but the chief stream is the Fough, or Owenriffe, which, collecting all the waters from the chain of lakes that margin the great road into Connamara, and especially those of Loughs Bofin and Glengowla, to

Corrib. These turloughs were famous waterfowl haunts in winter, and fine pasturage in summer; but since the drainage operations portions of several of them have been tilled. The term Turlough enters into many Irish topographic names. In Munster turloughs are called "blind loughs."

the east of the summit level, enters the lake at Oughterard. The Aughanure river also affords a full stream. From all this it will be seen that the chief supply to Lough Corrib is independent of springs, and hence the water is remarkably soft.

That portion of the lake bordering on the south and east is low and unpicturesque, especially along the baronies of Kilmaine, Clare, and Moycullen; but towards the east can from most points be seen the remarkable "Hill of the Plain," called Knockmagh, near Tuam—a locality very memorable in history, and to which we shall have occasion to refer in another place. The slope of the Moycullen hills, rising gradually into the great western peaks and highlands, and crowned by Carn Seefin, 1006 feet high, between Oughterard and Doon, relieves the monotony of the south-west bank; and the bold flat-topped outline of Benlevy, rising to 1019 feet, at the southern extremity of the Partry range, commences on the north-west the eminences that shelter the upper waters, and slope down to the wooded point of Doon. Towards the extreme north may be seen, on a clear day, the bulky form of Nefin; and, out-topping the deep blue range of Partry, the conical top of the Reek, or *Croagh Phadrig*, standing beside Clew Bay. And looking westward, as we pass between Inishamboe and Inchenquin, we obtain glimpses of the peaks of Bennabola, or the "Twelve Pins" of Connamara, steeped in purple, and draped with gold-fringed clouds, and the topmost of which rises to 2395 feet.* Viewed from any point in Mayo or Galway, on the radius of a circle thirty miles in length, as well as from the midwaters of the lake itself, the mountains that margin the upper portion of Lough Corrib present an outline of great beauty, and when approached nearer fully vie with those of Killarney and Glengariff.

Leackavrea†—the tortuous slate or flag—rising abruptly to a height of 1307 feet from the south shore of the upper lake, apparently bare, and barren even of heather, forms a step in the ladder of elevations that lead by gradation to Shanannafeola,‡ in the background of the picture, and on by

* *Bean-na-Beola*—"the Bens of the giant Bola"—corrupted by English-writing authors into "Pins." The term Ben, a mountain, is still of not uncommon occurrence; as in Ben Levy, Ben Bulbin, Ben Burb, Ben Lettery, formerly Bendowglas, &c. Roger O'Flaherty, in alluding to these alpine peaks, says that in his day they were "called by mariners 'the twelve stackes,' being the first land they discover, as they come from the main."

† Leackavrea is thus described to me by G. H. Kinahan, Esq., of the Geological Survey, and to whom I am very much indebted for information upon some subjects contained in this work:—"It is principally formed of quartzite or quartz rocks, which were originally aqueous sandstones, that by some metamorphic power have been changed into a compact rock; and as those quartzites, previous to being changed, were deposited, in lamina, they have the appearance as if they would split into flags, which is not the case, as they break into irregular lumps. This appears to be the reason for the name of the hill."

‡ Shanannafeolia—*Shan-na-feolla*—a name probably much corrupted from the original, is difficult to explain or derive. *Shan*, old; *na-feolle*, of meat, such as the flesh of deer or cows, of which animals it was the

Maam-Turk, Corga-more, and Ben-bawn, which attains an elevation of 2307 feet high. From the upper lake, in certain states of the atmosphere, we can see the outline of Moahlrea, "The bald King," that stands by the Atlantic, 2688 feet high, over the entrance of the Killeries, and the rugged scarped sides of the mountains overhanging Maam on the north; and which, when lighted by autumn sunsets playing on the russet tints of the projecting crags, produce flecks of a burnished coppery hue of surpassing loveliness. These brown hills slope gradually into the valley of Bealnabreac, towards the west; and on their south-east they end abruptly in the doon of Castlekirk, where the natural wood descends to the water's edge.*

favourite resort, may give some clue to the origin of this name; but the legends are so fast dying out, and the "old people" becoming so scarce, that topographical nomenclature has become very difficult. But for the labours of John O'Donovan during the continuance of the Ordnance Survey under the direction of Lieutenant, now Sir Thomas Larcom, K. C. B., the names of many places in Ireland would be little understood at present. There are several *Shans* in this neighbourhood—*Shan-Kinlougha*, at the head of Lough Bofin; *Shannaun-na-Geeragh*, "the old hill of the sheep," over the wood of *Shan-dilla; Shannan-na-Cloon*, "the old meadow;" *Shannaun-na-Keela*, "the old river ford;" and several others.

* The natural woods now remaining in the extreme West, and that more particularly come within the scope of this work, are Doon, Glann, Annagh, Bilberry Island, Gortdarragh, Kylebeg, and Kilroe, upon or around Lough Corrib; Ballykine and Kilbride, on Lough Mask. Erriffe, on the road between the Killeries and Westport, was probably originally

The lake naturally divides itself into four portions:—The upper or Connamara and Joyce Country portion, from Maam to Doon, placid, and untenanted by islands, save the bare rock on which the ancient Hen's Castle of the O'Conors and O'Flahertys stands; the narrow portion along Doorus and Cannaver; the broad "old lake," crowded with islands, that forms its middle portion; the rocky narrow gut that commences below Inchinquin, and, turning to the south, by the ferry of Knock and Kylebeg landing, opens opposite Portdarragh, into the broad expanse of the free lower lake that forms its fourth part, and sends its volume of waters through the Corrib and Menlough Rivers, and the "Friars' Cut," into the Gaillieve, and through it to the ocean, at the estimated quantity of 126,000 cubic feet per minute in summer. In the deeper parts the bottom is mud, and in the shallow ones gravel and rock.

The great carboniferous mountain limestone formation occupies all the eastern and southern shores, and the lower portion of the western, in a line drawn from Oughterard to

a natural wood; and the islands in Toneymore Lake are certainly so. In Connamara the chief remaining woods are those of Kylemore, (overhanging the beautiful lake of that name), Glendalough, Shandilla, Invermore, Inver na-Glearah, and Derryclare, as well as the Islands of Lough Inagh &c. Their timber consists chiefly of oak, hazel, birch, mountain ash, yew, holly, wild apple, and white and black thorn. But in most of those localities other timber has been introduced, especially alder, poplar, larch, and spruce, &c. See Appendix A.

Cong, occasionally cropping to the surface, and forming stratified fields of smooth bare rock, or where it meets the water being honey-combed like a cullender, and in other places grooved by the action of water, ice, or the attrition of harder bodies passing over it, generally in a south-eastern direction.

The geology of the upper lake is of a totally different character. At Oughterard, writes Mr. Kinahan to me, "the limestone becomes interstratified with sandstone; and immediately north of that village is replaced by granite, which at Glan gives place to fossiliferous Silurian rocks, that lie unconformably on older gneiss, schist, quartz rock, and primary limestone, with dykes and masses of various igneous rocks. On the north of the lake the geology is similar, fossiliferous Silurian rocks occurring at the north-west end of the Maam valley, and extending by Kilbride and Lough Mask to Benlevy and Cong, under which, bounding Lough Corrib, are found gneiss, schist, and primary limestone; and, extending from Benlevy Lodge on Lough Mask to Cong, the mountain limestone is found capping the primary rocks. In the small eastern tract between the River of Cong and the stream at Cross, a detailed list gives an epitome of nearly all the rocks entering into the structure of the district about Lough Corrib;—carboniferous limestone, yellow sandstone, and fossiliferous Silurian grits and shales in sandstone and a variety of whinstone similar to Cotta's description of diallage rock.

"In the townland of Gortachurra there are Carboniferous limestone, conglomerates, and diallage rock; and in that of Ballymagibbon South, and the islands adjoining, granite, gneiss, schist, fossiliferous Silurian grits and shale, with igneous (diallage) rocks, and conglomerates. There is also, in a boss of primary rocks at the north-west corner of this townland, a small mineral vein containing lead ore, and a trace of copper and mundic.

"Good Silurian fossils, supposed to be of Upper Llandovery age, have been found at Currareavagh and New Village in Glan, on the west of the lake; also at Kilbride, on Lough Mask; Benlevi, more especially about Coolin Lough, and from that to Ashford Demesne; also in Lisloughery, and Gortachurra townlands, and the adjoining islets. West of Ashford rare trilobites occur; and in the carboniferous limestone in that demesne I was fortunate enough to find a Chiton, this being the second locality where chitons are recorded as found in the carboniferous limestone, the other being near Rathkeale, Co. Limerick. Black limestone, that will take a fine polish, and form good marble, occurs at Menlough and Anglingham, which quarries are at present worked; also at Rushveala and Cregg, near Oughterard. The serpentine, or green calcareous rocks, commonly called 'Connamara marble,' are found in various places between Lissoughter and Clifden; and at present a company is about to open works on these at Lissoughter and Ballinahinch, from whence it is intended to carry the blocks to the sea, sea, and ship them at Cashel, near Roundstone.

"In the primary rocks, and in some of the carboniferous limestone adjoining the lake on the north, north-west, and east, mineral indications are frequent; but up to the present no deep workings have been carried out, therefore it is impossible to speak positively on the mineral resources of the district. In the carboniferous limestone, on the east of the lake, lead and sulphur ores have been found in the neighbourhood of Ballycurran; and on the west of the lake, at Gortmore, Drumeillstown, Moyvoon, Portacarron, Lemonfield, Ardvarne, and Eighterard, and in most of these places small trials have been made on the veins. In all the primary rock the indications of lead, copper, and sulphur are more or less plentiful, and small trials have been made in Doorus, and other places on the north of the lake. At Leackanvrea, and in Glann, Mr. Hodgson carried on mining operations for some time, and shipped some copper and sulphur ore from the port of Galway, having for the time a steamer plying on the lake to carry the ore to that port. During his operations the hills were burrowed in various directions, and more money spent than, if put in a deep working, would have proved whether the country contains good mines or not. The deepest working in the district is that at Glengowla, in Mr. O'Fflahertie's mine, where large bunches of lead were found some years ago." His mines at Cregg and Canrower are at present let to a Glasgow Company.

Bogs are scarce, and consequently fuel dear, on the south-east shore of the lower moiety of the lake, but plentiful on the west and south, and near Oughterard supply good turf in *puckauns*, or large lug-sail boats, to the surrounding districts, and even to the town of Galway, from whence they bring back cargoes of seaweed for manure. Turf is procured in three ways, according to the nature of the boggy material :—by the down cutting or foot *slane*, a sharp narrow spade, with a wing on one side; by the broad flat "breast slane," which cuts it out in front of the worker; and by raising, mixing, kneading, and forming into loaf-like lumps and then drying, the black mud of old cut-away bogs, and this is called "hand turf." There are several varieties of peat, either owing to the nature or age of the bog:—as *spoddagh*, a whitish towy stuff, composed of the latest layer of uncompressed sphagnum; brown turf; and black or stone turf, the latter being often used, when charred, for forge purposes.

I am indebted to S. U. Roberts, Esq., County Surveyor, Galway, for the following notes on the improvement of the drainage, navigation, and water power in connexion with Lough Corrib, by the Board of Public Works, between 1848 and 1857, under the provisions of the Drainage Acts:*—

* In 1837 a company was projected by Mr. C. Staunton Cahill and others, and a Bill obtained "to empower landed proprietors in Ireland to

"The result obtained by these works has been, first, to relieve 13,685 statute acres of the low lands, on the margin of Lough Corrib, and along the various tributaries which flow into it, from flooding; secondly, the connexion of the Bay of Galway with Lough Corrib, by a navigable canal, and the opening up of the navigation of the Lake; and, thirdly, the improvement of the water power of the River Corrib at Galway. Some idea of the extent and magnitude of the works necessary to effect any improvement in the drainage of Lough Corrib may be formed from the vast extent of the district which sheds its waters into the lake, and the volume of floods at its outfall, which sometimes reaches 800,000 cubic feet per minute.

"The level of the lake has been lowered three feet, and the rise and fall between summer and winter level is limited to three feet, which has been found sufficient to relieve the low lands in the district from injurious flooding, except under some very extraordinary circumstances. The summer level of the lake is fourteen feet above that of high water of ordinary tides in Galway Bay. The River Corrib, which connects the Lake with Galway Bay, is four miles in length, and the length of the Ship Canal is two-thirds of a mile; at the entrance is

sink, embank, and remove obstructions in rivers within the district of Lough Corrib, in the province of Connaught." The only work of any note, however, which that Company effected, was the formation of an embankment along the Terrilan side of the river, which was twice swept away. See evidence on Lough Corrib, printed by the House of Commons in 1847. See also page 13 of this work.

a tidal basin, 470 feet long, and 170 feet wide, with 1000 feet in length of quayage. The ascent from this basin to the level of the lough is accomplished by one lock, 130 feet long, and twenty-one wide, with a lift of fourteen feet. The depth of the navigation is six and a half feet. The water power of the River Corrib at Galway has been increased to an extent of about 1200 horse power; it formerly did not exceed 400. The surface area of Lough Mask is 22,000 statute acres."

The water has also been kept at a proper level by lowering the river bar at Galway, and constructing a regulating weir there. At the same time the navigation channel in the narrow rocky portions of the lake was deepened, the rocks raised; and by buoying and marking with pillars, rocks, and irons, the steamer's track, it has been rendered navigable from Galway to Cong, and also to Oughterard, and to within a couple of miles of Maam hotel. All the marks on the eastern side of our upward course from Galway are coloured white, and those on the western side dark. It will help to give confidence to our Lady friends, who can almost touch some of these marks, triangles, and gridirons, from the "Eglinton," to know that all these rocks were lifted by the present captain of the vessel, who was formerly employed here as a diver.

At the entrance of the Maam river a sandbank occurs, with only four or five feet of water over it in dry weather, which might easily have been removed, were it not considered that the floods of the Failmore and Bealnabreac rivers carry down such large quantities of sand and gravel, that the maintenance of a deep channel through the bar would be attended with considerable expense. The trial, however, should, we think, be made; and if the extraordinary tortuous course of the latter river at least, was straightened, it would not only help to keep the bar channel free, but relieve the low lands along its banks of winter floods.*

A project was entertained of opening up a free communication through the great chain of lakes—Corrib, Mask, and Carra—with the harbour of Galway (like the Caledonian Canal), and much expense was incurred in constructing a canal, locks, and other works for that purpose. Before they were completed it turned out to be a failure—not, however, like the Shannon works, which it is now said retain and retard the flow

* Not long since the bridge of Erriffe, on the main road between Westport and Clifden, which had been swept away by a great flood, was allowed to remain for some years unrestored, until the Grand Jury of Mayo could decide whether the cost was to be defrayed by the neighbouring barony or the county at large. And to this day we have another instance of either local or county economy at the short cut made by the Government for the relief of the famine-stricken people of Mayo and Galway, at Munterowen, between Maam and Leenane, where for nearly the past twenty years the traveller has had to climb a steep hill, and had formerly to run the gauntlet of a ragged village, because neither the barony nor the county at large would put a bridge, value £200, over a mountain stream that crosses a most admirable, straight, level road. During the past summer a portion of the parapet on the bridge of Cong, in the county of Mayo, was allowed to remain for months unrepaired!

of water; for it was discovered, that like many other undertakings, the great canal at Cong "would not hold water." There it remains among the ruins of Cong, so dry, that little boys may be seen playing marbles on the bottom. Even if it could be staunched, a fair excuse may now be offered for its incompleteness by the fact that at each end of this great water track, from Galway to Castlebar, there is sufficient railway accommodation to Dublin to warrant the abandonment of the original design.

The Eglinton Canal at Galway is, however, a work of great utility, both in draining and regulating the surplus waters of the lake, and permitting ingress from the sea. The lower lake empties its waters through a delta by three visible outlets into the Gallive; the natural and original shallow, tortuous, and rocky Corrib River, navigable only for very small craft and row-boats, on the west; the Menlough Creek, a small stream, on the east, now nearly filled up; and through the boggy island covered with sedge between these two, by means of the "Friars' Cut," a canal of about three-quarters of a mile in length, fifty feet wide, and twelve deep, through which the main stream passes. This latter is generally held to be artificial, and tradition ascribes its formation to the Friars of Clare-Galway; but it is remarkable that neither by Roger O'Flaherty or Hardiman, nor in any of the local records, is allusion made to it; while certainly a work of such magnitude and importance, if formed by the industrious and enterprising Franciscans, would have been referred to. On the contrary, O'Flaherty, writing in 1684, says expressly in his Iar Connaught, that "the River of Galway, whose channel is the conveyance of Lough Orbsen for four miles into the sea, slides with some meander windings in a slow and deep stream till it comes near the town of Galway;" and further adds, "there is an island, where the river issues from the lake now called Olen-na-mbra-har, or the Fryars' Isle, but anciently Olen-na-g-clereagh, *i. e.* the Clergy's Isle." This is still marked on the maps, although at present more of a peninsula. During the recent operations of the Board of Public Works, the Friars' Cut was cleared out by a steam dredge, and rendered navigable.

Besides these three streamways, there is a subterranean communication through the cavernous limestone, by means of "swallow holes," near Terrilan, on the eastern shore, which formerly carried off a large portion of the surplus waters of the lake, and discharged them into the sea near Oranmore, as already referred to at pages 14 and 32.

It is memorable that so early as 1498, about the time when the subject of the construction of canals occupied so much public attention in the Italian States, an attempt was made to unite the waters of Lough Corrib with the sea, through the Lough Athalia Estuary by a canal, taking the course of the Terrilan river, a small stream which runs into the Gallive. See M'Mahon's "Report on the Drainage of Lough Corrib."

The steam navigation of Lough Corrib was commenced in 1852, when a dredge was employed to clear out the Friars' Cut, and to assist in lifting the rocks that obstructed the shallow passes. About the same time, Mr. J. Stephens put another small steam boat, called "The O'Connell," on the lake, which carried passengers; and the year after, Mr. Hodgson procured a steamer, "The Enterprise," and afterwards "The Lioness," for carrying down mine to Galway. The first effort, however, to establish a regular traffic and passenger boat on the lake, is due to the patriotic exertions of the Rev. Peter Daly, after whom it was called "The Father Daly."

For the Zoology and Botany of the district, see Appendix B.

CHAPTER III.

GALWAY TO ANNAGHDOWN.

PARISH OF ST. NICHOLAS. TERRILAN CASTLE. ANNALS OF GALWAY. THE DE BURGOS. MENLOUGH. PARISH OF ORANMORE. THE LOWER LAKE. CLAREGALWAY PARISH, CASTLE, AND CONVENT CHURCH. ANCIENT PLOUGHS. KNOCKNATUATH; THE BATTLE OF THE CHIEFTAINS; THE IRISH AGAINST THE IRISH; THE BOOK OF HOWTH; THE ENGAGEMENT, AND THE ROUT. CREGG CASTLE; ATHCLOIGGEEN; THE HAG'S CASTLE.

"Now then, time's up—strike the bell—stand by good people, the gentlemen don't want any more lobsters at sixpence a piece—shove along that vagabond pig—get these barrels and meal bags forward—pull in the gangway—throw off the line—move her ahead." We are afloat on the River Gallive, with our larboard side to the deserted breweries and never completed factories, by which runs to waste upwards of a thousand horse power in the rapid river—with our starboard along side Terrilan, *Tir-Oillen*, the pass or "ford of Oillen"—the ruined castellated mansion, figured in the following cut, 75 feet long by 25 broad, and said by tradition to have been one of the earliest locations of the Earls of Clanricade. It possesses little architectural or picturesque interest, as, like most ruins in the neighbourhood of crowded localities, every accessible quoin or dressed stone has been removed, to assist in erecting whatever structures not composed of mud may be seen in the neighbouring cabins of Bohermore, and other equally classic suburban villas on the south slope of the heights of Caher Gallive; and no fostering ivy has as yet thrown a green mantle over its bare grey walls.

Numerous are the legends still repeated of the prowess of the De Burgos, and the wiles and daring of the O'Flahertys, in connexion with this castle, erected to defend the river's ford at this point. It is frequently alluded to in the "Annals of the Four Masters,"* and in other authentic histories, and so late as 1641 it was garrisoned by Dermot O'Daly.

Where the earliest Castle of Galway absolutely stood, unless at this spot, it is now difficult to determine. Turgesius, the sanguinary Danish commander, overran Connaught in 835, and "the ancient town of Galway was destroyed." Hardiman says, the Castle *Dune-bun na Gaillve*, or the fortification at the mouth of the Galway river, was erected soon after the defeat

* Early in the seventeenth century a learned Irishman, Hugh Ward, head of the Franciscans at Louvain, sent Michael O'Cleary, a lay brother of that order, and a distinguished scholar and hereditary antiquary, to Ireland, to collect materials for lives of saints, which, after Ward's death, were used by Colgan in his "Acta Sanctorum." Michael associated with him two other scribes, antiquarians, and genealogists of his tribe, Conor and Peregrine O'Cleary, and also Fearfassa O'Mulcorey, or Conry, and O'Dugan, &c.; and, besides other works, they compiled from all the then available sources a book of the "Annals of Ireland," from the earliest period to the year 1616, and which they completed at Donegal, in 1634. Colgan, writing of this work shortly afterwards, styled it, *Annales Quatuor Magistrorum*, and hence the appellation of the "Four Masters," in imitation of a similar term employed by early medical writers. See the author's description of the Annals of Ireland, in the "Census Reports for 1851," vol. v. published in 1856.

The learned Dr. O'Conor published an annotated version of a portion of these annals, and Professor Connellan translated and published those from 1171 to 1616. Subsequently all these annals were translated into English, and copiously annotated, by the late John O'Donovan, and now form seven large quarto volumes, published by Hodges and Smith; and it may fearlessly be asserted that they are the most extensive, truthful, and learned historic and topographical work of their kind in Europe.

of the Danes at Clontarf; and then its erection, and the improvement of the town, were a source of jealousy to the people of Munster, between whom and those of Connaught there had long existed a considerable degree of competition. Conor, King of Munster, in 1132 despatched a body of troops by sea, commanded by Cormac Mac Carthy, who besieged and took the Castle. Again, in 1149, Turlogh O'Brien, King of Munster, invaded Connaught, and destroyed the town and Castle of Galway, which ravages, however, appear to have been soon after repaired. In 1230 Hugh O'Flaherty, the chief of his name, fortified himself in the Castle of Galway, which, by his spirited resistance, he was able to keep against De Burgo.

The foregoing references to castles and fortified houses (neither uncemented Duns, Cahers, nor Cashels, such as shall presently engage our attention), out of hundreds which could be adduced of fortifications, churches, and bridges, erected by Irish chieftains long prior to the date of the Anglo-Norman invasion, are here worthy of notice, and might afford materials for a dissertation, if the question required further proof. Yet still some of the architectural lights from across the water, unfamiliar with our early history, occasionally propound the doctrine that the Irish were unacquainted with the use of mortar until taught by the invaders of 1172. Our traditions are to be approached with reverence, and investigated with care; and there can be no doubt that the eclectic examination made of our annals during the last thirty years, and a comparison of the ancient literary records, or the story of the shannaghie, with the existing monuments, have largely tended to confirm the truth of Irish history; nor have we any doubt that they will be still further elucidated, when a more extended examination of the three memorials of the past—the record, the legend, and the existing monument—shall have been made by learned, faithful, and unspeculative scholars and antiquaries.

The subject of this digression introduces to us a family which, of all the Anglo-Norman chieftains who came over at the time of the invasion (except the Geraldines), exercised most influence, retained most territory, and still possess most power in Ireland. The descendants of William Fitzadelm De Burgo, who arrived with Strongbow Earl of Pembroke, in 1172, acquired more land, built more castles, and left a more widespread name than most of those whose ancestors had conquered Harold on the battlefield of Hastings—a fact which may be accounted for by the circumstance of their having been among the very first of those who earned the title of *Hiberniores ipsis Hibernicis;* having as frequently been found fighting side by side with the Celt as taking part with the Saxon: although members of that family were more than once the English King's Deputy in Ireland. Sir William Leigh De Burgh, who died in 1324, and was interred in the Abbey of St. Francis, at Galway, left seven sons, the eldest of whom, Sir Ulick of Annaghkeen, was the first Mac William *Oughter*, or of the "upper" or Galway Connaccan territory; and from his son Rikard has descended the family of the Clanricarde, one of whom, Walter De Burgo, who was styled Earl of Ulster, in right of his wife, daughter of Hugo de Lacey, was assassinated at Carrickfergus in 1333. Another branch of this family, descended from Edmond Albanagh, or "The Scot," possessed the lower or Mayo territory, and took the title of Mac William *Eighter*, from whom the Earls of Mayo have descended. Both the De Burgos, however, in the early part of the fourteenth century, shook off obedience to the English laws, renounced their allegiance to the Crown; and, "in order to conciliate the natives in their favour, discontinued the use of the English language, threw off their English dress, and adopted both the language and apparel of the Irish, embraced the Irish laws, and transmitted their possessions in the course of tanistry and gavelkind." So much for the De Burgos, now called Burkes or Bourkes—a name of very frequent announcement in the entire West of Ireland, and especially along the shores of Lough Corrib.

Passing up the river by Jordan's Island, we steam past Menlough Castle, the picturesque residence of Sir Thomas Blake, Bart., standing on the water's edge, with the remains of the outer walls on the south, and presenting to us, as shown by the subsequent cut, one of the handsomest of the inhabited old castles of Ireland. Neither the family records, nor any of the published histories, afford a clue to the date of its erection; but the Menlough family founded one of the tribes of Galway, and are connected with, if not descended from, the English Blakes of Cumberland.

At the rere of the castle may be seen the village of Menlough, one of the largest collections of cabins in Ireland, and the inhabitants of which formerly exercised, in conjunction with those of the Claddagh, so potential an influence upon the return of the member for Galway. The inhabitants of this village amounted in 1841, to 1100; in 1851, to 764; and in

1861 they had fallen to 682. What a source of wealth the children of this village could be made to some enterprising manufacturer, who might employ them, and hundreds of others in the vicinity, at from three to sixpence a day!

Around the village of Menlough we see nothing but stones, stones, stones; but on the opposite bank we have Dangan, the original seat of the Martins, lately converted into a nunnery, but now deserted even by the benevolent sisters; and also Bushy Park, and other residences of the neighbouring gentry.

So far on our course we have passed through the barony as well as the county of Galway—between the parishes of Rahoon on the left and St. Nicholas on the right; and in the latter, besides that of Terrilan, already described, we have the ruins of Castlegar, Ballybrit, and Merlin Castles; but they are not of sufficient importance nor vicinity to the lake to merit a detailed description, or require illustration.

The large parish of Oranmore, through a portion of which we passed on approaching Galway, and which contains the castle and townland of Menlough, here runs down to the lake margin between those of St. Nicholas and Clare Galway; but its early inhabitants seem to have concentrated their energies more upon its sea-board than its lacustrine border, and have left us nothing worthy of attention at this end of it, except the ruins of the square Castle of Cloonacanneen and that of Carrowbrowne.

Here, as we pass upwards, the Corrib River diverges to the west; and, being too shallow and rocky for the passage of the "Eglinton," we enter, through a deep sedgy marsh or bog, about a mile in length, the canal traditionally called the "Friars' Cut," as explained at page 36. Leaving behind us the long curling sludgy waves that rush like serpents along the banks, as if to overtake us, as we pass through this Cut, we emerge into the broad blue waters of the Lower Lake. On the left, or western side of our course, may be seen the ridge of hills that stretches from Galway to Oughterard; and along their slopes the demesnes of Woodstock, Farm, Danesfield; and also the village of Moycullen, now the property of Lord Campbell; beyond which appear, as we proceed, the woods of Drimcong, Knockbane, and Ross.

Putting on full speed as we leave the Friars' Cut, and pass into the broad uninterrupted space of the lower lake, we have on our right the marble quarries of Angliham, and soon get a glimpse over the low limestone plain, eastward of our course, of the butt of the old castle, and the tall slender tower that rises from the centre of the Abbey or cruciform church of the Convent of Clare-Galway, which, although at some distance from the water's edge, is not without our prescribed parochial limits, and is of too great beauty and importance to be omitted; and, moreover, it is on the highroad between Galway and Cong, being but six miles' distance from the former. A more picturesque group of ruins, or one comprising a greater variety for the display of the artist's pencil, can scarcely be found, even amidst the multitudinous remains that crowd the parishes abutting upon Lough Corrib, than this scene presented in former days—with its little mill, and slow winding river passing under a long, low, many-arched bridge, but which is now replaced by a canal, and a single formal arch.

The massive square ivy-clad keep of the castle, now used as a barn, stands on the east of the roadside, and was formerly the residence of Mac William Oughter De Burgo, as stated by the Four Masters, under the date 1469, in which year it was burned by Hugh Roe O'Donnell. As it was contiguous to the famous battle-field of Knocktuagh, fought between the Earls of Kildare and Clanricarde in 1504, it was occupied by the Irish party; and in 1512 it was again the seat of war. It is at present 63 feet high, 20 long, and 20 broad, and partakes of the general characteristics of such buildings in the West—consisting of a pointed-arched entrance to the porch, within which is the usual *Poul-na-morrough* or "murdering hole," an aperture in the thick vaulted roof above, through which missiles could be showered on assailants who had gained an entrance through the outer door. A winding stone staircase leads from story to story, the lower one of which was usually stone-arched, and over it an upper apartment with a large handsome chimneypiece, and illuminated by mullioned or decorated narrow lights; and, as here, a corbelled projection all round for supporting a wooden floor, or sometimes a stone-arched one; and above that the parapet, either plain or corbied, and having one or more turrets at the angles; while the prison, gardrobe, and some secret hiding holes, were usually placed in the thickness of the northern wall. In addition, this castle had a portcullis, the groove of which shows long and constant usage.

In a document styled "The Division of Connaught, A. D. 1586," now in the British Museum, no less than thirty-three castles are enumerated in the barony of Clare, chiefly of De Burgo origin; but all are now either in ruins, or their sites only discernible by heaps of stones.

Writers on domestic and defensive architecture, alluding to these castles, erected in Ireland between the fourteenth and sixteenth centuries, are too much in the habit of looking upon our castellated mansions as mere guardrooms for the security and defence of the soldiery by which they were garrisoned, without taking into consideration the artistic skill and taste with which many of them were adorned; nor remembering the ladies bright and accomplished, who "walked in silk attire;" the bards and minstrels, with their harps, and songs, and legends; the scholars learned, the clerics pious, as well as the valiant knights and nobles, in their burnished armour and nodding plumes, by whom they were tenanted, but of whose social life and habits we know little. In looking back upon those ages, it is scarcely possible to disassociate from skill, taste, and refinement in architecture, similar personal culture and costume; but until some gifted poetic child of Erin, with an eye to see, and a pen to paint the beauties of both nature and art—observation to appreciate and display the workings of the human heart—dramatic—learned in the history of the past—antiquarian in knowledge, and patriotic in feeling—and, above all, possessing that rare gift of fusing fiction with fact, and weaving the romance with the legend, as Scott did for the history and monuments of his native country—the castle may crumble, the abbey moulder, the warrior lie unremembered, and the lady fair unwept for, in this land so fertile in imagination, and so profound in pathos. And until the proprietors who own these castles feel proud of their heritage or their acquisition, and the clerics who claim by transmitted hereditary right these abbeys, and who perhaps hope to claim them on a future day, take some interest in their preservation, the most the modern writer can do is to invoke public opinion; while the tourist will still have, for yet many a day, to grope his way among these crumbling walls, through mud and briers, and to disturb the bullock calves, and fat wedders, that may almost invariably be found desecrating the tombs that pave these sacred aisles, and disturb the goats that take occasional shelter even underneath their high altars.

The records state that about the year 1290, John De Cogan built a Monastery at Clare-yn-dowl for Franciscan Friars, in a very elegant style, and at great expense. A few brothers of the order performed service in the small northern chapel within the last six years; but all that now remains of recent occupancy within these consecrated precincts are a cowhouse and pigstye.

Although the modern name of this parish is CLARE-GALWAY, it is called in Irish *Bailie-Clair* or *Bally-an-Clare*, the Bally or town of the *Claire* or "flat"—a title which it well deserves. There are several Clares and Bally-Clares in Connaught—and it requires some topographical knowledge to distinguish which is the one referred to in the annals and histories; but this particular locality is styled, in most ancient documents, "*Clare-en-Dowl*," "the Devil's Flat," or board, because, according to the local traditions, the rapid river at this place was formerly crossed on planks supported on pillars.

The ruins of the Abbey or Convent Church stand on the right or northern bank of the river, a little below the Castle; and, like most other structures which came from the hands of those noble church-builders, the Franciscans, it is characterized by a taste and elegance which neither time, nor the rough hand of the despoiler, nor even the gross neglect of modern proprietors has been able to efface. It was originally cruciform; and from the intersection of nave, choir, and transepts, was reared, on high pointed arches, a tall slender tower, that for graceful proportions may vie with, if indeed it does not surpass, any other of its kind in Ireland.

When the sun breaks forth after a passing shower, brightening up a side of this tower, and throwing out the gorgeous colours of golden lichen clothing its grey time-beaten stones, and contrasting with the brilliant green of the pellitory and umbelliferous plants that cluster on its string courses, and around its windows and corbied parapet, a more glorious effect, and at the same time a more beauteous harmony of colour and form, can scarcely be imagined. The illustration of this ruin in the following page has been taken from the south-east, and represents, besides the tower, which is seen from a great distance all round, the dilapidated east window, the northern arches of the nave, and the small chapel, in which the friars had service

within the last few years. The entire length of this church was 142 feet, and that of the transept, 112. The height of the tower is probably 80 feet. Among the references made to this place by our annalists and ecclesiologists, it is said, under the date of 1296, that Philip de Blund, Archdeacon of Tuam, during the time of the dispute respecting the episcopacy of Enachdun, took by violence from the friars of Clare-Galway, in which place they had been deposited, the pontificalia, consisting of the chest containing the "episcopal mitre, together with the pastoral staff, and sundry other things," of the neighbouring cathedral.

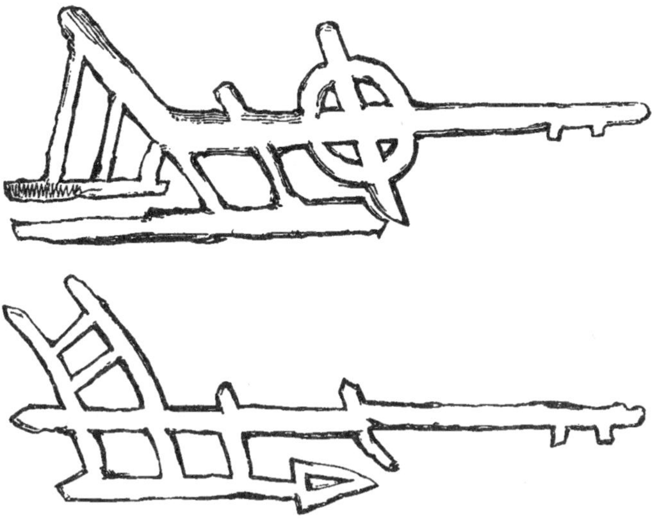

There are not now many tombs of note within the precincts of this venerable and still beautiful pile; but among the well-cut flagstones paving the aisles of nave and transept, may be seen early indications of the agricultural skill of the people of this great fertile plain or *Clare*, in the number and variety of ploughs carved upon them. They bear date from the middle of the seventeenth to the end of the eighteenth centuries; and the two preceding *fac-simile* cuts, selected out of eight, represent that early civilizer as it existed in Galway, the upper one in 1696, and the lower in 1773. Neither seems to have been drawn by the horse's tail, against which so many enactments had been made in former days; but which practice, it is said, had not been altogether discontinued in Erris at the early part of the present century.

Upon the left or southern bank of the river stands a large ecclesiastical ruin, surrounded by a graveyard.

About eight miles from the City of the Tribes, and behind, and somewhat to the north-east of Clare-Galway, rises a sloping green elevation, crowned by the dilapidated mansion of the late Major A. Kirwan, and which is known as Knocktoe, or *Knoc-na-tuadh*, "the hill of the hatchets" or battle-axes, from the following circumstances; although the name is probably older than the assigned date. At the beginning of the sixteenth century, Gerald, eighth Earl of Kildare, was the English King's (Henry VII.), Lord Deputy in Ireland, and had married Eustacia, one of his daughters, to Ulick Mac William De Burgo, Earl of Clanricarde; but, according to the narrative, she "was not so used as the Earl [Gerald] could be pleased with, and he said he would be revenged upon this Irishman [Mac William], who stood at defiance with the Earl and all his partakers." The Deputy thereon assembled a great army, and marched into Connaught in August, 1504, bringing with him O'Reilly, O'Conor of Ofaley (it is said O'Neill), Sir Nicholas Lord of Howth; the Barons of Delvin, Gormanstown, Killeen, Slane, and Trimbleston; with Hollywood of Artane, and other nobles and gentles of "the best men in all the English Pale." Some border chiefs also flocked to his standard—as O'Hanlon, O'Farrell, Mac Mahon, OBeirn, and, according to some writers, Hugh Roe O'Donnell; and "he was joined by the forces of almost all the Northern half of Ireland." Some of the Connaceans likewise joined the Viceroy's army—as O'Conor Roe from Sligo; The Mac Dermot of Moylurg; and even the Mayo or lower branch of the De Burgos, the sons of Mac William *Eighter* and all the O'Kellys, from the neighbouring territory of Hy-Many; for, according to the statement in the "Four Masters," the true cause of quarrel and immediate excuse for this rising was, that O'Kelly had complained to the Lord Justice that Ulick, third Earl of Clanricarde, had demolished three of his castles; and we read elsewhere that the Clan-Rickard Burkes, being "of Englishe nacion, berith mortal hate to the Kellys," who were of the old Irish stock.

There also came with the King's representative several bishops, clerics, and lawyers. On seeing which class of non-belligerents, O'Neill is said to have thus addressed his chief at a council of war, held within a short distance of this hill on the day before the battle:—"My Lord of Kildare, command the bishopps to go home and pray; for bishops' councells ought not to be taken in matters of warr, for their profession is to pray and preach, to make fair weather, and not to be privy to manslaughter or bloodshed, but in preaching and teaching the Word of God." And with respect to the men learned in the law O'Conor said:—"Wee have no matters of pleading, nor matters of arguments, nor matter to debate, nor to be discussed by pen and ink, but by the bow, speare, and sword; and the valiant host of gentlemen and men of warr, by their fierce and lofty doings; and not by the simple, sorry, weak, and doubtful stomachs of learned men; for I never saw those that were learned give good counsaile in matters of warr; for they were always doubting, staying, or persuading men in frivolous and uncertain words. Away with them! they are overbold to press among this company; for our matter is to be decided by valiant and stout stomachs of prudent and wise men of warr, practised in the same faculty, and not matters of law nor matters of religion."

On the other side Clanricarde mustered a great army to give them battle, among whom, with their clans, were Turlogh O'Brien, Lord of Thomond, and his brother, with all their forces; the Siol-Aedha, or the Macnamaras; and Mulrony O'Carroll, Lord of Ely, with all his clans and chieftains, who were joined by the nobles of Ormond and Ara.—See Annals of The Four Masters.

The Irish held possession of the hill; and the battle was fought, on the 19th of August, in the plain that slopes by the north-east to Turloughmore. Both sides had cavalry, and the English at least had archers; but the chief stay of both armies were the gallowglasses, with their bright battle-axes, and the De Burgo contingent of which was headed by the redoubtable Mac Swine, so famed for his prowess in the use of that weapon.

By the so-called English army the battle was "sett" by placing the horse on the left or southern wing, under Baron Delvin; "the bowmen [were] put in two wings, of which the Lords of Gormanstown and Killeen had the charge, being good men that day; the billmen in the main battle, of which the Lord of Howth was leader, and in the vanguard himself."

The Connaught and Munster men, or so-called Irish Army, says the chronicler, in the "Book of Howth," spent "all that night watching, and drinking, and playing at cards, who should have this prisoner or that prisoner, and thus they passed the night over; and at morrow they prepared for battle in such order as their custom was. * * They set forward their gallowglass and footmen in one main battle, and all their horse on their left [or northern] side, and so came on."*

The Lord Deputy, "a mighty man of station," who rode

* The "Book of Howth" is a MS. of the sixteenth century, now in the Carew Collection preserved in the Lambeth Library. See Hardiman's notes to O'Flaherty's "H-Iar Connaught," p. 154, from whence the foregoing extracts have been taken. See also the "Annals of The Four Masters" under A. D. 1504; O'Donovan's Letters on Galway, in Ordnance Collection, in Library of Royal Irish Academy; and Gilbert's "History of the Viceroys of Ireland," p. 468. A remarkable discrepancy occurs between the Howth and Donegal Annalists, the former of whom, writing earlier than the latter, states that O'Neal was with Kildare at Knocktuadh, and ignores the presence of O'Donnell. The latter enumerates O'Donnell among the advisers and chief supporters of the Deputy, but says that O'Neill was not there. See also the latest description of the Battle of Knocktoe, in Haverty's History of Ireland, 1860, p. 343.

upon a black horse, made the following oration just before the engagement: "Here is against us a great number of people without weapons, for a great number of them have but a spear and a knife; without wisdom, or good order, they march to battle as drunken as swine to a trough, which makes them more rash and foolish men, than wise and valiant. Remember, all that we have done rests upon this day's service, and also the honour of our Prince ; and remember how we are in a country unknown to the most number of us, and farr from our towns and castles." When the Earl had proceeded thus far, three great cries were heard, probably of *Gall riagh aboo*, the battle cry of the De Burgos, as *Crom a boo* was that of the Geraldines. "The English archers lent such a shower of arrows, that the weapons [of the Irish gallowglasses] and their hands were fastened together. Mac Swine struck Darcy such a blow upon the helmet, that he put him upon his knees. With that, Nangle, Baron of the Nowan, being a lusty gentleman that day, gave Mac Swine such payment, that he was satisfied ever after. They fought terrible and bould awhile, [but] the Irish fled." A Dublin soldier struck an Irish horseman "with a gun, with both his hands, and so let out his brains." This is the only notice of firearms recorded in any of the narrations of the battle ; and the gun, which was probably a matchlock, seems to have been used more as a shillelah or *clath-alpeen*, than as a chemical explosive projectile.

Far from the field of action, wrote the Donegal Annalists—possibly quoting or paraphrasing some of the grandiloquent descriptions of the contemporaneous poets or prose writers of the locality—"were heard the violent onset of the martial chiefs, the vehement efforts of the champions, the charge of the royal heroes, the noise of the lords, the clamour of the troops when endangered, the shouts and exultations of the youths, the sound made by the falling of the brave men, and the triumphing of the nobles over the plebeians. The battle was at length gained against Mac William, O'Brien, and [the chiefs of] Leath Mhogha, and a great slaughter was made of them; and among the slain was Murrough Mac-I-Brien Ara, together with many others of the nobles. And of the nine battalions which were in solid battle array, there survived only one broken battalion."—Annals of The Four Masters.

"The young Gerot [Kildare's son, who had been stationed with the reserve], seeing the battle join, could not stand still to wait his time, as he was appointed by the Earl his father, but set on with the foremost, in such sort that no man alive could do better with his own hands than he did that day for manhood of a man. But by reason of his hastyness, not tarrying in the place appointed, all the English carriage was taken by the Irish horse, and a few of the English gentlemen taken prisoners."—Book of Howth.

The numbers slain in this battle are variously stated—some writers asserting that the Irish lost 9000, and others only 2000. It was evidently a hand-to-hand fight without firearms, and only lasted a few hours before the rout commenced ; and it is scarcely possible that 9000 persons were killed on either side. Some writers have fallen into the error of styling this memorable battle an engagement between the English and Irish; whereas it was neither more nor less than the result of a personal quarrel between two rival Norman-Irish Chieftains, the Geraldine and the De Burgo, who, having their own aggrandizement in view, used the "mere Irish" to assist them in their personal quarrels and family feuds. The battle of Knocktuath was not fought between English and Irish, but between the *Leath-Chuinn* or Northern chieftains, assisted by the Easterns, and the *Leath-Mhogha*, or the Southern or Munstermen, together with those of the western portion of Connaught—in which the latter were defeated, as they probably might be in later times. Kildare and his army proceeded to Galway, "carrying with them as prisoners the two sons and a daughter of Mac William;" probably from Clare-Galway Castle.

Passing along the road from Clare-Galway by Leacht-George (for which see description of Castle Creevy at page 78), and northwards towards Headford, we cross an angle of Lackagh parish. Upon the left of the road stands a very fine liss or earthen fort; and on the right are the young woods of Baunmore, the property of Richard A. H. Kirwan, Esq. We then proceed by Cregg Castle, the seat of Francis Blake, Esq., which with Menlough is one of the few old castellated mansions still inhabited in Connaught. It was erected by Patrick

Kirwan in 1648, and stands in a spacious well-wooded demesne, and was the birth-place and formerly the residence of the distinguished philosopher, and President of the Royal Irish Academy, to whom allusion has been already made at page 10.* Within Cregg demesne there is a small ruined church, and to the south-west is seen the tower of Liscanniaun Castle, and more to the west stands Drumgriffin held by Ullig Reogh in 1586.

Outside the north side of the demesne is a pretty bit of landscape, and a "flash" of water called *Ath-cloiggeen*, or the "ford of the little bell;" and beyond it the mills of Cregg, near which the tourist, if travelling by the road, can turn down to the lake side by Winterfield, through the parish of Annaghdown; but, to pursue our lacustrine course, we must rejoin the steamer, and, passing up through the lower lake, approach the group of ruins which stands beside the landing place of Annaghdown.

As we leave the Friars' Cut, and steam through the lower lake, and also while passing through the narrow rocky portion ahead of our course, the long, low sterile district of Gnomore and Gnobeg, with the flat, lake margins of the parishes of Moycullen and Killannan come into view on the west; and as the eye traverses this apparently sterile region, it rests occasionally on the chimney of the lead mine at Gortmore, and the grey side wall of Tolokian Castle, popularly called

* See Mr. Donovan's Memoir of Richard Kirwan, in the Proceedings of the Royal Irish Academy, vol. iv., page 480—lxxxi.

Caisleau-na-Cailliaghe, or the Hag's Castle and of which the accompanying illustration, from a drawing made by Mr. Wakeman for the Ordnance Survey, many years ago, gives a good idea. This castle is called Tullokyne on the Ordnance Map, and it must not be confounded with the Caislen-na-Caillighe on Lough Mask, referred to in the Donegal Annals, under A. D. 1195. In 1586, Muriertagh O'Conor held the castle of Tullekyhan.

Of its origin, or true history, we know nothing; but it is mentioned by O'Flaherty in 1684, when a similar structure, a few paces distant, existed, but which was blown down by the great storm of January, 1839. They were called, says Hardiman, "the Castles of the two Sisters, of whom some romantic tales of former days are still current." Among these, the people state that when these old maids were too old to visit, they built these castles in such close contiguity in order that they might daily "barge" one another from their respective windows. At long run, however, the dame that owned the present ruin cut short the dispute by killing her sister.

CHAPTER IV.

ANNAGHDOWN TO KYLEBEG.

ANNAGHDOWN PARISH, AND ANCIENT BISHOPRIC; ST. BRENDAN. THE DESMOND AND O'DONNELL COSTUME. THE MONASTERY AND ABBEY. ANCIENT TOMBS. THE NUNNERY. WINDOW OF MODERN CHURCH. THE CLOIC-THEACH OF ANNAGHDOWN. THE CASTLE AND HOLY WELLS. CASTLE CREEVY. KILCOONA PARISH; CHURCH, AND ROUND TOWER. HISTORY AND WRITINGS OF ST. COONA. PARISH OF KILLEANY. CLOCH-AN-UAIBHER CASTLE. LEE'S ISLAND. KNOCK FERRY AND KYLEBEG.

ANNAGHDOWN, Annaghdune, or Enough-Duin, the dun or "fortress of the bog"—and in modern Irish, Enagh-coin, "the fort of the bog," or possibly of St. Coona—giving name to a large parish in the barony of Clare, about twelve miles from Galway, is the first stopping place of the steamer, and contains the chief group of ruins that occur on the eastern shore of Lough Corrib, on our upward route. They consist of, a picturesque tall square castle, still in fine preservation, the walls of the Bishop's residence, with the wells of St. Brendan, the founder, and St. Cormack, on the south; and the extensive remains of an Abbey and Monastery, and also a Nunnery, and other ecclesiastical buildings, on the north side of a rocky inlet of the lake, into which a small stream pours its waters. In early Christian times this was the site of the fifth Bishop's See in Connaught, the boundary of which was coextensive with the seigniority of Iar Connaught, and in the territory of the chiefs of Hy-Brien Seola, the progenitors of the O'Flahertys, ere they were driven by the De Burgos and other English settlers westward, across the lake, into the baronies of Moycullen and Ross.

It is stated in the "Book of Ballymote" that Aodha, son of Eochy Tirmacarna, King of Connaught, bestowed Enaghdun on God and St. Brendan of Clonfert; and it is probable that the ancient see of Cong was transferred here early in the twelfth century.

St. Brendan, having established a nunnery, and placed his sister Briga, a canoness of the Augustinian order, over it, died here, but was interred at Clonfert, A.D. 577. Several of its bishops are mentioned in the Irish Annals; but the episcopal lords of the neighbouring diocese of St. Jarlath, and especially Archbishop Mac Hugh, feeling perhaps some jealousy on the subject, induced Pope John XXII. in 1321 to issue a bull to suppress it, and join it to that of Tuam; and many of its revenues and valuables were transferred to the collegiate church of St. Nicholas in Galway. The mandate of the Pontiff does not, however, appear to have been implicitly obeyed either by the Irish or English; for some of its bishops are enumerated after that date; and, so late as 1484, Richard III. "dispatched to Ireland Thomas Barrett, a cleric of Somerset, who had been appointed to the bishopric of Enagh-dun, in Connaught, to instruct the Deputy Kildare by all possible means to bring into the King's power the Earldom of Ulster, then almost entirely possessed by the native Irish." And in order to conciliate the Desmond of the day, the Bishop brought a royal message that he should "renounce the wearing and usage of the Irish array;" and presented him with the King's livery, consisting of a collar of gold, weighing twenty ounces; and from the King's wardrobe a long gown of cloth of gold lined with satin, doublets of velvet and crimson satin; stomachers, shirts, and kerchiefs; hose of scarlet, violet, and black colours; bonnets, hats, and tippets of velvet, &c.* But, gorgeous and enticing as this English "array" was, it will not bear comparison with that of Cormac Mac Art many centuries before, as related in the "Book of Ballymote;"† nor of O'Donnell, respecting whose costume the Lord Deputy St. Leger, when that Irish chieftain requested "Parliament robes," informed the King that—"At such time as he mette with me he was in a cote of crymoisin velvet, with eggletts of gold, xx or xxx payer. Over that a greate doble cote of right crymoisin satin, garded with black velvet; a bonnet, with a fether set full of eggletts of gold, &c." And, as regards the twenty ounces of gold sent to tempt the Desmond, we had, and still have, far finer and more costly gold orna-

* See Gilbert's "History of the Viceroys of Ireland," p. 415.

† See O'Curry's "Lectures on the Manuscript Materials of Ancient Irish History," p. 45.

ments even of Pagan times; and only the other day an antique gold ornament, weighing twenty-six and a-half ounces, was procured by the Royal Irish Academy from the county of Tipperary.

Eventually, the bishopric of Annaghdown was incorporated with that of Tuam; but it does not appear, from the histories, to have been given up without a struggle; and the adjoining castle, which is probably of De Burgo origin, was significantly placed on the south shore of the little creek between the residence of the diocesan and his cathedral: while, at the same time, it commanded an extensive view of the country of the O'Flahertys towards the west. When the Monastery of Annaghdown was suppressed, it was granted to Richard Earl of Clanricarde.

Not many years ago there was an extensive village here, nineteen of the inhabitants of which and the adjoining townlands were drowned near Menlough, when sailing in a rickety old boat with their sheep to Galway fair, which event gave origin to one of the most mournful of the Irish laments of recent days. Now there is but one house remaining, inhabited by the man who attends the steamer, and who will act as a guide to persons anxious to explore the ruins.

Passing up the road to the east, we reach the crumbling walls, constructed chiefly of round, undressed stones, of an extensive monastic building, of which the succeeding illustration is a faithful representation.

Attached to the north side of the monastery is the Abbey

Church, the west gable and the north walls of which are still standing, as also a portion of the south walls at the west, where it is supported by a remarkably well-built buttress of dressed stone, evidently of much later date. The entire length of this *Domhnach-mor*, or large cathedral church, is 108 feet 9 inches, by 21 feet 2 inches broad in the clear, of which space the chancel occupies 17½ feet by 14½, having a reveal of four feet on each side.

The northern entrance, near the western end, which is still intact, has a deeply-moulded pointed arch; but that on the south, which was probably nearer the east, for the accommodation of

the clerics, is undistinguishable. The choir arch has also been completely destroyed; but several of the stones of the clustered pillars that supported it can be seen strewn around, or forming headstones to modern graves. Owing to the luxuriant growth of the dwarf elder, which has overgrown all the ground in and around the ruins, it is difficult in summer time to discover or explore the plan of these, as well as those of other ruins that are now choked with brambles and underwood.

During past times here and elsewhere, religious fanaticism, and the ignorance and want of taste in the gentry and farming classes, or the mischievousness of peasant boys, injured many of our most beautiful sacred edifices; and now, when improved education among the former, and depopulation among the latter, have arrested these desecrations, weeds, brambles, and wild shrubs hold undisputed rule among the historic landmarks of the past. Visiting the cultivated demesnes often located in the immediate vicinity of some of these Irish ruins, and admiring the carefully-shaven grass-plots and highly cultivated gardens and parterres, the antiquary cannot help wondering why a few pounds have not been expended upon the preservation of edifices once devoted to the service of religion, illustrative of the greatest architectural period of the country, and frequently containing the mausolea of the ancestors of their proprietors. And when, again, we see large sums of money expended on erecting ugly unarchitectural structures for religious worship, we cannot help asking ourselves why the clergy of Ireland, no matter what their special persuasion may be, have done nothing to re-edify or restore these monuments of the past.

Clearing away some of the rubbish that had accumulated under the site of the chancel arch, we lately discovered two remarkable tombstones, both unhappily broken, and without inscriptions; but each significant of its date and origin—probably of the fifteenth century. The succeeding cut is that of an unhewn, irregularly shaped flag, 27 inches by 20, lying underneath a sycamore tree, that nearly fills the choir; and the other, bearing a fleur-de-lis ornament, may be seen at a short distance from it. They were both, probably, those of ecclesiastics, many notabilities of which class, especially of the O'Malley and Mac Flynn families, were buried here. There is one small trefoil-headed window in the north wall of the long nave, and another narrow light in the chancel of this church; but the south light in the latter part is still in partial preservation, and its lion's-headed impost on the east side is uninjured. A large chasm in the wall marks the site of the east window.—See page 71.

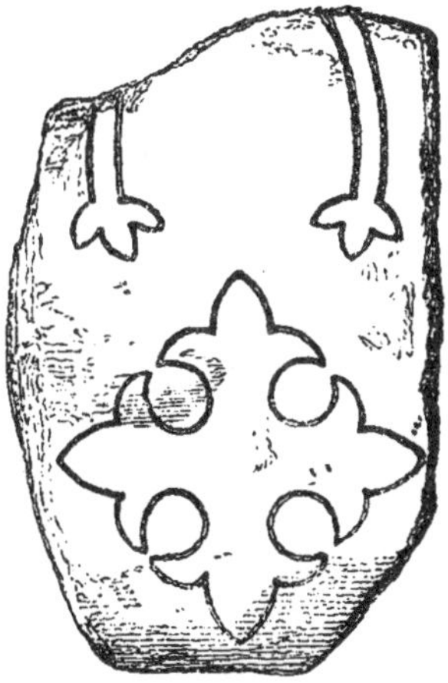

Archdall, in his "Monasticon Hibernicum," published in 1786, mentions the nunnery at Annaghdown, which, together with the town of Kelgel, was, by a bull of Pope Celestine III., granted, in 1195, to the nuns of the Order of Aroacea; likewise the Abbey of St. Mary *de Portu Patrum*, for white nuns of the Premonstre Order (probably the present ruin), a Franciscan friary, and the college of St. Brendan.

To the north-east of the abbey is the nunnery church, undoubtedly the oldest structure now remaining at Annaghdown, and the west gable of which, with its small bell tower, is shown in the general view of the ruins, at page 67. It possesses no architectural attraction, nor any means of judging of its precise date, except a Gothic pointed doorway in the north wall, which portion is still standing, and measures 90½ feet on the outside. Around it on all sides are vestiges of stone foundations; but whether they are the remains of the ancient fort or dun, from which, according to some interpreters, the place derived its name; or, as is more probable, the walls of the nunnery buildings, it is now difficult to determine.

Still more to the east, and adjoining the road, is St. Columbkill's tree, the legend of the miraculous jump of which may be learned from the guide; and to the south stands the roofless walls of the parochial Church of England edifice, the intervening space between it and the nunnery being used as the comparatively modern burial ground.

After frequent and careful examinations we have been unable to discover any architectural feature claiming a greater antiquity for any of these ruins than the fourteenth or fifteenth century—no small primitive Pelasgic church, with its square-headed western doorway—no angular-topped window, nor any remnant of that peculiar masonry that marked the period when St. Brendan died here, or when St. Meldan was abbot or "bishop of Lough Orbsen," although it is more than probable that the present edifice stands on the site of the old. It is stated in the records, that the church of Annaghdown was built by Hugh Mor O'Flaherty in 1400, and that it was burned eleven years afterwards; but, possibly, the former entry may refer to its re-edification.

The east window of this cathedral church has been long since removed, and nothing now remains there but an irregular gap in the wall; there can, however, be little doubt that every stone of that beauteous specimen of mediæval Irish work is still in existence; and thanks to the taste, if not the honesty, of the architect of the adjacent Protestant church, it will there be found, presenting interiorly, as perfect a condition as when the adjoining church was unroofed. This building, like every other ecclesiastical structure at Annaghdown, is a ruin: and its last use—that of a ball-alley—has been discontinued for want of Sunday occupants; and the present parish church is some miles distant. This window consists of a deeply-splayed circular-headed light, 8 feet high in the clear of the opening, and 12 feet high internally. The accompanying illustration, from a photograph by Mr. Allen, for which I am indebted to the Earl of Dunraven, who lately accompanied me to this locality, expresses better than words the skill of the artist who designed the neighbouring abbey. It was drawn by Mr. Wakeman, and

it has been beautifully engraved by Mr. Oldham. On each side of the half round moulding, where the deep splay of the window joins the church wall, there is a line of decorated chevrons, in the angles formed by which on both sides, are sixty-six floral ornaments, still quite sharp, and each different from the rest, and showing the marvellous fertility in conception and design of our Irish artists, which are so well seen in metal-work and enamel on several of our most ancient shrines and croziers, and in the tracings on manuscripts, as well as in the limestone decoration of many of our churches and castles. Of the latter we have a notable example in the banqueting hall at Aughnanure, on the opposite shore of the lake, to be described further on. The annexed cut shows the base of one of the angles in this window. The church itself, which cannot be 200 years old, is, with the exception of its northern doorway, otherwise wholly undecorated. Architects acquainted with early church architecture cannot but regard this window as one of the most perfect and beautiful specimens of decorated stone work now existing in the island.

In the "Annals of the Four Masters" we find the following entry:—"A.D. 1238, the *Cloictheach* of Annadown was erected." This is the latest notice of a *Cloic Teach*,* "bell

* The term *Cloic-Teach*, Bell frie or Bell's house, for the Round Towers was first promulgated by Sir Thomas Molyneux in 1725; and he was very near to the discovery of all their true uses, although he fell into the error propagated by Lynch ("Cambrensis Eversus") and Walsh, as to their Danish construction. His words respecting the "*Clogacha*, the

house" or round tower, erected in Ireland, and antiquarians have anxiously sought for it; but after a rigorous scrutiny on several occasions, we have not been able to discover the slightest vestige of any such structure in or about the ruins of Annaghdown; and the hypothesis that the foregoing notice might refer to a square belfry like that at Clare-Galway Abbey, is quite untenable. We think the difficulty can be solved, by introducing to the reader or tourist the remains of the beautiful round tower of Kilcoona, in the adjoining

name by which they are still called among the native Irish," are—"Now the Irish does plainly owe its etymology to *Clugga*, a German-Saxon word, that signifies a bell, from whence we also have borrowed our modern word, a clock. This appellation also shows the end for which these towers were built,—for belfries or steeples, where was hung a bell to call the people to religious worship; but the cavity or hollow space within being so narrow, we may conclude the bell must needs be small, one of a larger size not having room to ring out or turn round, which argues, too, they are ancient; for the larger bells are an invention of the later times, and were not used in the earlier ages of the Church."—See his "Discourse concerning the Danish Mounts, Forts, and Towers, in Ireland," which, although first published in 1725, and afterwards with Boate's "Natural History of Ireland," was written in 1711, as appears from his manuscript which was in my possession when I wrote his memoir in the "Gallery of Illustrious Irishmen," No. XIII., which appeared in the "Dublin University Magazine" in 1841. The passage from that memoir, quoted by Dr. Petrie at page 10 of his great work upon "The Origin and Uses of the Round Towers of Ireland," does not particularly refer to the Cloicṫeach, but concerns the stele, or monumental stones or pillars of sepulchral origin, and the "mounts erected over soldiers killed in battle."

small parish of that name, and which has heretofore been unnoticed by any writer on the subject.—See page 78.

Passing round the little creek to the south of the ecclesiastical ruins, we reach the walled-in bounteous well of St. Brendan, and gain access to the tall, square tower-castle figured below, that forms so conspicuous and attractive an object, both from the lake and land sides all round. It is exceedingly well built, and, like all the castellated remains in this district, batters gradually at the base. The entrance, on the south face, is by a pointed-arch doorway, strongly fortified by all the defensive contrivances of the period, and the character of the warfare of the time. To the left of the porch is a long flag-

roofed guard-room and square door. Two other doorways, with angle-arched heads open, one into a small chamber, and the other into the winding stone stairs that gave access to the upper portion of the building. In the roof of the porch is the usual *poul-na-morrough*, through which missiles might be poured on those who had so far gained access to the inside.

In the thickness of the wall is a square tube leading from the outer door-jamb, and which was probably used for communicating with those beyond, like a modern acoustic apparatus. Other flues of a like nature, but larger, exist in different parts of the building, and also passages formed in the thickness of the walls. The corbels that supported the floors and the chimney breasts are still *in situ*, and the garde robe is on the north face. Mr. Parker, in his "Essay on the Domestic Architecture of Ireland," has given an architectural "elevation" of the interior of this castle, from a drawing by Mr. Hills. In 1586 "Nicholas Lynch [held] Anaghcoyne."

To the south of the castle are the remains of an old house, said to have been that of the diocesan; and on the shore, to the south-west, is St. Cormack's Well, where "stations" are still occasionally performed on Sundays and Fridays. From a point between these two last mentioned places, the best view of the Annaghdown group of ruins may be obtained.

Besides those just described, this extensive parish contains several other objects of antiquarian and historic interest; in fact—to use the parlance employed in other writings—"too numerous to mention," unless in a minute parochial survey. It abounds in raths; and among its ruins may be mentioned—besides Drumgriffin, referred to at page 61—the tall, well-built Castle of Drumboo, with its adjoining Well of St. Cyprian, Mace Castle, the old church of Killian, and the circular-towered Castle Creevy; but, except the latter, they are either too far distant from the lake to be accessible to the tourist, or not of sufficient interest to be dwelt upon.

To the north-west of the village of Correndulla, in this parish, upon a scarped bare rock, surrounded by a dilapidated village, stand the ruins of Creevy Castle, originally square, with massive circular towers at the corners, somewhat like that of Dunmo, upon the left bank of the Boyne; portions of two of these towers still remain, and are well worthy of examination. Many legends attach to this old castle, and many romantic tales of Creevy-ny-Bourke and her husband, George Barry, are still related by the neighbouring peasantry to somewhat the following effect:—This chieftainess and her husband not agreeing, she sent him down to his fortress near Castlebar. Now in the neighbourhood of the castle, in the low, boggy district between it and Annaghdown, still exists the enchanted lake, called Lough-a-Foor, where lamentations are heard in the summer twilight, every seventh year. Out of this lake, one summer's day, a young water-horse—the Each or Coppul-uisge of Irish fairy tales—coming out to disport itself, was captured by the lady's retainers, who carried him off to the castle, where he was shut up in the stable for some time; but no one could be found to ride him. So the lady had to send for her discarded spouse, who was a celebrated equestrian. He came; and some green moss was tied on the eyes of the water-horse, so that he might not see where he was going. Off rode the horseman; and, finding the beast willing and fleet, was unwise enough to take the covering from off its eyes, upon which it dashed forward, and slew the rider, leaving portions of him at different places, and the remainder at Leaght George, referred to at page 60, where his *leaght* or stone monument was erected that has given name to the locality. It then dashed back to Lough-a-Foor, and, having plunged into the waves of its native element, has not been seen or heard of since. These legends respecting the Irish water-horse will be more particularly described in the Appendix upon the Zoology.

A deep bay borders the north-west margin of Annaghdown parish, as far as the mills of Killroe, where the parish of KILCOONA abuts upon Lough Corrib. Passing eastward from which, and crossing the main road from Galway to Headford, by Ballinduff, the seat of Mr. Gunning, and near Cahermorris, the residence of Mr. Crampton, through a country studded with raths and cahers, we reach the little church and burial ground of St. Coona, nearly in the centre of the enclosure of which stands the "butt" of the Round Tower, which I am inclined to believe is that referred to by the annalists as having been erected in 1238; and the illustration of which, from a photograph taken under the direction of Lord Dunraven, on the occasion of our visit in September, 1866, is here afforded. It stands upon a double plinth, and is now 8 feet high and 52 feet 9 inches in girth; and when I say that it was originally one of the most beautifully built round towers in Ireland, I do not think I will be accused of exaggeration by those who have given the subject consideration. The stones, some of which upon the lower course are 5 feet 2 inches long, of a yellowish white limestone, are dressed, cambered on the outside, and laid in regular courses; and in some instances, as may be seen in the engraving, cut into each other,

after the manner of the ancient Cyclopean masonry. No vestige of the doorway remains, as the present top is below the level of the usual site of that portion of a Cloictheach or Irish round tower, but it was probably on the east face. The interior of the tower is at present a solid mass of clay and stones, from which some luxuriant ivy has thrown its projecting arms around the ruin, and at the same time added to its picturesque effect. A few of the dressed stones of the tower form the headstones to modern graves; but Mr. Gunning, the present enlightened proprietor of the property on which it stands, has kindly undertaken to restore them to their original sites, and thus preserve this ancient monument from further destruction for centuries to come.

We abstain from all discussion respecting the origin and uses of the round towers of Ireland, as it remains for those who dispute their Christian origin—now so generally accepted by the learned—to answer, in the first instance, the as yet uncontradicted statements and arguments so forcibly brought forward by the late Dr. Petrie. It is questionable whether the round tower of Kilcoona was ever completed; but at present we are unable to adduce any fact, or offer any argument thereon. Is it the veritable *Cloightheach* referred to by the Four Masters, as having been erected at Annaghdown sixty-six years after the Anglo-Norman invasion? There is every probability of such being the fact; as Kilcoona parish was in the diocese and immediate district of Annaghdown, and about three miles in a direct line from the cathedral. The single entry referring to it is very short and meagre, and merely mentions the locality as Enagh-dun, and may refer to the diocese or district where there are several Enaghs or Annaghs giving names to townlands, as well as to the locality of the abbey and nunnery upon the shores of the lake.

The long, narrow parish of Kilcoona, running nearly north and south between those of Annaghdown and Killeany, occupies about two miles of lake shore, and is crossed by the high road between Galway and Headford.

It is remarkable that neither in the maps nor letters connected with the Ordnance Survey, nor any work published previous to this, has the round tower of Kilcoona been noticed. A few paces to the north-east are the ruined walls of a church, 66 feet 5 inches long, and 24 feet wide outside, with the gables still standing; but there are no carved stones throughout the building that afford us any means of conjecturing its date. Archdall says: "Tipraid, Prince of Hy-fiachria, granted the abbey of Killchunna to St. Columb, who placed St. Cuannan over it; he was maternal brother to St. Carthag, and was afterwards removed to the abbey of Lismore. This is now [1786] a parish church."

St. Cuanna, or Coona, who was born towards the close of the sixth century, was a son of Midarnus, son of Dubhratpa, son of Ennius, son of Niall of the Nine Hostages, the great King of Ireland. His mother was Meda, or Finneda, daughter of Fingen, a nobleman in the western district of Munster, and whose origin was derived from the tribe and territory of Corca-duibhne. She is said to have been the mother of four distinguished men, the first of whom, Carthagius, son of Findallus, was Abbot of Rathen, in Meath, and afterwards Bishop of Lismore, in Munster. The second, St. Cuanna, whose festival and natal day is the 4th of February, from being a monk of Lismore, became "Abbot of the Monastery of Kill-chuanna, in the western district of Connaught." He is said to have died about the year 650, and is reputed to have written a chronicle of his own time, or Annals of Ireland, up to A. D. 628; for Sir James Ware, in his "Writers of Ireland," thus refers to him—"Cuan, or Cuanach, is an author often quoted in the Annals of Ulster as low down as the year 628, but not afterwards, by the name of the Book of Cuan, or Cuanach, from whence I conjecture that he was the author of a chronicle, and flourished about this time." There were, however, other Coonas of a later date. In the fragments of his history collected in the *Acta Sanctorum* many prodigies are recorded, especially as to his manner of crossing the lake upon a flat stone with his followers from Gnomore; but it is also stated that he collected around him, at his church and monastery of Kilcoonagh, a great number of learned Christian men, when the whole of this region, from Clare-Galway to Cong, was fertile with piety, learning, and art. Some members of the reformed churches may sneer at the history of those good men, who, professing the pure faith and doctrine of Patrick, "once delivered to the saints," went forth as missionaries among the wild, half pagan natives of the West, to Christianize, civilize, and instruct; and who left their names, and in many instances their monuments, in these parishes. But sifting the marvellous from the probable, or possible, and allowing for the age in which these facts or traditions were written, it may possibly appear that those missionaries were as pure in their lives, as unselfish, as scriptural in their doctrine, and as useful in their generation as those sent out at immense expense in our own days to Christianize the Pagan, the Mahometan, or the Buddhist.

The local tradition is to the effect, that Saints Eany and Fursæus, who gave names to the adjoining parishes, were sons of Meda, and brothers of Cuanna, but the hagiology is is not clear upon the subject. The saint's well, called *Dabhach Chuana*, formerly much frequented by pilgrims, lies in the adjacent townland of Knockreen.

Within Mr. Gunning's demesne of Ballinduff stands an old castle of the Skerritts, where a fierce contest took place in 1469 between Clanricarde and O'Donnell; and in 1586 it was held by "Mac Walter, called Thomas M'Henry." Not far distant, in the wood by the roadside, is shown a stone bearing the footprint of a bull, concerning which there are many legends afloat.*

* The tale is by popular tradition brought down to a late date, when Donnall Cam, who was cowherd to the lord of the neighbouring castle, and one evening saw a strange bull visiting one of his cows. It left its track in the rock, where it is still seen; and the herd having related the circumstance to his master, he was desired to keep the "beastings" for him; but, tasting some of them himself, he became a prophet or soothsayer, or was endowed with the gift of second sight. According to another version, this bull and cow were the first seen in that part of the country. This story adds another to the many legendary tales respecting cattle in Ireland.—See the Author's "Essay on the Unmanufactured Animal Remains in Ireland," and also that upon the "Ancient Oxen of Ireland," in the Proceedings of the Royal Irish Academy.

With reference to Castle Creevy, referred to at page 77, the following version of the legend has been furnished me:—George Barry was the son of the Widow Burke, who had a farm convenient to Lough Afoor, the land of which she had well cultivated. When the corn grew up, it was terribly damaged every night, although no one knew what ate it. The

To the north of Annaghdown, and the west of Kilcoona, is the parish of KILLEANEY, which, although not large, occupies a considerable extent of the lake's margin. It derives its name from Eidhne, or Eaney (a very common name formerly in the West), who, as already stated, is said to have been the brother of Coona and Fursæus; but, after investigating the subject, O'Donovan has left the following record:—"This St. Einne is the famous Endeus of Aranmore." The parish is sometimes called *Cloch-an-Uabhair* (pronounced Clough-an-our), "The Stone of Pride," which, with the adjoining castle of the same name, can be seen on the roadside, between Clare-Galway and Headford; and there is a tradition of a celebrated witch, called *Cailleach-an-Uabhair*, "The Hag of Pride," who cast this stone hither from a distant hill, and left the marks of her thumb and three fingers upon it.* It

field was watched; and then, in the dead of night, a number of horses were seen to rise out of the lake, and come to graze on the young corn. The watchers captured one of them, which remained at Castle Creevy for a year and a day, until taken out to hunt by the young master; and, having got a glimpse of its native element, it became furious, and perpetrated the catastrophe referred to in the text. Shortly afterwards a female was seen rising out of the lake, who told the neighbours that the horse was enchanted; and that, if it had been kept one day longer in confinement, the enchantment would have ceased.

* These ancient stone markings, cups, foot and finger prints, circles, lozenges, volutes, &c., such as I figured and described many years ago upon the monuments of the Boyne, are now receiving the attention they deserve; and the subject has lately been investigated with great care by Sir James Y. Simpson, Bart., of Edinburgh, in his beautiful work upon "Archaic Sculptures," just published.

lies a few paces to the south of the castle. The old church and saint's well are to the south-east of the castle, but present no features of interest. Near this castle passes a very "tempting" stream for the angler, which carries off the water from Doolough, and some of the eastern turloghs, and delivers itself into a deep adjoining bay of Lough Corrib.

At the northern extremity of this parish, and on the high road from Galway to Cong, although not within the parochial boundary, stands the little town of Headford, still called in Irish *Ath-Cuinn*, "The Head of the Ford," which contained 993 inhabitants in 1861. Beside it is the beautiful residence and extensive demesne of R. M. St. George, Esq.

Near the shore, opposite Lee's Island, which the steamer passes on the starboard side, there is an ancient stone fort called Caher-Aidne, and, like all the other parishes along the lake, numerous caves, lisseens, raths, and cairns can be seen therein. The island contains 47½ acres, and was in former days a scene, as well as the cause, of a memorable dispute between the O'Flahertys and the O'Lees.

We now pass between the parishes of Cargin and Killannin, and approach the Ferry of Knock, where the lake narrows to about a quarter of a mile in width. This was formerly the chief passage between Iar Connaught and Connemara, on the south-west; and the barony of Clare, in Galway, and the Mayo side of the lake, on the north-east. Upon the northern side there is a low shrubby growth of hazel, giving it the name of Kylebeg, or "the little wood;" and at the pier here the steamer stops for a short time. It is in the parish of Cargin, which will occupy our attention in the next chapter. The transit here was formerly effected by a large flat-bottomed boat or float, capable of holding carriages and cattle; but foot passengers were taken across in small boats. It has been proposed to construct a causeway and bridge at this point, and such would certainly be a great convenience to the counties of Mayo and Galway on either side of the lake; but at the same time it is fair to add, that it should be an imperial, or at least a national, not a local undertaking. There are also some engineering objections to the proposed site; but these might be got rid of by choosing a better one, a little to the north-west. Should, however, the distress which, it is said, now threatens West Connaught and Connamara, extend, no more useful public work could be desired for this district.

CHAPTER V.

KYLEBEG TO INCHIQUIN.

CARGIN PARISH, CHURCH, AND CASTLE. KILLEENS. INISCREAWA. ANNALS OF LOUGH CORRIB. IRISH PAGAN AND CHRISTIAN ARCHITECTURE. CAHERGAL. CLYDAGH. KILLURSA PARISH. HISTORY OF ST. FURSA. INCHIQUIN. CASTLE OF ANNAKEEN. CAIRNS. GIANTS' GRAVES. CHURCH OF ST. FURSA. EARLY IRISH CHURCH ARCHITECTURE. ROSS-ERRILLY. THE LOCUST PLAGUE. MOYNE CASTLE. THE BLACK RIVER.

THE parish of CARGIN, although small in extent, is one of great interest in an historic and pictorial point of view. It extends eastwards between that of Killeany, on the south-east, and Killursa, on the north-west, over a space about three miles long, and one broad; but, owing to the wooded promontories of Kylebeg and Clydagh, its shore margin is of much greater extent; and between these projections, a deep bay passes inwards for about three quarters of a mile.

The old church of this parish is of no great interest or antiquity, and neither to it nor to this parish itself is the term "Kill" applied, but the ruin is called *Seipul-a-Cargin*, "The Chapel of Cargin," and in all probability it was a chapel of ease to some of the saints' churches in the neighbouring parishes. Around it are the remains of a circular rath, and beside it a *Killeen*, or children's burial ground, of which class of cemetery there are great numbers in the West, but especially along the shores of Loughs Corrib and Mask.*

The ruined Castle of Cargin, here presented, stands on an eminence at the extremity of the little bay, and, with the adjoining islet, helps to form, with its ivy-mantled walls, a very picturesque group when viewed from the steamer's deck. Thanks to the good taste of the present proprietor, the con-

dition of this castle forms a striking contrast with that of the great majority of ancient castles along our route, which

* *Killeen*, a "little church"—applied to diminutive graveyards, nearly always used for children, and generally for those who have died unbaptized, respecting which many curious popular superstitions are still afloat in the minds of the ignorant.

for the most part are used as barns, stables, or cowhouses. There is no history, nor are there any legends attaching to this ancient castle, which measures externally 40 feet by 30.*

In the little bay in front stands Iniscreawa, or "wild-garlic Isle," where, says O'Flaherty, in his "West Connaught," "the walls and high ditch of a well-fortified place are still extant, and encompass almost the whole island. Of this isle Macamh Iniscreawa, a memorable antient magician, as they say, had his denomination. Anno 1225, the Lord Justice of Ireland, coming into the port of Iniscreawa, caused Odo O'Flaherty, Lord of West Connaught, to deliver that island, Kirke Island, and all the boats of Lough Orbsen, into the hands of Odo O'Connor, King of Connaught (Cathald Redfist's son), for assurance of his fidelity."

The great uncemented Cyclopean stone fort to which this ex-

* In the State Paper styled "The Division of Connaught," already referred to at page 49, it is said that in 1586 William Gaynard held the Castle of Carigin; Mac Reamon Cloghenwoyr; Moyler Mac Reamon, Anaghkyne; Tybbot Lyogh, Loscananon; Ullig Rogh, Drumgriffin; "Walter fitz-Ab, fitz-Ed., Masse;" and M'Walter's sept, Cahrmorise; all of which are referred to in this work.

tract refers still encircles the brow of the little island, as shown in the foreging illustration, for which, as well as that of Cargin Castle, the author is indebted to Miss E. Lynch-Staunton; but the scrubby brushwood around it partially obscures the masonry, which stands over a deep trench or fosse, that must have rendered its capture a matter of much difficulty before the general introduction of fire arms. In all probability it served like a crannoge to guard Cargin Castle, or as a safe refuge for the persons and valuables of its inmates, or those of the surrounding country. There can, however, be no doubt that this structure belongs to the days of the unmortared duns, cahers, and cashels long prior to the date of the Anglo-Norman invasion. The walls average 6 feet thick, and are still 10½ feet high; but the stones of which they are composed, owing in all probability to the fact of their having been carried from the neighbouring mainland, are of comparatively small size. They enclose an oval space of 144 yards in circumference; and the doorway is on the east or land side, where the ditch is level to afford means of access. The present name of the island on the Ordnance Map is Illaun-Carbery, because a fanatic named Carbery lived for many years during the last century in a hut he built for himself within the enclosure.

To the foregoing notice of the depredations upon Lough Corrib in early times may be added the following, A. D. 929:—"The Danes of Limerick took possession of Lough Orbsen, and pillaged its islands." A. D. 1061 the O'Flahertys of the adjoining territory of Magh Scola, already referred to at page

19, took possession of Lough Orbsen, and expelled Hugh O'Conor; and in 1224, after the death of Cathal Crovedearg, the red-handed son of King Turlough, and during the contentions between the O'Conors of Connaught, Hugh, the son of Cathal, compelled the O'Flahertys to deliver up this island, as referred to in the foregoing extract.

In 1233 Felim O'Conor, King of Connaught, "demolished the castles of Kirk Island, Galway, Hag Island, and Donoman." Again, "in 1256 Walter De Burgo, Lord of Connaught, and first Earl of Ulster, marched against Roderick O'Flaherty, plundered the territories of Gnomore and Gnobeg, west of Lough Orbsen, and took possession of the lake, its islands and castles. These he fortified, and by that means considerably increased the power of the English in Connaught." In all probability it was at this period, and from thence up to 1450, that the great majority of the De Burgo castles in this western district were built or remodelled.

As this ancient fortress of Iniscreawa is the first of its class to which the visitor or the reader has been introduced, a word respecting the style of architecture of its period may not be out of place. The ancient architectural remains which occur in our route are of two classes—Pagan and Christian. The former are chiefly monumental, sepulchral, and military, or that form of building that served for domestic and defensive purposes, and most of them belong to the prehistoric period; so that of the precise date of their erection, or even the many centuries included in the cycle during which they were constructed, we have no more means of judging than we have of those of Stonehenge, or of similar structures elsewhere throughout the world. A few are referred to in history, but the chronology of the annalists as to the period of their construction is questionable. The space of time over which they extend must have been very great, but they are nearly all of the same type: cairn, circle, cashel, cave, cloughaun, and pillar stone, are but repetitions of the same idea, and show no material advance, nor any progress towards the development of a higher order of art, or greater aptitude of purpose in their construction, from century to century. They were all built without mortar or cement, and usually of very large blocks of stone. That some of them were occupied and defended, even after the Anglo-Norman invasion, there can be no doubt, as such circumstances are stated in history. The earthen raths and lisses are in a like category. The opinion as to the Danish origin of these ancient structures, which has so long obtained credence in this country that it has become a "popular superstition," is beginning to fade; and will in time, as investigation extends and knowledge increases, be obliterated.* If by "Danes" are meant the very early fair-complexioned Tuatha de Danann colonists, who, it is said, came back to us from the north of Europe, the association

* See the Author's "The Beauties of the Boyne," 2nd edition, p. 70.

may be congruous; but if by the Danes is implied the Norsemen, who commenced their invasions in the middle of the ninth century, and held sway in parts of Ireland until conquered at Clontarf, it is an egregious mistake.

Of the latter, or Christian edifices, we have the ruins of the ancient castles, or fortified dwellings, extending from the twelfth to the seventeenth century, and some few of the modern mansions of the present time; but the objects of most interest in this class are the ecclesiastical remains of oratories, churches, abbeys, convents, monasteries, crosses, and monumental stones, &c.; and to many of these we are able, either from an examination of their architecture, or from absolute history, to assign a date. Of late it has become the fashion to ignore early Irish architecture, and assign a twelfth century date, and a Norman origin to every carved, moulded, punched, or chiselled stone found in connexion with our ecclesiastical and Christian monuments. That there was a very wide-spread and improved taste in ecclesiastical architecture and stone decoration throughout North-western Europe from the year 1000 to 1200, and that it was chiefly exhibited in Normandy, is admitted: and that that taste found its way into Ireland, and subsequently influenced artistic design here, is equally true. But so long as the elaborately decorated doors and sculptured effigies on some of our round towers, and the sculptured crosses at Monasterboice, Cashel, Clonmacnoise, Kells, and other places, some of them bearing inscriptions denoting the date of their erection, remain; and so long as we possess the early churches of Raheen, Killaloe, Cormac's Chapel at Cashel, and the church at Inniscaltra, which it is said was remodelled by Brian Boromhe in the early part of the eleventh century; and while there are before us the sculptures on Devenish Tower, Donoghmore, and (very probably), those in the Saint's Church at Inchangoill; and until we find a counterpart, or even the crudest idea elsewhere, of that peculiar Irish tracery which adorns same of our early churches, crosses, tombs, shrines, and crosiers, &c., it may be assumed that during the three centuries preceding 1172 we had in Ireland men with taste and wealth to pay for, artists capable of designing, and tradesmen competent to the task of producing such works, in either stone, metal, or enamel. Our still remaining specimens of early Irish art afford irrefragable proofs of such culture; and until it is proved that the pre-Christian antiques in the Museum of the Royal Irish Academy are of foreign origin; or until those "twelfth-century" advocates have controverted the foregoing statements, it is unnecessary to descant further on the subject in a work merely intended to direct the steps of the tourist through a region hitherto but scantily explored, and to rescue from oblivion, or preserve from desecration, some of the historic monuments of the country.

About two miles east of the lake, in this parish, stands *Cahergal*, or "Whitefort," one of the finest specimens of ancient military architecture on the mainland of Ireland, and which can easily be reached by the roads leading from Kylebeg or Clydagh to Headford. From its colour it gives its English name to the townland, as, for similar reasons, we meet with the names of Roundfort and Darkfort, &c., in other localities.

This magnificent circular Cyclopean building, a portion of the external face of which is well shown in the subjoined illustration, encloses a space of 137 feet in diameter; and its massive

walls of unhewn stone, of a whitish hue, from the lichens covering them, are 9 feet 4 inches thick, and, although lowered in many places, still average 7 feet 7 inches high.

The entrance on the south-eastern side, over the road leading to a farm house, is 7 feet 6 inches wide; its external jambs, measuring 5 feet 8 inches over ground, are each 5 feet broad, and 21 inches thick. Inside, on the south-east, is a flight of three massive steps, figured on the next page, which probably led to a parapet, as at Stague fort, in Kerry. Within the enclosure there are the remains of several intersecting walls; but, as the space is grass-grown, it is difficult to say whether they are the ruins of *Cloughaunes,** or the top structures of caves, of the existence of which there is a tradition.

Of this class of defensive building, erected, in all probability, in the days of the Belgic and Danann colonization, like those in the western Isles of Aran, no question need be asked the peasant; for his only reply will be, "Ogh, sure, it was med by the giants in ancient times, or maybe by the Danes; anyway it's there as long as I remember, or my father afore me, or any of the ould people about." Fairy occupation is never associated with these structures, although every green fort, rath, and lisheen (probably of earlier origin), is still in the imagination and traditional folk lore of our remaining rural population inhabited by "the good people."

In the valley to the south of this great caher (which term is fully explained by this structure), there is said to have

* Cloughaunes are small uncemented, or dry-wall huts, generally circular or oval in shape, and having their domed stone roofs constructed with flags gradually projecting inwards like those of some of the Pyramids—and the tumuli of Newgrange and Dowth, &c. They abound in the Aran Isles, and in Kerry.—See Mr. Du Noyer's account of the city of Fahin, and the author's Catalogue of Antiquities in the Royal Irish Academy, &c.

existed two similar stone works, the sites of which are pointed out; and it is reported that one of them afforded building materials for the barracks of Headford, some years ago.

To return to our itinerary—on the northern shore of the little bay containing Iniscreawa, and turning round by the south-east margin of the lake, with a sloping green sward running down to the water's edge, and surrounded by well-grown timber, and tastefully laid out pleasure grounds, stands Clydagh, the handsome residence of George Lynch-Staunton, Esq., of which the subjoined woodcut, taken from a photograph, is a faithful representation.

Mr. Lynch-Staunton descends from the ancient Anglo-Norman family of De Staunton, of whom Sir Malger was the head in 1129. The present proprietor of Clydagh assumed (under the will of his relative, Sir G. Staunton, Bart.), the name of Staunton, in addition to that of Lynch, in 1859.

We read, that "Among the Englyshe greate rebelles of

Connaught in 1515 were Syr Myles Staunton's sonnes." Some of the Stonduns of Mayo, after the death of Edmund Burke, in 1338, were so much ashamed of the transaction, that they assumed the name of Mac Evilly—*Mac a Mhilid*, "Son of the Knight."*

A part of the extensive demesne of Mr. St. George, of Headford, already referred to at p. 85, is within this parish; and to the west of the Galway road, near where it joins that of Killursa, may be seen a remarkable ancient enclosure, with several standing stones circling the brow of a small hill, and called *Lisheennabasty*, or the "little fort of the serpent," or worm.†

KILLURSA—properly *Kill-Fursa*, in commemoration of Fursæus, a celebrated Irish saint and traveller—margins Lough Corrib, in continuation of Cargin, on the south; and forms the terminal parish of the barony of Clare, and county of Galway, on its eastern shore. Its northern boundary is the Owenduff, or "Black River," which, passing under ground below Shrule, rises again to the surface to the east of the castle of

* See description of Oilean-an-Iarla in Lough Mask; also Hardiman's Notes to O'Flaherty's "H-Iar Connaught," p. 47.

† *Peast*, "a worm," serpent, or beast, like the Latin *bestia*, is a term that frequently enters into topographical names in Ireland. Worm holes—*poul na peasti*—are common, and applied to deep caverns with water at bottom. Although St. Patrick "gave the frogs and toads a twist, and banished all the varmin," there are still traditions of water serpents in abundance; but, like the great sea serpent, these animals have not been seen of late.

Moyne, and, running by the ruins of Ross, enters the lake about a mile beyond the castle of Annakeen. Irish hagiology abounds with notices of the Christian celebrities of this district in the sixth and seventh centuries. In the large Island of Inchiquin, belonging to this parish, and now on our starboard quarter, it is stated that St. Brendan founded a religious establishment, which was afterwards increased by St. Meldan, of the Hua-Cuinn family, from whom the Island of *Inch-in-Cuinn* took its name. Fintan, King of Munster, with his Queen, Gelgies, daughter of the King of Connaught, in consequence of some troubles in his province, fled to Lough Orbsen, and was hospitably entertained by his relative, Brendan; and while residing with him in his *Cella Hospitum* at Rathmath, in Inchiquin, had a son, who was christened Fursa, or Fursæus. He flourished between A. D. 584 and 652, and his festival is kept on the 16th of January; but several other days are given in Irish ecclesiastical writings for that event. He is said traditionally to have had two brothers, Eidne or Ainey, and Coona, who have given names to the adjoining parishes of Killeany and Kilcoona, as stated at page 83.

Killursa is now united with Cargin, and also with Killannin on the opposite shore of the lake, in the Roman Catholic Union of Headford, at present occupied by the Rev. Peter Conway, to whose zeal and energy his parishioners are indebted for the erection of St. Mary's at Headford, one of the handsomest rural chapels in Ireland, built at a cost of about £4000, chiefly collected in America.

The steamer, in her course along the lake, approaches sufficiently near this parish to give us a good view of the castle of Annakeen, especially in the down trip; as, passing upwards, a knoll of land projecting into the lake obscures the prospect. Landing in a small bay, guarded on the north by the little bluff island of Bull's Eye, now quite green, but the major portion of which is probably artificial, and which, in all like-

lihood, occupied towards the adjoining castle the same relation, as regards defence and security, which Iniscreawa did with respect to the castle of Cargin (see page 89), we stand upon the parish of Killursa; and a few paces bring us to the walls of this very ancient castle, figured in the preceding cut, taken from a photograph by Mr. O'Reilly, kindly supplied by the Rev. Mr. Conway

It is a square keep, the outer walls of which are perfect, except upon the north side. That upon the lake or west side is 46 feet long; and that on the south, here represented, is 50 feet. There are also some remains of the outer enclosure, and the whole is surrounded by a very beautiful park of the finest land, ornamented with some aged ash. Of all the castles surrounding Lough Corrib, this would appear from its masonry to be the oldest; for, although it has not been dilapidated for building purposes, it is not possible to find in or around it a single dressed stone of any description! the quoins, doorways, and window openings being, with the walls, both within and without, all formed of undressed stone. Perhaps there is not in the British Isles a similar example of such admirably constructed masonry of its class and period. At the north-west corner there is a square tower, and probably a similar one existed on the north-east. All the outer walls of this structure are six feet thick, and contain passages leading to the upper apartments and the parapet. Some of the arches of the windows and doors are circular, and others pointed; but all ingeniously constructed with stones to which a hammer or chisel was never applied—in like manner as in the arch of the east window in the beautiful old church of Cross, and as we find in other localities where the great abundance and variety in form of the surrounding limestone afforded ample materials for any description of building, and the ingenuity of the artists was equal to the task of rendering them subservient to architectural purposes. Even to the present day, every man in this and the adjoining limestone districts is more or less a mason.

Among the structural peculiarities of this castle is that of having upon the outer face of the ground story small, low, arched apertures leading into guard rooms or sentry cells, but in other instances communicating with the walled passages above. The marking of the wattled centring upon which the arches were laid, so many centuries ago, shows the great strength of the mortar used at the time of their erection; for it is as hard and sharp as when the basket-work, on which it was raised, was removed; and in the upper apartment of the north-west tower the roof is perfectly flat.

As there is no stone now remaining at Annakeen to afford us a clue to the date of its erection, neither is there any history which throws much light upon the subject. That, however, it was a place of note in very early times, may be learned from the fact that in 1324 Sir William, or Ulick De Burgh, the first Mac William Oughter, son of Sir William the Grey, and the progenitor of the Clan-Rickard, was called "*Ulicus de Anaghkeen;*" and certainly the architecture of the castle may with safety be ascribed to a date five and a half centuries ago.*

* In 1586 Nicholas Lynch was possessed of the Castle of "Annaghcoyne;" and when, in 1619, James I. confirmed the possession of the Castle Hacket estate to the Burkes of that place, as was done to all Irish proprietors who

In the immediate vicinity stands the unfinished residence of B. O'Flaherty, Esq., of Galway; but the lord of the soil is Captain Carter, whose family once possessed the greater portion of the lands in this locality, and the unfinished house of one of whose ancestors, called by the country people *Teach Carter*, may be seen on the lake shore opposite Inchiquin.

Here, as elsewhere throughout Ireland, the ruins are grouped with others of different eras and uses. A little to the east of the old castle there are the vestiges of the church and burial ground of St. Cronin; and a short distance to the north-east thereof a considerable cairn, which may be seen from the lake, crowns an eminence in a neighbouring field; while, following the inland road, we soon arrive at Doonaun Fort and Eynagh graveyard, in the townland of Carrowakil, on the south of the road opposite which there is one of those early Pagan structures known as "giants' graves," and here significantly called by the people *Leabhy-an-Fear-mor*—the bed or "grave of the big man." The fort has recently been in great part obliterated, although a few of the large flagstones are still standing; and, as it is asserted that human bones of large dimensions were found in it, I may here remark that no human bones of a gigantic size were ever found in an Irish burial place, either ancient or modern. The Leabhy crowns a little mammillary

surrendered their estates for the purpose of getting a new title to them, and erected the same, the Manor of Castle Hacket, the castle and lands of Annakeen are included in the list of lands forming it.

elevation, and consists of an oblong enclosure, running nearly east and west, and having at the eastern end several of the large upright flagstones still remaining. These "giants' graves" are not uncommon, although not of such frequent occurrence as the stone circles, the inner enclosure of which originally supported the hive-shaped domes.

Passing beside Clover Hill in an easterly direction, by St. Kieran's Well, and through a group of ancient forts and raths, we reach the extensive graveyard and ruined church of Killursa, erroneously styled on the Ordnance Map Kildaree, from the neighbouring townland of that name, although O'Donovan, in his letters, has given a distinct description of it, as well as a drawing of the western doorway, which forms a remarkable feature of this ruin. All the walls are still standing, although considerably dilapidated; it was of the *Daimhlaig-mor* class of church, and measures 70 feet 6 inches, by 24 feet on the outside. The southern doorway is a pointed arch; and the east window, which, compared with the extent of the building, is of unusual height, was a fine specimen of pointed Gothic architecture, and was probably erected in the sixteenth century; it is 11 feet 6 inches high, and 3 feet 4 inches in the clear. The well-cut stone mullions still remain; but the outer spaces were built up years ago, when, perhaps, the poverty or persecution of the parishioners prevented its repair. A cross wall cuts off 9 feet 4 inches of the western end, which portion was probably occupied in later times by the officiating priest or friar. A similar wall exists in the little church of Ross Hill, at Lough Mask.

The characteristic feature of this church is the small square-headed sloping-jambed doorway, near the southern angle of the western gable, of the great antiquity of which there can be no doubt; and which is probably a remnant of the early church founded here by St. Fursa, when, disgusted with the state of affairs at Inchiquin, he came over to the mainland, and established a religious house in this parish. The dimensions of this doorway are—5 feet 4 inches in height, 2 feet wide at top, and 2 feet 5 inches at the bottom. Nearly all the stones of its sides occupy the entire thickness of the wall, which here measures 2 feet, and are undressed on the ends; but upon the inside they are all perfectly smooth, as if they had been first put in their places in a rough state, and were then sawn or rubbed down into their present condition. The lintel, which is a rough, unhewn, weather-worn flag, 3 feet 8 inches long, does not appear to have been part of the original structure, and is quite incongruous with the rest of the doorway, in openings of which class the lintel is generally of great size and thickness. The probability is that, in the original church, this doorway stood in the centre of the west gable; and that when, in the process of centuries, the present church was reconstructed on the site of the old, it was enlarged towards the north, as well as in length, the doorway being left *in situ*, and the present lintel placed upon it.

These square-headed, so-called Cyclopean doorways, with sloping sides, are characteristic of our very early Irish churches; although, as in the case of that at Inishmain, on Lough Mask, they are occasionally associated with the florid architecture of a much more recent period, and evidently of foreign introduction. They abound in the Lough Corrib district, as at Kilcathail, below Knockdoe,* Kilfraughaun, Inishmain, Ross Hill, Inchangoill, and Killannin.

There are no materials whereby we can reproduce a picture of Irish public or domestic architecture beyond that of the dun, cashel, cave, fort, caher, or cloughaun, the togher, pillar stone, Druidical religious circle, the cromleach, or the sepulchral monument, at the time when St. Patrick served as a bondsman or swine feeder to Milchu, one of the chieftains of Dalaradia, in the beginning of the fifth century. The people worshipped in the open air, under the spreading oak, around the stone enclosure, or beside the hallowed well; the laws were administered by the Brehon from the fort or rath; the kings and chieftains were inaugurated standing upon, or beside, the consecrating stone; the games and festive meetings were all outdoor transactions; the great as-

* Kilcathail, the church of St. Cathaldus, stands by the road-side, about four miles from Clare-Galway, on the way to Tuam.—See "H-Iar Connaught," p. 369. O'Donovan has given a drawing of it in his Ordnance Letters on Galway. By an oversight the window in Annaghdown, figured and described at p. 72, is stated to be 8 feet high. It is 6 feet 8 inches high, and 2 feet 10 inches wide in the clear of the opening.

semblies were held in wattled halls; and the people lived in stone-roofed houses, caves, cabins made of tempered clay, or wattled structures, either on the mainland, or in crannoges or lacustrine habitations, and were buried beneath the cairn or tumulus, &c. Thus, when the early Christian missionaries, in the days of Pelagius and Patricius, wished to erect a church in Erinn, the domestic cloughaun and the wattled hut furnished the types from whence the stone oratory or monastic cell, and the wooden *Duirteach* were derived—partly church, and partly dwelling-house for the officiating cleric—as at Gallerus, Kells, and Kilfrughaun.

There are, however, special characteristics by which such primitive Irish or Pelasgic churches as now exist may be distinguished. These features may be summed up by size, form of masonry, and the shape and position of their doors and windows. In size they vary from 15 to 35 feet long, by from 6 to 15 broad. The smallest, as well as the most beautiful structure of this class, is that of Teampull Benan, standing on the height over Killeaney, in Aranmore, and which is but 15 feet long on the outside. The walls of these little churches are generally constructed of large stones, not laid in courses, nor yet what is termed Cyclopean, but irregularly, as the material offered to hand; and sometimes at the angles, in that description of work called "long and short," such as distinguish the early Saxon churches of Britain. Except on the inside of the door jambs, or the reveals and arches of windows, they seldom bear the mark of a tool.

Although they may be considered the first mortared buildings in Ireland, there is at present very little appearance of such externally. The mortar of that period, of which the lime is said to have been so good from having been burned with charcoal, was evidently used in a semi-fluid state, and perhaps poured in as a grouting. In position these little churches are not always placed due east and west; and St. Benan's Church (just referred to) stands north and south; but there the altar occupies a position in the north-east angle, and has over it, facing the east, the only window in the church. It is thought that the great church builder, the Gobaun Saer, and his pupils, in laying out these churches, were guided by the sun's rising and setting at the time of the year in which the building was commenced.

The windows are comparatively small, but usually splayed, and either circular-headed or rectilineally pointed; the former was often cut out of a single stone; and the latter, which was that most usually employed at the east end, was constructed of two stones meeting at an angle. A divided or many-lighted window is unknown in these early churches, which are totally devoid of architectural ornamentation, or of carving, with the rare exception of a cross or a small human figure in relief, as at the little church of Killarsagh, in the parish of Cong, described at page 158. Some doors were surrounded with projecting, and others with recessed bands.

The chief distinguishing mark of these early churches is,

however, the doorway, with inclining jambs, which invariably occupies the centre of the west gable, and is always square-headed; the lintel, from 4 to 5 feet long, being usually very massive, and in several instances covering the entire thickness of the opening. This doorway is, on an average, 5 feet 6 inches high. The inclining sides, in the Egyptian fashion, leave the opening about 2 feet 3 inches above, and 2 feet 8 inches below, or in that proportion. These square, semicircular, and angle-headed openings, are likewise found in some of our oldest round towers, with the erection of which structures they were probably contemporaneous, and in some instances antecedent to.

It is very questionable whether the most ancient of our Irish small churches were divided into nave and chancel; and it will still require careful and extended research to determine when the latter was added; and, where it exists, whether it formed part of the original plan of the building, or was added subsequently, say in the eighth or ninth century. Almost invariably the little chancel is narrowed about 2 feet on each side. It is also questionable whether these divisions in the plan of the church necessitated the erection of a choir arch, and it remains to be shown that any such structure in Ireland is older than the ninth century.

Some of these *Daimhliags*, or primitive "stone churches," called by the people *Teampulls*, were roofed with the same material, as may be seen in the groovings for the flags in several of their high-pitched gables; but others were covered with wood, and perhaps thatch.

We have a starting point for this early church architecture in the Irish Christian era, towards the end of the fifth century; but when it ended, or was modified by the introduction of the pointed or Gothic style of doors and windows, or the more florid style known as Norman, it is difficult to determine. John O'Donovan—no mean antiquary, and whose local knowledge, acquired by his personal examination of nearly every ancient church in the north and west of Ireland, while engaged upon the Ordnance Survey, was unsurpassed—held that this form of ecclesiastical building was maintained until the tenth century, if not later.* On the other hand, our great ecclesiologist, Dr. Petrie, was of opinion that in and after the seventh century a Romanesque style of building, with decorated semicircular arches, and ornamented windows and doors, some of the latter being placed in the north and south walls, was gradually introduced, as in the *Domhnach*, or *Teampull mor*, "the big church," with its choir arch and decorated stone work. This seems the most probable; but more modern authorities hold, as already stated, that all decorated or or-

* Mr. Wilkinson, in his valuable work upon "Practical Geology and Ancient Architecture of Ireland," published in 1845, says that the pointed arch was in Ireland practically applied before the introduction of the pointed style through England; and that it resulted from a progressive improvement in constructive arrangements.—See p. 140.

namented stone work in our churches, is of "twelfth-century origin." It is more than probable that the transition from the severe Pelasgic style through the Romanesque into the Roman Gothic was gradual.* In addition to the Daimliag, or stone church, or the Domhnach-mor, or Cathedral, we had, in very early times, wooden ecclesiastical structures, used either as oratories or penitentiaries, and probably also employed as dwellings, and called *Diur-teachts*, "tear houses," or *Dear-teachts*, "oaken houses," and of the burning of which we read in some of our early Christian annals. It is probable, however, that during what may be termed the Irish mediæval times these gave way to stone structures, and were only roofed with timber. This church of Killursa, as well as others, shows that many modifications, additions, and reconstructions took place; for it is quite impossible to believe that this straight-lined western doorway was coeval with the pointed southern entrance, and the large stone-mullioned east window. As an exception to this general rule may be cited the church at Inishmain, on Lough Mask, already referred to at page 106, where there is a square-headed doorway on the north side, adjoining a choir arch supported by clustered pillars, with floral capitals. In the "Saint's Church," at In-

* O'Donovan's opinions and arguments are stated at length in his letters preserved in the Ordnance Books already referred to, and date so early as 1839. The same works contain Dr. Petrie's letters in reply; but his more matured opinions will be found in his "Round Towers," published in 1845.

changoill, however, the building partook in size, masonry, and position of doorway, of the primitive type.

Looking north-eastward from Killursa Church into the fertile valley through which the Owenduff flows, the eye rests on the picturesque ruins of Ross-Errilly, depicted below; which, although at a distance of more than three miles from the lake, are of too great beauty and importance not to be included among the ecclesiastical structures along the shores of Lough

Orbsen. Upon a slight elevation on the Galway bank of the river, surrounded by fat pasture lands, and approached by a long avenue, or causeway, on the south, stand the extensive ruins of this Franciscan convent and church, and which are thus referred to by the Donegal Annalists:—"A. D. 1351, The monastery of Ros-Oirbhealagh [afterwards called Roserrilly], in the diocese of Tuam, was erected for Franciscans." And when, in 1604, Brian Oge O'Rourke was buried there, the name had changed to Ross-Iriala.*

The following legend still exists:—The building was commenced at Ross-daff, on the north or Mayo side of the river, when three swans came and perched on it, and having remained some time, flew to the other side with some *ros*, or flaxseed, which there grew up forthwith; and then the former structure was deserted, and the present commenced, and called *Ross-an-tree-Olla*, "the flaxseed of the three swans," which, in course of years and mispronunciation of the language, became Ross-Errilly.†

* See O'Donovan's translation of the Annals of the Four Masters. Archdall, who had not access to these great historic repertories, states in his "Monasticon," that it was erected in 1498, by a Lord Gannard; but who he was had not then been ascertained. Sir B. Burke, our present Ulster King of Arms, in answer to my question on the subject, says that "there never was an English Lord Gannard;" but conjectures that the name should be Gaynard, and has furnished me with the following passage from an Inquisition taken at Galway, 29th January, 1584:—" . . . . fitz. Gerr. et Gaynard et Richardus fitzWillem Gaynard, cum consanguineis de nomine et stirpe de les Gaynard erant seit de feodo de 15 qr terr vocat 'the Gaynard land,' &c. &c. et 2 qr de Bredaghe unacum Insula de Inishcreas, in Stagno quæ vulgarit dict Logh Corbo," &c. And this is the more probable, because, in the "Division of Connaught," in 1586, we find that William Gaynard possessed the Castle of Cargin.—See pp. 49 and 88.

† The derivation of Rosserrily has not been given; if not that mentioned in the text, possibly it may be a corruption of Ross Iarla—the Earl's Ross, or peninsula. By an inquisition on the 22nd April, 1636, "this monastery is called Rossryally, and placed in Mointermoroghow, in the territory of Clanrickard."—See note to Annals of Four Masters, A. D. 1604.

The illustration has been taken from the south-east, from which point the best general view of this charming group of ruins may be obtained. The house to the extreme right of the picture, called "Castle Burke," was probably the private residence of the Guardian, or the Provincial, who occasionally resided here. The church was not built cruciform, as in the case of its brethren at Kilconnell and Clare-Galway, but the high central tower, supported on pointed arches, springs from the junction of nave and chancel. The gables on the left are those of additions, and that in the centre, of a mortuary chapel. Popularly, but erroneously, this building is styled an "abbey," as in the instances of the two last named edifices; but an abbey can only appertain to a community governed by an Abbot, which office did not belong to the Franciscan order. Before examining the ruins in detail, let us read what was written of them 250 years ago. In 1617, two Irish Franciscans, Fathers Purcell and Mooney, were resident at Louvain, where they and their order had, after their expulsion from Ireland, been protected by Albert and Isabella, then joint sovereigns of the Netherlands. Mooney, at that time Provincial, and far advanced in years, had been in early life a soldier, and served in the Desmond wars. Purcell was a man of great learning; and, from materials supplied him by his superior, wrote, partly as a dialogue, a Latin history of his order, so far as it related to their Irish establishments. This interesting MS., the original of which is in the Burgundian Library at Brussels, the

Rev. C. P. Meehan, of Dublin, lately translated and published.* Mooney's recollections of this monastery are thus afforded by his ancient scribe and modern commentator :—

"Never was a more solitary spot chosen for the habitation of a religious community than that on which Rosserilly stands; for it is surrounded by marshes and bogs, and the stillness that reigns there is seldom broken, save by the tolling of the church bell, or the whirr of the countless flocks of plover and other wilds birds that frequent the fens which abound in that desolate region. Another remarkable feature of the locality is, that the monastery can only be approached by a causeway, paved with large stones, over an extent of fully two hundred paces, and terminating at the enclosure, which was built in 1572 by Father Ferrall Mac Egan, a native of Connaught, and then Provincial of the Irish Franciscans. He was, in sooth, a distinguished man in his day, far-famed for eloquence and learning, and singularly fond of Rosserilly, which he used to compare to the Thebaid, whither the early Christians fled for prayer and contemplation. He died in our house of Kilconnell, where he made his religious profession, and there he awaits the rusurrection—peace to his memory! As to the church of Rosserilly, it is indeed a beautiful edifice; and the same may be said of the monastery, which, although often

* See his "Noctes Lovanienses," in "Duffy's Hibernian Magazine," for 1860 and 1861. A transcript of the original is now in the Library of Trinity College, Dublin.

garrisoned by the English troops during the late war, is still in excellent preservation. Cloister, refectory, dormitory, chapter house, library, and lofty bell tower, have all survived the disasters of that calamitous period; but, in the twenty-sixth year of the reign of Elizabeth, the friars were forcibly expelled from their beloved retreat."

The friars, however, soon returned, and remained in quiet possession for long after, till Sir Arthur Chichester, then Lord Deputy, directed O'Donnell, Archbishop of Tuam,* to turn them out; but that good and learned Protestant sent them word privately of his intention, and they saved themselves and their effects by flight. One good turn deserved another; and this kindness was repaid in 1641, when, after the massacre at Shrule, Father Brian Kilkelly, then Guardian of Rosserilly, hearing of the atrocities which were enacting

* Dr. William O'Donnell, F.T.C.D.—or, as he is styled by English writers, Daniel—who died Archbishop of Tuam in 1628, was a very learned man, and thoroughly acquainted with the Irish language. He translated the Book of Common Prayer from the English into our native tongue; and is also said, by Ware and others, to have translated the New Testament Scriptures from Greek into Irish. This latter statement is not, however, strictly correct, as the author has shown in the account he published in 1841 of the translation and printing of the New Testament Scriptures, in his Memoir of Sir Thomas Molyneux, referred to at pages 74 and 123 of this book.—See "Gallery of Illustrious Irishmen," No. XIII., in "The Dublin University Magazine," for September, 1841, p. 308. The men who assisted O'Donnell were—Miles Mac Brody and Daniel Inigin, and their labours in translation were fully acknowledged by the learned prelate.

within a few miles of him, hastened to the spot, succoured the wounded, and brought the Bishop of Killala's wife and children to his monastery, and treated them with the greatest kindness. See Otway's "Tour in Connaught."

Great changes have taken place in the surrounding scene since Father Mooney's description was written. This site was in all probability a *Cluain*, an "isolated meadow," or oasis; and there was originally a water course leading from some springs, pools, and turloughs, on the south-east, which supplied a stream that turned a small mill, the foundations of which still exist, and then passed by a conduit through the kitchen on the northern side into a fish tank, or circular reservoir, within the walls, the cut stone margin of which remains; so that the fresh trout and curdy salmon from the neighbouring Owenduff prevented the worthy friars from feeling the effects of abstinence on fast days.

This kitchen is a spacious apartment, fitted up with oven, extensive fire-place, and an aperture through which the smoking savoury viands could be passed at once into the refectory, which adjoins its eastern side, and had all the other appliances which the gustatory taste of the period could suggest; so that, if the Franciscans did not exactly fare "like sons of Irish kings," they certainly lived like gentlemen, and much good may it have done them. In the north-east corner of this refectory is a sedile, with a handsome slender pillar support, in which the reader, in sonorous tones, read to the fathers as they were regaled from the produce of the adjoining kitchen. Wandering among these noble ruins, evincing so much taste, if not luxury, one cannot help peopling them, in imagination, with the inmates of four or five hundred years gone by; when, after dinner, the brown-robed friars strolled in the adjoining cloisters, of which several of the arches are quite perfect. But the picture dims as we proceed from that portion of the ruins allocated to the creature comforts of the clergy, to those devoted to the service of the Most High; for, passing into the great church by its western entrance, amidst heaps of human skulls and bones, into the great aisle or nave, we are at once met by droves of sheep and oxen, that rush from off the altars, or from out of the tombs, or from within the precincts of the small chapels around us. It would not be profitable to either reader or tourist to depict the amount of desecration which the author witnessed in this abbey on several occasions, but especially in July, 1866. Here, in former times, were interred, with pomp, while bells tolled, friars chaunted, and chieftains clad in all the panoply of funereal state assisted at the ceremonial, the mortal remains of the O'Flahertys, O'Donnells, Kirwans, Lynchs, Brownes, Mac Donnells, Burkes, Kilkellys, and other Connaught notabilities, whose tombs stud the walls or pave the aisles of Ross-Errilly, but which are now the habitation of rabbits, sheep, and oxen.* The total length of this great church is 128 feet, and its breadth 20½ feet. The arches between the nave and side aisle on the southern side, as we

* This is not the first notice of the desecration of Ross-Errilly, and the indecent exposure of the vast multitude of human remains within and around

enter from the west; the tall tower, 70 feet high, supported upon pointed arches, that separates the nave and chancel; the beauteous four-lighted east window, partially deformed though it be by the unsightly modern tomb that occupies the situation of the high altar; the coronetted tomb of the founder, recessed into the northern wall; the low, deeply-moulded arches that lead into the side chapels; the history of the families to whose memory the different mortuary chapels were erected, and all the architectural details of this memorable place, would occupy many pages to describe; but possibly the foregoing will be sufficient for the purposes of this

the ruins; for, twenty-eight years ago, the Rev. Cæsar Otway produced at the Royal Irish Academy a human skull from Ross-Errilly, upon which long shaggy moss had grown, and feelingly remarked upon the circumstance here referred to. He afterwards alluded to it in his "Tour in Connaught," already referred to at p. 116. Not long since, Mr. Bevan, the writer of Murray's valuable "Handbook for Travellers in Ireland," has thus described it:—"It is the cemetery of many good Connaught families, and probably contains more grinning and ghastly skulls than any catacomb, some of the tracery of the windows being filled up with thigh bones and heads—a not uncommon way of disposing of these emblems of mortality in Irish abbeys." Father Conway has also drawn public attention to the subject in a letter recently published in the "Freeman's Journal."

Mr. Oliver Burke, of the neighbouring family of Ower, a gentleman who takes much interest in antiquarian matters, did good service to these ruins very lately, by removing the obstructions from between the mullions of the beautiful windows, and also by making several repairs in the tower, and thereby rendering it accessible to the top; he also caused some good photographs to be made of the interior.

work.* There are many interesting and peculiarly Irish architectural details in this ruin, among which are the decoration of the bolt-hole in the western door-way, which resembles some of the Newgrange carvings; the beautiful cross, a fragment of which has been erected over a grave adjoining the modern western wall; and the form of an ancient hatchet or *Tuath* figured on the tomb of the Tnuhils in 1617, who probably derived their name from that implement. The great bell, with its silver tongue, is, it is said, occasionally heard to chime in its deep bed in the adjoining river.

From the rolls of the order we learn that in 1647 a chapter of Franciscans was held here under the presidency of the Very Rev. Anthony de Burgo; and also that it was occupied until 1687, when the Rev. P. O'Neill was elected Provincial, and the Rev. B. O'Flaherty Guardian; and the friars prayed for James II. and his consort, and his Irish viceroy, Tirconnell.—See Appendix. It is said that at a later period Lord St. George aided the friars by placing some looms in the church when the government sent down orders to dispossess them.

* Irish ecclesiastical history ought to have been pretty well determined in the middle of the nineteenth century. Ussher, Ware, King, Harris, Lanigan, De Burgo, Archdall, the O'Clearys, O'Donovan, Petrie, Todd, Reeves, O'Curry, and the Transactions and Proceedings of the Royal Irish Academy, and the Archæological and Celtic Societies, have illustrated the subject so far as probably it is possible. What then will be thought of a work published in New York, in 1854, entitled, "History of the Irish Hierarchy," full of gross errors, strong anti-English prejudices, and innumerable plagiarisms, in which the following description of the ruins occurs:—"Ross, a monastery . . . .

The following circumstance serves to show how far the legend, the fairy tale, the local tradition, or the popular superstition may have been derived from absolute historic fact. A gentleman residing in the neighbourhood lately told the author that about 200 years ago it was mysteriously communicated to the people of the district, that the fairies of Knockmagh were, upon a certain day, to have a battle at Ross with the fairies of Scotland. Thither flocked the people from all quarters, and great was the excitement. Well—they waited at the abbey all that long summer's day until sundown, in anxious expectation of the prodigy, and were about returning home, when, lo, and behold, in the twilight the sky became darkened, and a great humming noise was heard in the air, and then the forces of Fin-Varragh, in the form of *Primpiollans*, or beetles, met those of the hostile fairy chief from the other side of the Channel, and a terrific conflict ensued. Thousands of

founded . . . in the diocese of Tuam, A. D. 1431. It *is* a very solitary place, surrounded on all sides by water. Rosserrilly, in the barony of Clare, situated on the river of Ross. The Lord Granard founded this monastery for the strict observants, A. D. 1498. A. D. 1604 the Roman Catholics repaired the Abbey of Rosserrilly; its ruins, which still remain, show it to have been a very extensive building." Now, every word of the foregoing, erroneous as it is, is extracted, without acknowledgment, from the "Monasticon Hibernicon," the labour of the Rev. Mervyn Archdall, the Protestant writer of 1786; but the Rev. Mr. Walsh, his American commentator, has added to the foregoing the following passage:—"It has been lately purchased by the Archbishop of Tuam." If it had, we would have expected a better preservation of this ancient ruin; but it belongs to a gentleman living a long distance off, on the south-eastern border of the county of Galway.

them fell dead all round; and others, rushing into the church and monastery, strewed the sacred edifice with the slain. Such, without variation or adornment, is the tradition still current in the locality.

The informant was not a little surprised when told that the narrative was founded on fact; that the author knew all about it, and had published an account of it many years ago. It is this :—In 1688 a swarm of locusts, so called, invaded Connaught, and are thus described by Sir Thomas Molyneux :—

"They appeared on the south-west coast of the county of Galloway: from hence they made their way into the more inland parts, towards Headford, a place belonging to Sir George St. George, Bart., about twelve miles north from the town of Galloway; here, and in the adjacent country, multitudes of them showed themselves among the trees and hedges in the day-time, hanging by the boughs; thousands together, in clusters, sticking to the back one of another, as in the manner of bees when they swarm. In this position, or lying still and covert under the leaves of the trees, they continued quiet, with little or no motion, during the heat of the sun; but towards evening, or sunset, they would all rise, disperse, and fly about, with a strange humming noise, much like the beating of drums at some distance, and in such vast, incredible numbers, that they darkened the air for the space of two or three miles square.

"So complete was the devastation occasioned by this insect, that in a short time the whole face of the country presented the appearance of winter, though it was then the middle of summer—every green thing having been devoured by them.

"Nay, their multitudes spread so exceedingly, that they disturbed men even within their dwellings; for out of the gardens they got into the houses, where numbers of them crawling about were very irksome, and they would often drop on the meat as it was dressing in the kitchen, and frequently fall from the ceiling of the rooms into the dishes as they stood on the table while they ate, so extremely offensive and loathsome were they, as well as prejudicial and destructive."*

Such is the account given of this invasion by the great Irish physician and antiquary. The insect was not the true locust, such as occasionally devours every green thing in eastern countries, and as once invaded England from the coast of Normandy, but a description of cockchafer, the *Melalontha vulgaris*, or summer beetle, that buzzes past us on calm evenings as the harbinger of fine weather, and which is known to the peasantry by the Irish name of *primpiollan*. No doubt can be entertained on the subject, for Molyneux has given a faithful engraving of

* See a letter to St. George Ash, Bishop of Clogher, giving "An account of the swarms of insects that of late years have much infested the province of Connaught, in Ireland," which was printed in the "Philosophical Transactions," No. 234, and was republished in Boate and Molyneux's "Natural History of Ireland." See also the Author's Memoir of Sir T. Molyneux, Bart., M. D., in the "Dublin University Magazine" for December, 1841.

the animal. In winter they retired under ground, where it is thought they hibernated; but there they deposited their eggs, and their larvæ destroyed even more than the parent animals, for they ate up the grain in the ground, and the crops of the ensuing year completely failed wherever these insects existed. A famine seemed to threaten the whole of the province, and it became the cause of much and just alarm throughout the entire kingdom. A long continuance of wet weather and high winds, however, checked their further spread, and timely aided in averting the expected calamity. They were also eaten in large quantities by pigs and poultry, and, according to the narrator, were even used as human food. Large fires were likewise kept up in different districts, with the hope of arresting their progress, and towards the end of the following summer their numbers had greatly diminished. They, however, continued their progress in an easterly direction, and in 1697 "they reached as far as the Shannon, and some of the scattered, loose parties crossed the river, and got into the province of Leinster, but were met there by a stronger army of jackdaws, that did much execution among them, killing and devouring great numbers." Their main body still kept in Connaught, and were last heard of "at a well-improved English plantation not far from the River Shannon, called Air's Court, where they found plenty of provision, and did a great deal of mischief by stripping the hedges, gardens, and groves of beech, quite naked of all their leaves." Had we this animal in Ireland before 1688; and may it not again increase and devastate?

About a mile to the north-east of Rosserilly, but upon the Mayo side of the river, and in the parish of Shrule, stands the old castle of Moyne, and a little beyond it the ruins of an ancient church. Besides these different places already referred to or described in the parish of Killursa, the following may be noted. The site of the ancient "Church of the two Kings," *Kill-da-Reigh*, from which the townland of Killdarre has been called; Ardfintan and Caher-Fintan, which also gives name to a townland to the north-east of Killursa Church, where also several raths and forts exist, and which is so called after the ancient king already referred to at page 99; *Cathair-na-hailighi*, now called Cahernally, where the Kilkellys of old resided; and near the church the remains of a cromleagh, termed—as such structures usually are, *Leabha-Dearmid-agus-Graina*—the bed or "resting place of Dermod and Grace" during the period of their courtship and flight from Tara; its top stone is 9½ feet long. There are also forts and raths along the shore, which are well worthy of inspection, especially Lisheennakirka. The church of St. Fursa is on the property of W. G. Burke, Esq., of Ower.

Appertaining to this parish, near its north-western end, and about half a mile off shore, is the long, low Island of Inchiquin, running nearly north and south; which is upwards of a mile and a quarter in length; it contains 229 acres, and is the largest island in Lough Corrib. "On that island of Insequin," O'Flaherty says, as already referred to at page 99, "St. Brendan built a chappell, and worked divers miracles. In the same island St. Meldan, whose festival day is on the 7th of February, was abbot of a famous abbey about the year 580. He was spiritual father to the great St. Furse, of Perone, in France, who carried the relics of this saint along with him, and enshrined them at Perone." The local habitation of these early saints on Inchiquin was *Rathmath*, "the rath of the field" or plain—a name that has become very celebrated from its frequent mention in Irish hagiology. Its outline still exists, but scarcely a vestige of the walls of the ecclesiastical structures remains; the site is, however, still used as a burial ground. Possibly the dilapidations commenced here when "the isles of Lough Orbsen were pillaged by the Danes." Its Irish name is *Inis-Mac-Hy-chuinn*—the island of the descendants of Con, Monarch of Ireland in the second century; and it was so celebrated, that the entire lake is said at one time to have been called Inis-ui-chuinn. Three Cons have been celebrated in Irish history, and Con-Cedchathact, here referred to, was the ancestor of St. Meldan. It is said, traditionally, that Roderick O'Conor, when on his way to Cong, after his abdication in 1183, rested at this island; but, finding a favouring breeze, he said, "Well, if the land is against me, the wind is with me;" and so set sail sail for Illaunree.

Having advanced thus far in the footprints of the early founders of Christianity in the west, and traced the early Irish and the Norman chieftains through their forts and castles, the question naturally arises, when looking to the present sparsity of population in the same districts—where the population came from, and what was its amount, to whose spiritual necessities these early missionaries ministered, or for whose defence or governance these cahers and cashels were erected. To the troglodyte people, whose subterranean dwellings will be described farther on in this book, it is here unnecessary to refer; but that long subsequent to their period there must have been a very great population in Ireland is shown by the vast number of earthen forts, raths, and lisses with which the country in certain fertile localities, is studded. Even in this far western district we have examples of this; for, in a comparatively small space upon the Ordnance Sheet 56, including portions of the junction of the parishes of Killeany, Kilcoona, and Annaghdown, there are no less than 50 raths and circles marked; and, as the author has shown elsewhere, certain districts in Kerry presented a greater amount of population than at present exists in any *rural* part of Ireland of the same extent. Each of these forts was either the habitation of a large family, or sometimes a village; and the larger ones belonged to chieftains, or persons of rank. But then, it must be remembered that there were no large towns or cities in those days.*

* See the Author's Lecture upon "Ireland Past and Present—the Land and the People," delivered at the Metropolitan Hall, Dublin, in 1864, and published by M'Glashan and Gill, p. 19.

CHAPTER VI.

INCHIQUIN TO INCHANGOILL AND CONG.

COUNTY OF MAYO. THE ISLANDS OF LOUGH CORRIB. INISHANBOE. PARISH OF SHRULE. BALLYCURRIN, BALLISAHINEY, AND MOCEARA CASTLES. FORTS. PARISH OF CONG. INCHANGOILL. ST. PATRICK'S, AND THE SAINT'S CHURCHES. STONE OF LUGNAEDON. SOUTH-EAST BORDER OF CONG PARISH. CASTLETOWN. INCHMICATREER. CROSS. ANCIENT CHURCHES OF KILFRAUGHAUN AND KILLARSAGH. MOYTURA. LACKAFINNA. LISLOUGHRY. CONG ISLANDS. KINLOUGH. ASHFORD. STRAND HILL. CONG.

Returning to our steamer from the point where we landed, at Annakeen Castle, to investigate the extensive parish of Killursa, and continuing our north-west course, we steer by the south-west corner of Rabbit Island, from whence glimpses of the grand mountain view already referred to may be descried. And here, as we enter the broad waters of the upper lake, a word about the islands which cluster around us may be useful.

The islands of Lough Corrib are so numerous, that the people of the district say they number. 365, or one for every day in the year, and that an additional one rises on leap year; and as many as 145, independent of rocks and shoals, have been named. The largest are those of Inchiquin, Inchmicatreer, Doorus, Inchangoill, Cannaun, Lee's Island, and Illaunaconaun. Passing the narrow channel through which the steamer darns its tortuous path, amidst the intricate navigation of rocks, shoals, and breakers, and getting into the open space of the large or middle lake, we are struck with the curious appearance of the groups of islands in threes and fours, arranged in lines, as if marking the ancient boundaries of the lake beach. Such may be observed in those running nearly north and south, from Bilberry Island to Cussafoor, and from Coad to Inishbeagh, both to the west of the steamer's track; and from Carrickaslin to Inchbiana, to the east of that line; and again a group of five, stretching from the north-east point of Inishdoorus, by Cleenillaun and Ardillaun, to the west of the Cong River. The west face of several of these small islands is truncated, the alluvial soil and gravel having been cut down by the winds and waves of thousands of years.

As we are now passing Inchiquin, already twice referred to, we must again, in fancy, if not in fact, land our tourist freight for a short digression to the mainland. Before, however, we take leave of the Galway waters, or pass into those of Mayo, we must introduce the accompanying vignette of the Rev. John D'Arcey's pretty cottage upon Inishanboe, "the island of the old cow," that just now appears in view, among the cluster of small islands to the west of our course. It is so called on account of the usual tradition or cow legend of which the tale will be told when describing Kilcummin, the parish to which this island belongs.

We now enter the county of Mayo portion of the lake, and pass along the south-western boundary of the extensive parish of SHRULE—Shruille—in Irish, *Struthair* or *Srutho-fuile*, "the bloody stream"—which is next in succession to Killursa, on the eastern shore of the lake. It spreads along the coast for about two miles, and proceeds inland in a south-easterly direction for nearly five miles, except where it includes the small parish of Kilmain-beg. Although possessing several objects of historic and antiquarian interest, especially the fine old castle at the village of Shrule, they are not sufficiently near Lough Corrib to bring them within the pale of this work.

This parish is situated in the south-west corner of the barony of Kilmain, and county of Mayo, and extends from the Black River, which divides it from the county of Galway, to the stream at the mill of Ballynalty, which separates it from the parish of Cong. The vicinity of this little country mill is a noted spawning ground for *Salmonidæ*, and around it grow, in great profusion and luxuriance, the bushy shrubs of the *Potentilla fructuosa.*

Besides the great tower at Shrule, there are several ruined castles in the western extremity of this parish, of which the most extensive and best preserved is Ballycurrin, within view of the steamer, and in connexion with the beautiful residence of Charles Lynch, Esq., as figured in the subjoined illustration, taken from the south-east.

This old tower-house, or defensive mansion, consists of a quadrangular ivy-mantled keep—now somewhat altered for modern purposes—64 feet long on the south, 39 on the west face, and 47 feet high; but possessing no architectural memorial by which to assign even a probable date to it, as the dressed stones are not chiselled, but punched, or what is styled "sparrow-picked;" massive defence and security having evidently been the main objects of its founders. Both it and the modern residence are most pleasingly situated on a green slope, rising from a sheltered little bay, and surrounded by a large park of well-grown timber. There is no reference to this ancient building in our histories or inquisitions; and the only legend attaching thereto is, that it was built in the "ould times" by one of three brothers, the two others of whom erected those of Ballysnahiney and Moceara (possibly *Mac-Ceara*), with which it forms a triangle. After the Milesian invasion, our bardic histories say that one of that race, named "Caicer, erected a castle at Dunn Inn, in the West of Ireland." Upon the shore adjoining Ballycurrin there exists a mound, or earthen tumulus of that name, about 30 feet high, and occupying nearly a rood of ground, which Mr. Lynch thinks may be that referred to above, and mentioned in Keating's History of Ireland. There is, however, no mortared structure in Ireland older than the Christian Era. And he is also of opinion that Ceara, one of the artificers said to have come over at that time, left his name to many localities in Connaught—such as Lough Ceara, Castle Ceara; and in this immediate neighbourhood, *Tobar-Ceara* and *Gorren-Ceara*, or Ceara's well and garden. In the old quit rent receipts Ballycurrin is called Ballycar, possibly a corruption or Anglicized version of Bally-Ceara. In the vicinity was found a collection of amber beads, and several bronze antiquities, now in the Collection of the Royal Irish Academy.

In the south-east of this parish, and to the right of the road between Moyne and Cross, there are several objects worthy of inspection, especially the great Pagan forts of Cahermore and Cahernahilk, &c.

We are still in Mayo waters: in the barony of Kilmain, and legally within the limits of the extensive and celebrated parish of CONG, which forms the entire northern boundary of Lough Corrib in both counties, and extends from its junction with that of Shrule to near the bridge of Maam, a distance of about twenty miles. As the nearest point of land in this parish is immediately on the larboard or western side of our track, we will conduct our readers to it.

Inchangoill—*Inis-an-ghoill-Craibhtheach*, "the island of the devout foreigner," *Gael*, or Gail, as all strangers were formerly styled—which now rises its long green ridge-like back to the west of our course, is by far the most interesting island on the lake; and, if we said one of the most remarkable spots on Irish ground, we should not fear to take up the gauntlet in its favour, for picturesque scenery, grand mountain view, and existing historic monuments.

In an undulating slope, where the island narrows towards its centre, an extensive graveyard, in an ancient ecclesiastical enclosure, marks where, so long as there were any of the name left in the country, the Kinnaveys, Conways, Sullivans, Murphys, Lyddans, Butlers, and others, interred their dead; and many a wild wail of the Irish keen has floated over the surrounding waters, as the funeral procession of boats, with their picturesquely clad freights, approached the shore of this sacred isle.

Within this graveyard, lately enclosed by its present proprietor, Sir Benjamin Lee Guinness, Bart., the restorer of St. Patrick's, stand the ruins of two exceedingly ancient churches, both of the small Irish type, already noticed at page 107, but of far different styles and dates. That to the north-east, which is much the older and plainer, bears all the characteristics of its period in its narrow square-headed doorway, with inclined jambs, and the Cyclopean style of its masonry. It was not built due east and west, but inclines to the north of the former, and south of the latter, as sometimes occurs in our very early Irish churches.* This little *Teampull Phaidrig*, or "St. Patrick's Church," which is 34 feet 7 inches long, measured by its outer wall, is divided by a slight recess into a nave and chancel, but there are no vestiges of a dividing arch; and it is questionable whether any very early church of this

* As already stated at page 108, many of our old Irish churches are not built exactly east and west. Cormac's Chapel, at Cashel, and the adjoining cathedral, present strikingly different bearings. The old Gobaun Saers, when laying a church foundation, assumed as east and west the points in the horizon where the sun rose and set at the time. This would account for a multitude of differences in the *cast* of such buildings.

class had originally a choir arch.* Its internal dimensions are, 29 feet 7 inches in the clear, of which 17 feet 11 inches by 11 feet 10 inches are occupied by the nave; the chancel is 11 feet 7 inches by 8 feet 8 inches. There are no remains of the altar or the east window, nor of any side light. The massive walls, now about 9 feet high, of what is termed Cyclopean work, show no signs of morter except in their interior. The stones of the south-western portion of the wall of the gable have lately been carefully replaced; and the square-headed doorway in it, figured at page 142, is of the true primitive type, and about 6 feet high; its jambs formed of square, but uncut stones, incline inwards, from 24½ inches at the sill to 22½ inches under the massive lintel, which is 4 feet 8 inches long.† "That this church," says Dr. Petrie, "is of the age of St. Patrick, as is believed in the traditions of the country, and as its name would indicate, can, I think, scarcely admit of doubt."—Round Towers, page 163.

What gives the most special interest to this locality is the preservation there of a monumental stone, containing, un-

* The choir arch in the little church called St. Kevin's Kitchen, at Glendalough, may be cited as contradicting this statement; but it is probably not so old as that at Inchangoill; and, besides, such arches may have been superadded to the original building. Why are such structures styled by writers, "triumphal arches"?

† See a view of this doorway in Petrie's "Round Towers," p. 163; and Wakeman's sketch of it as it stood in 1839, in the "Galway Ordnance Letter Book," vol. iii., p. 47; and in his useful little book, "A Week in the West."

doubtedly, one of the very earliest Christian inscriptions in Ireland. It is a single four-sided obelistic pillar, of hard, greyish Silurian stone,* unhewn, slightly cambered, broad at the base, where it measures 10 inches, and gradually decreasing from 6 to 5 inches on the inscribed side, which faces the south-west end of St. Patrick's Church, and from which it is distant a few paces. This monolith now stands 2 feet 4 inches over the ground, as a headstone to a grave, but that such was not its original position is manifest; and it has all the appearance of having been one of those corbel stones so often seen projecting in old Irish churches, and of which there is an example in the north-east angle of the gable of the neighbouring "Church of the Saint." It has at top two crosses on the west, two on the east (as shown in the accompanying illustrations), two on

* Professor Haughton, who examined a small fragment of this fossiliferous stone for the author, reports that "It is a fine-grained micaceous sandstone, coloured green by silicate of iron; it contains fragments of *Orthis*." There are other similar *stele*, but uncarved, throughout this graveyard.

the south, and one on the north face, which may be regarded as examples of the most ancient carvings of that sacred emblem now to be found in the British Isles, or perhaps, if we except those in the Catacombs of Rome, anywhere in Europe.

On the east face is an inscription, in the Uncial or old Latin character, which is reduced from a most careful rubbing lately taken by the Earl of Dunraven.* It reads perpendicularly, and was first published in 1845 by the late Dr. Petrie, in his celebrated work upon "The Ecclesiastical Architecture and Round Towers of Ireland," as *Lia Lugnaedon Macc Lmenueh*, "the Stone of Lugnaedon, son of Limenueh," the sister of St. Patrick. Taking the authorities in consecutive order, it may be observed that Roderick O'Flaherty, who first informed us of the ancient name of this island, makes no allusion to this monolith. In 1810 an officer quartered in Galway described it in a local newspaper, and an Irish-speaking soldier of his regiment gave a fanciful interpretation of its inscription.†

In 1839 our great topographer, John O'Donovan, then

* At Llandewi-breefi, in South Wales, there is a somewhat similar stone, with a like character of inscription, said to be of the fifth century.

† See the "Hibernian Magazine," edited by the redoubted Watty Cox, and quoted by Dutton in his "Statistical Survey of the County of Galway."

In 1824 Dr. Petrie, in company with Samuel Lover, was in the West of Ireland, and visited Inchangoill, where he had an opportunity of examining this stone.

employed upon the Ordnance Survey, visited the island, along with Mr. Wakeman, who made most careful drawings of the stone, and all the other objects of antiquarian interest in connexion with these two churches; and O'Donovan's illustrated communication of the 27th of June in that year is preserved in that great repertory of Irish history, "The Ordnance Letters on the Antiquities of the county of Galway," vol. iii., page 46, now in the Library of the Royal Irish Academy.

With reference to this stone he writes thus at page 50:—It "exhibits a very ancient inscription, in the Roman characters, of the fifth or very beginning of the sixth century;"* and adds, "That this Lugnoedon Macc Lmenueh was no other than Præsbyter Lugnath, who was the son of Liemania, otherwise Darerca, the sister of St. Patrick, is highly probable, though we have no account of his having lived or being buried in this island. According to the 'Book of Lecan,' fol. 51, p. b. col. 5, Presbyter Lugna (otherwise called Lugnath), was the alumnus of St. Patrick, and son of his sister; and he was located at a place called Fearta, in Tir Fheg, on Lough Mask, where Duach Teanga Umha, King of Connaught, gave him and his fellow-labourers the lands extending from that part of Lough Mask called Snamh Tire Feig to Sail Dea. In the same MS., fol. 45, a. 1, he is called St. Patrick's *Luamaire* or navigator. The Irish

* O'Donovan likewise gives, in proof of this opinion, examples from an alphabet of the seventh century, furnished by Astle "On the Origin and Progress of Writing," p. 96. Lugnaedon's stone is also figured in his Irish Grammar.

authorities are not, however, all agreed upon the history of this saint, some making him the son of St. Patrick's sister Lupita, some of his sister Darerca, and others of Liemania! But this stone is a cotemporaneous monument, and should be received as historical evidence to prove that he was the son of Liemania. This inscription is the oldest Christian monument I have yet seen; and, whatever doubts there may be about the history of this saint, as given in the Irish MSS., there can be none about the authenticity of this inscription." O'Donovan also gives the various authorities from the Irish hagiology, and Eugene O'Curry's extracts from the Book of Lecan, and other Irish MSS. bearing on the subject.*

Subsequently our great ecclesiologist, Dr. Petrie, published, as already stated at page 137, a drawing of this inscribed stone,

* The foregoing references to the ancient monuments in the island of Inchangoill, contained in the MS. Ordnance Letters, now amounting to 137 thick quarto volumes, are here specially introduced in order to show the great value of these productions. With Larcom directing the survey, maps, and topography—Petrie, with an office in Dublin, and a staff, in which were Eugene O'Curry, George Downes, Clarence Mangan, O'Keeffe, and others, searching the ancient records, and transmitting to the fieldworkers the results of their labours; and with O'Donovan, O'Connor, and others, investigating each parish and townland in Ireland, exploring its antiquities, jotting down its local history and legends, and attended in many localities by draftsmen of the first character—Wakeman and Du Noyer, both pupils of Petrie—who made most graphic sketches, some of which have been already published—a work was produced unsurpassed by anything of the kind in the world. The 137 volumes of manuscripts to which we have referred, and which are deposited in the Library of the Royal Irish Academy, are no longer a sealed book, but are freely open to all students of Irish history.

and gave a learned dissertation upon it, which confirms O'Donovan's opinion, and said, "that the most ancient authorities which make mention of Lugnat, concur in stating that he was one of the seven sons of the Bard or Lombard — as in Duald Mac Firbis's compilation of ancient genealogies, and that the most of those authorities state that these seven sons of the Lombard were St. Patrick's nephews," and quotes in support thereof the *Leabhar Breac*, which states that "Cruimther Lugnai (*i. e.*, the foster-son of Patrick and son of his sister) was the seventh son of the Bard, and located at Ferta of Tir Feic, on Lough Mask."*

Of this inscription, says the Rev. Dr. Todd, in his work on the Life and Mission of "St. Patrick, Apostle of Ireland," its character may, with almost certainty, be regarded as not later than the beginning of the sixth century; and he observes, that "Lugnaedon is the Celtic genitive of Lugnad, or Lugna, the name given to the youngest of the seven sons of Limanin," of which Limenue is also the genitive. The inscription, of which the foregoing is a *facsimile*, is, however, still susceptible of further elucidation.† No matter what interpretation

* Where Tir Feig is, unless it be the very ancient square-headed church at Ross Hill, also called *Teampull Phaidrig*, is unknown.

† In the Appendix to his "History of the Ancient Churches of Armagh," the Rev. Dr. Reeves writes :—"Of Lupeit, or Lupita, St. Patrick's alleged sister, there is no notice in any of the Irish calendars. The tract on the mothers of the saints of Ireland, ascribed to Aengus, the Culdee, says, Lupait, sister of Patrick, was the mother of the seven sons of Ula Baird [an Irish chieftain]; namely, Nectan, Dabonda, Mogorman, Darigue, Ausille, Sechnell, and Crumtha Lugnadh."—See also the "Tripartite Life of St. Patrick," p. 235; and the "Irish Book of Hymns," p. 34.

may be given of the second line, no doubt can exist that Petrie and O'Donovan were correct in stating that this was the monumental stone of Lugnad, or Lugnaedon—the former of whom inclined to the opinion that he was the son of Restitutus, the Lombard, and Lemueh.

A short distance to the south-east is the second building—*Teampull-na-Neave*, "the Church of the Saint," probably Lugnad; and an ancient flagged way, 79 yards long, leads between the two. It is a more modern and highly decorated structure than that called after our great Irish Missionary, and lies nearly due east and west. It measures 38 feet 1 inch from out to out, of which 26 feet 4 inches is the length of the wall of the nave, and 11 feet 9 inches that of the recessed chancel, which is 5 feet 11 inches wide at the eastern end. The masonry of this church is, to a certain extent, laid in courses, except a portion of the south wall, which is very massive, or what is usually called Cyclopean; but the quoins and several other stones were dressed. Projecting from the north-east angle of the wall of the nave is a remarkable corbel-shaped stone, 2 feet 4 inches long, that reminds one strongly of the Lugnaedon pillar, and strengthens the opinion given at page 136.

Here, in juxtaposition, but in chronological and architectural contrast, are shown, on the two next pages, the doorways of the Inchangoill Churches. The first, taken from a photograph made last year, represents the plain, severe, square-headed doorway of the very early primitive church, or *Teampull Phaidrig*, described at page 135. And on the opposite side we have represented the beautiful, highly decorated, circular-arched, cluster-pillared doorway of *Teampull na*

Neave, now for the first time brought before the archæological world; and between the erection of which and the former, some centuries must have elapsed. This marvellous doorway, which is a grand specimen of early Irish decorative art, is decidedly anterior to the date of the Anglo-Norman conquest. Like its elder brother adjoining, it is placed in the western gable, and its jambs slope slightly inwards.* Its dimensions are 5 feet 11 inches from the lower edge of the arch to the sill, 2 feet 2 inches wide at bottom, and 2 feet at top—almost the same as that of its primitive

neighbour, previously described. The entire thickness of this doorway is 39 inches; it is formed of a reddish drab

* The doorway of the church of Dysart, near Currofin, Co. Clare, adjoining the round tower there, presents features similar to the foregoing, especially in the row of heads surrounding the arch.

coloured sandstone, such as that found on the Cong side of the lake; where, as here, it has become porous or pitted with small depressions, as if eaten by the Pholas. It has also suffered much generally from the weather; and although the author remembers the lower portion of the arch perfect in the days of his boyhood, the two external or upper bands had fallen, and their stones were strewn about.*

Fortunately, nearly every stone was forthcoming, and it has been skilfully restored by the present proprietor within the last few years. The jambs are formed by columnar pilasters, which are crowned by human-face capitals, from which springs the arch, the middle portion of which is carved into deep, horizontally projecting chevrons, over which is a row of faces, each differing from the other, and which may, for aught we know, have been portraits; but all are now so much defaced by weathering on the surface, and by the pitting already alluded to, as to efface their individuality.

* When O'Donovan was here in June, 1839, he wrote as follows—"The west gable contains the doorway, which was highly finished, very like that in the church of Kelleshin, near Carlow, but now much injured. It consisted of three concentric arches, formed of red gritstone, but the two external ones are now nearly destroyed." To this description in the "Ordnance Letter Book for Galway," vol. iii., p. 49, is added a charming pen-and-ink sketch of the doorway, as it then existed, by W. Wakeman, who accompanied him. All the lower member, and a portion of the left-hand side of the middle, a chevron ornament, were then *in situ.*

The impost capitals are of exceeding interest, as they show a form of beard plaiting and knotted hair work, which, though rarely represented in sculpture, were in all likelihood the Irish fashion of its day. These, on the north and south sides, are most faithfully represented in the annexed cut.

Such may have been the pattern of the beard of Restitutus, the Longo-bardic father of Lugnaedon.* A similar form of decoration is to be seen on the fillet underneath the cap of

* A photograph does not bring out the beauties of this doorway as well as the pencil. When the foregoing illustration was made by Mr. Wakeman, the declining sun, then gradually throwing into relief the special peculiarities of this great work of early Irish art, served to produce the effect shown above.

the Round Tower of Devenish on Lough Erne, which is probably of contemporaneous antiquity. Another and later form of plaited beard is shown in the figures on the grand shrine of St. Monchan.* The entire space included by the pillars and mouldings cf this entrance is 4 feet 10 inches.

Upon entering the church, the view here figured, faithfully drawn from a photograph kindly furnished by the Earl of Dun-

* See the restored model of this shrine, made by the author, and now in the Kensington Museum.

raven, presents us with the low undecorated chancel-arch, altar, and deeply splayed round-headed eastern light. This arch measures 8 feet 7 inches in span; and from the keystone to the flagging beneath is 9 feet 7 inches.

The nave is 21 feet 7 inches by 12 feet 9 inches in the clear; and in the south wall there is a small, narrow, round-headed light, 6 feet from the ground, and deeply splayed inside. In the western corner of that wall may be seen one of the most remarkable pieces of carving on the island. It consists of a flat, irregularly-shaped, reddish stone, 2 feet 2 inches high, and 3 feet 10 inches wide, built into the masonry in this Cyclopean wall, of which it evidently formed an original part. About thirty years ago a considerable portion of this stone was covered with plaster, so that it is evident, not only that it formed part of the original structure, but that its carving was antecedent to its present purpose. Indented upon its surface is the very ancient Greek or Byzantine cross here figured, the base or skeleton of which is of the same type as that on the stone of St. Brecan, at the Seven Churches in Aranmore, and on

many ancient Irish tombstones. It is said that a similar cross exists at Ard-Oilean, or "High-Island," opposite the coast of Connamara.

The stone altar of this church is still perfect, and measures 4 feet 7 inches, by 3 feet 4 inches wide, and 1 foot 10 inches high. Upon it are two remarkable indented stones: one has an oblong quadrilateral hollow, 6¾ inches long, by 4 wide; the other, placed immediately under the small, eastern, round-headed single light, is a smooth stone, with an oval-shaped depression, 6 by 4 inches in diameter, capable of holding the closed fist—probably a very early font. It belongs to that class of cupped stones called in Aran, where they abound, *Bullauns*, and of which there are many at Glendalough, in Wicklow, of which "the deer stone" may be cited as an example. —See page 164.

On a stone of the ancient flagged way leading up to the western end of this church, is carved a square cross, with fish-tail terminations, like those on Lugnaedon's stone, and which is, no doubt, of great antiquity also.

Outside the north-east angle is a piece of square masonry, 10½ feet by 7 feet 8 inches, and about 4 feet high, believed to be the tomb of Muirgehas O'Nioc, Archbishop of Tuam, who died here in 1128.

O'Flaherty, in whose footsteps we have been treading, wrote thus of this island in 1684:—"Inis an Ghoill, so called of a certain holy person who there lived of old, known only by the name of An Gall Craibhtheach, i. e. the devout foreigner; for Gall (i. e. of the Gallick nation), they call every foreigner. So Inis an Ghoill, or the foreigner's island, between Ross and Moycullen barony on Lough Orbsen, contains half a quarter of pleasant land belonging to Cong Abbey, and hath a fine chapell therein, which is not for the buriall of any body." And further adds, that it "hath two chapells, the one dedicated to St. Patrick, the other to the saint of whom the island is named, which admits not the buriall of any body, but in the first it is usuall to bury." Very few interments now take place in the ancient cemetery of this island, portions of which, with the adjoining islets of Burr and Inishannagh, are planted, and will in time present a very picturesque appearance.*

In pursuance of our route consecutively round the lake we must return to the south-east corner of Cong parish. Viewed from the steamer's deck, or from any northern or western point, the hilly district, where the parishes of Shrule and Cong meet, presents a most dreary aspect; bare, brown, and crowded with intersecting walls, with scarcely a tree or house to relieve the eye; but along the water's edge the view is diversified with foliage and the evidence of human habitation, especially Castle-

* Although the perusal of the foregoing description of Inchangoill may while away the time spent in passing it, the details of this memorable locality are well worthy the tourist's attention. It can easily be visited from Cong village, to which we are now hastening, and to the Galway portion of which parish it belongs.

town, the residence of Mr. Story, which forms a conspicuous object from all parts of the lake in any way west of it. It takes its name from an old castle, now so ruinous as not to afford materials for a sketch.

Running out from the land in a western direction, and about a mile in length, is the long, low, narrow Island of Inishmicatreer, containing a few cottages, the meagre ruins of an ancient church, and also a burial ground. Of this ecclesiastical building we have no account; and there is not a single stone left whereby to judge of its style. It is, however, probable that on this island, as well as on the neighbouring one of Inchiquin, to which it is second in size, may have been erected one of those religious establishments referred to the times of Brendan, Meldan, and Fursæus; for there is great difficulty in determining the precise topography of many of the places in this district mentioned by the hagiologists; and when Colgan wrote he was evidently not personally acquainted with the locality, and his sources of research were chiefly Continental. The shores of this island abound with those peculiar perforated limestones already referred to at page 29; and at the eastern end they form a causeway, which, with the aid of "a plank," connects it in summer time with the mainland. This peninsular position may afford a derivation for the name of *Inish-mic-treer*, or *tier*, "the island of the land."*

* By one of those extraordinary inconsistencies in Irish topography, this island, which is in the Mayo waters, and can be reached dryshod

Taking up our itinerary where we left it, at the north-western angle of the parish of Shrule, we meet the little churchyard of Billapark, one of a group of several such which stud this corner of the parish of Cong. Then we approach Houndswood, the seat of John S. Dawson, Esq., a little to the north-west of which commences, with Caher-Mayo, that vast assemblage of stone forts, cairns, and circles, that culminate at Nymphsfield; and to which, occupying as they do the site of the great battle of Moytura, it will be necessary to devote a special chapter.

The river of Cross, already alluded to at page 23, opens into the northern end of a deep bay, surrounded on the north by the woods of Ballymagibbon, the residence of the Fynn family. In this deep bay there are a great number of small islands, upon one of which (Gibbs'), near "The salt house,"† there are persons now living who remember the timbers of a

from the parish of Shrule, forms a part of the parish of Killannin, nearly ten miles distant across the lake, on the Galway shore. It is said that, when the O'Flahertys were driven from their territory of Magh Seola, on the east, to Gnomore and Gnobeg, on the west of Lough Corrib, "they took their islands with them," or retained possession of them, and this may account for the isolated position of this portion of Killannin.

† "The Salt House," a very notable building on the shore of Lough Corrib; is so called from one of the author's ancestors having erected it when salt was very scarce in Connaught for the manufacture of that material. Sea water and rock salt were brought from Galway, and here turned by evaporation into the edible material. The salt pans existed within the last twenty years.

surrounding stockade rising above low water ; so that it may fairly be conjectured, that crannoges existed here and in other parts of Lough Corrib in early times.

Two roads on the west, and two others on the east, uniting at acute angles on each side of a small river running into Lough Corrib, give, together with a mill, dispensary, bridge, schoolhouse, a couple of shops, some cottages, a forge, and a public house, &c., the name of "Cross" to a village of some note and antiquity.

About half a mile to the north-east of this village, on the Kilmain road, stands an antique quadrangular tower, commonly known as "The Castle of Cross ;" and attached to its eastern side are the ruins of an early, and in some of its architectural details rather interesting church, of which the two following cuts are highly illustrative, although it has not been thought worthy of recognition on the Ordnance Maps. The tower, which is exceedingly massive and well built, is now 22 feet high, and measures 25 feet on the east, and 16 on the south side: and its walls are 3 feet 3 inches thick. It has a narrow light on each face ; and its pointed doorway, leading from the church, opens into a stone-roofed apartment, topped by another similar chamber, the only access to which is by a square aperture in the floor over the outer doorway, like those seen in secular defensive edifices. In all probability this tower, which was evidently constructed along with the church, was used not merely as a belfry, but as a residence for the clerics, and in troubled times a place of security for the people and the ecclesiastical valuables, just as it is believed the round towers were. A great many churches

in Ireland of the same architectural character as that of Cross are furnished with towers; and, as if carrying out the idea of the primitive round tower, their architects have almost invariably placed their doorways at a considerable distance above the ground. A striking example occurs at Corcomroe, in Clare, where the only opening giving access to the belfry tower is a square-headed doorway, placed about twelve feet from the ground. The church itself is 40 feet long and 19 wide, on the inside. Its northern wall is 13 feet 6 inches high, and the east gable is still standing, but formed of small stones, undressed, except at the angles, and in the double-lighted eastern window. The latter is deserving of a careful inspection, as its masonry exhibits a curious instance of economy and adaptation. The superincumbent weight of the gable is relieved by a solid arch of undressed stone below. Although the division between the lights, and also their outer edges, are all composed of chiselled stone, their inner jambs, a portion of the splays, and all the soffit and arches, are ingeniously constructed of carefully-selected blocks, that do not show the slightest trace of either chisel, punch, or hammer, as may be seen in the accompanying illustration. Although there are many legends afloat anent caillaghs, witches with black hafted knives, "weird sisters," and belated travellers, there is no real history of this building. It is situated in the townland of "Attyickard," as it is spelled on the map, but the proper name of which is *Ath-Teach-Ricard*, "The site of Richard's House," probably because a Burke had a hand in the construction of its castellated tower. To the south and west may be seen in a few minutes' walk several ancient remains—circles, forts, traces of Pagan sepultures, and caves—one of the latter in particular sunk in the middle of a fort, adjoining the site of the dilapidated village of the same name as the townland, is worthy of inspection.

Returning to Cross, and in the grounds of Thomas Gildea, Esq., at Dowagh, we must visit one of the very oldest primitive Cyclopean churches in Ireland, and undoubtedly the most remarkable that occurs in our route—that of St. Fraughaun, the square-headed western doorway of which is here faithfully shown. Its walls are now 7 feet high on an average, and 2 feet thick; its length is 18 feet intside, 12 wide at the west, and 14 in breadth at the east end—a remarkable peculiarity. There are no remains of window apertures, as the east gable is no longer standing. The doorway here figured is 5 feet 8 inches high, and 2 feet 3 inches wide at bottom, the jambs inclining to 1 foot 11 inches at top, where they are covered by a massive lintel, 3 feet 5 inches long, which spans the entire wall. The inner faces of the jamb stones are smooth, as at Killursa.

That this building is a representative of the primitive Oratory and dwelling house of an early Irish saint, there can be no doubt. It was divided into an upper and lower apartment by a flat floor, some of the corbels of which yet remain; and the space between this and the roof was, no doubt, the saint's sleeping apartment. We find the same arrangement in St. Kevin's Kitchen, St. Columba's House at Kells, Molua's House, and other buildings of the same peculiar class. The only difference between Kilfraughan and the others just mentioned is, that it had a dividing floor of timber, and the others one of stone, resting upon a barrel arch. This charming little ruin, which stands in the middle of a very ancient burial ground, and is surrounded by antique hollies and thorns, is highly venerated by the people, among whom there is a tradition, that from it was brought the clay with which the Abbey of Cong was consecrated.

Of St. Fraughaun, if such a personage existed here, we know nothing; and our annals, calendars, martyrologies, and the saints' lives make no mention of him. The ancient name of this church, and one which is still living among the old people, is *Kill-ard-creave-na-Naoimh*—literally, "the church of the high branch of the saints." Below its east end is a spring well of never-failing purity and supply, which, in fine weather, when the great turloughs are dry, affords water for the neighbouring mill, and pours its stream into the Cross river.*

* Within the precincts of this little church stands the tomb of a very memorable man in his day and generation, and by his life affording a type of many of the gentry of the West during the past century and a half. Well, with all your faults, Dick Blake, I cannot but remember how well you taught me to ride, keeping my "hands low down on the saddle"—what skilful di-

To the north of this locality is Garracloon, the property and residence of Colonel Veitch.

Continuing our route on to the village of Cong, through the great cairn-studded plain of Moytura, we meet another small ancient church called Killarsagh, in the townland of Ballymagibbon, of which 12 feet high of the east gable, with a small, round arched window in it, still remains, as shown in the accompanying cut; as also so much of the side walls as to give the measurement of its interior as 24 feet long by 16½ feet broad.* Again, a little nearer the lake, in the village of Gortachurra, "the field of the curragh" scrub or bottom, there formerly existed the ruins of a very small church, some of the large stones of which

may still be discerned in the adjoining walls and cottages.

From the hill of Tonlegee, overlooking this latter locality, was taken the accompanying view of Moytura House, the re-

rections for shooting, and training setters and pointers, you gave me; and with what pride you used to see me shoot the rising trout from off the bridge of Cross . . . . years ago. —W. R. W.

* In the wall of this church there was, a few years ago, a carved stone, having in relief the figure of a child. It is now built into a coach-house in the vicinity.

sidence of the Author, erected in 1865; and so called after the ancient battle-field on which it stands, with Benlevi Mountain in the distance, and Lough Corrib in front. The tower with the flagstaff stands within the enclosure of one of the ancient

cahers of the battle field. This house commands a magnificent prospect to the west, south, and east, and can be seen from most parts of the middle lake. To the west of Moytura is Lackafinna—"the white flagstone"—the residence of Ormsby Elwood, Esq.; and still nearer to Cong, over a small bay of the lake, stands Lisloughrey—"the rushy liss," or earthen fort—the residence of William Burke, Esq.

We have passed the last navigation mark, and laid our course nearly due north towards the Cong river. From this point the mountain view presents one of its best aspects; and the shores of Mayo and Galway, sloping down to the water's edge, are in many places pleasingly wooded. Leaving Coad Island on the left, we get among a group of islets at the mouth of the river, the outermost of which, Illaunree, or "the king's island," was said to have been a favourite retreat of O'Conor, the last Irish monarch, while sojourning in the neighbouring abbey; and nearer the shore are Inish-Cong and Illaundarra.

Now, dividing the waters of Mayo and Galway, we pass Cannaderry, "the peninsular headland," and enter the principal streamway which conducts the waters of Lough Mask into Lough Corrib. Well sheltered, wooded on both sides, having Kinlough on the right, the demesne of Ashford on the left, and Standhill, the seat of the Elwoods, in front, with the pretty spire of the parish church in the distance, it forms a picture of great beauty. The following illustration, taken from the eastern shore, represents the "Eglinton" passing under the demesne of Ashford, the noble seat of Sir B. L. Guinness, M. P., with his recently erected tower rising over the surrounding woods.

Our steamer has been warped round the little island, and brought to her berth alongside the quay.* We leave her for the present; and, starting for "The Carlisle Arms," in the village about half a mile distant, may visit two of the natural caves for which this locality is celebrated—The Lady's Buttery

* In the river opposite Kinlough, the residence of Mr. Moran, at a place called *Cushatruffe*, "the foot of the stream," there is a small island round which the steamer is usually warped, but the removal of which would form a basin in which the vessel could easily turn.

and the Horse Discovery, which both adjoin the road. Here, as we pass along by the canal referred to at page 35, we get a good view of the parish church,* the Roman Catholic chapel,

and the eastern gable and window of the abbey, which with the history and antiquities of this ancient locality, will be described in the next chapter.

* The simple architectural church of Cong, to which the lord of the soil has added a well-proportioned spire, is very well placed in an island between the land and two of the rivers. The chapel, for which a beautiful site was lately offered in the village, is placed within the abbey grounds, and is at present in process of reconstruction.

CHAPTER VII.

CONG.

CONG VILLAGE. RIVERS. ANNALS. ST. FECHIN. THE ABBEY, AND ITS HISTORY. THE O'DUFFYS. IRELAND'S LAST MONARCH. ASHFORD. THE STREET CROSS. THE IRISH LANGUAGE. RELIQUES; THE TRUE CROSS; THE TOOTH OF ST. PATRICK. THE BLACK BELL. WAYSIDE MONUMENTS. THE CASTLE OF AUGHALARD. CAVES. THE PIGEON HOLE.

CONG—in Irish, *Cunga*, "a neck," so called from its situation upon the isthmus that here divides Lough Mask from Lough Corrib, and also *Conga-Fechin*, in remembrance of its patron saint—is an island formed by a number of streams that surround it on all sides. There is water everywhere—gliding by in the broad river; gushing from the surrounding rocks; boiling up in vast pools that supply several mills; oozing through the crevices of stones; rising in the interior of caverns; appearing and disappearing wherever its wayward nature wills; passing in and out everywhere, except where man tried to turn it—into the monster dry canal. The village, which is approachable by four bridges, and occupies a small hill, is T-shaped, and consisted in 1861 of 88 houses, and 469 inhabitants. It is a market town, and was formerly a great milling depot; to which latter circumstance, and the patronage of the adjoining extensive ecclesiastical establishment, it no doubt owed its origin. As the tourist approaches it, a good view of the eastern end of its old abbey is presented; and, turning up by the main street, he has before him the base of the ancient cross, figured and described at page 185.

Outside the confines of this village, the scene presents a remarkable contrast—upon the south and east, all is bare, grey limestone rock; while on the west and south lies a beautiful, well-wooded, and highly cultivated demesne, through which glides the clear stream of the Cong River, up the lower portion of which we passed in the "Eglinton." The eastern roads lead to The Neale, Ballinrobe, and Kilmain, and by Headford to Galway; and its south-western to Lough Mask, and through the Joyce's Country by Maam into Connamara. The northern and western streams divide the village from the county of Galway.

The Annals of Cong, which, if all collected, would almost form a history of Ireland, might commence with the battle of Moytura, stated by the bards, and believed by the early writers, (where they assign dates to events), to have been fought in the year of the world 3303. For some centuries after that period, and down to the Christian era, the great plain to the west and north immediately adjoining this village, and on which the battle took place, was thickly studded with inhabitants, whose dwellings and monuments the tourist is now about to visit, and which are certainly amongst the most remarkable in the British Isles. It does not appear, either from history or tradition, that St. Patrick or his attendants visited Cong, or that his immediate successors approached nearer to it than Inchangoill; but, in the seventh century, St. Fechin of Fore, struck, perhaps, with the extraordinary resemblance which the natural features of Cong, and its underground rivers, &c., bore to his ecclesiastical home in Westmeath, is said to have blessed this neck of land, from which the extensive parish of Cong still takes its name, and to have erected a church here; and the good man left his track, and gave his name to several holy wells and churches in the district westward of this village.

It is also said that, so early as A. D. 624, an Irish king, Domhnall Mac Aedh Mac Ainmire, founded an abbey here, and that St. Fechin was its first abbot. The hagiologists, or saints' historians, must settle this question. Colgan also states that Cong was "celebrated for divers churches, as their walls and remains at this day testify." Such may have been the case at the beginning of the seventeenth century, but they no longer exist, and the name of only one remains, attached to the field of the *Killeen-breac*, or "little speckled church,"

* St. Fechin died of the great yellow plague, or *Buidhe Chonnaile*, that twice devastated Ireland, first in 539, and then in 664; for which, and other pestilences, see the Author's collected references in his dissertation on the subject in "The Tables of Deaths," published among the Census Reports for 1851, Part v., vol. i., pp. 50 and 416, &c.

to the south of the present abbey grounds. There is, however, a stone near the river side, in an old garden to the left of the second eastern bridge, which takes precedence of all other stones in Cong, upon which the craft of man had been exercised in Christian times, and which, as known by the Irish name of *Leach-na-poll*, or the "flagstone of the holes," is here figured. It is a large triangular red grit flag, 2 feet thick, and 8½ feet long in its greatest diameter, from under which a never-failing limpid spring issues. Its upper surface is hollowed into five

basin-like smooth excavations, averaging 12 inches wide, and 4½ deep, and usually known as *Bullauns*, from the Latin *bulla*, a bowl; and which, from their being invariably found in immediate connexion with the most ancient churches, may be regarded as primitive baptismal fonts.—See page 147.

What description of church St. Fechin erected here and dedicated to the Virgin before his death, in 664, or where it stood, is unknown, although Colgan states, in the *Acta Sanctorum*, that it was "his own monastery." But in truth the Irish church of that period was but the daimliag, or domhnach, already described at page 107; and the Culdees or early ecclesiastics lived either within it, or in stone cells, or cloghaunes, or in wooden houses, in the surrounding enclosure, and occasionally in the adjoining round tower.

Cong was originally a bishopric, and with those of Tuam, Killala, Clonfert, and Ardcharne, was named among the five sees of the province of Connaught, regulated by the Synod of Rath-Breasill, in Leagh (the present Queen's County), in the year 1010;* but, as stated at page 64, the see was shortly afterwards removed to Enaghdun. Keating also styled it a bishopric.

In 1114 the Annals of the Four Masters state that Cunga, with Kilbanon and several other ecclesiastical establishments, "were all burned this year." The bishopric removed, and the cathedral burned; but the odour of sanctity still clinging to the venerable locality, hallowed by the remembrance of St. Fechin, a fine opening offered to the Augustinians to display their architectural taste, and to establish their ecclesiastical power in Connaught—so that probably between the former date and 1127–28, when the deaths of two of its Airenaghs (or conventual superiors), Gilla-Keerin O'Roda, and O'Draeda, are re-

* "This synod made the following decree respecting Connaught:—'If the clergy of Connaught be satisfied with the division, we are well pleased; but if not, let the division be made according to their own pleasure, onlie they shall have but five bishops in the province of Connaught.'"—See Hardiman's additional notes to O'Flaherty's "H-Iar Connaught," p. 155.

corded, the abbey and monastery were founded. This magnificent establishment was erected for Canons Regular of the Order of St. Augustine, whose vast territories and rich possessions extended not merely throughout Connaught, but into several counties in the South and East of Ireland;* in whose keeping were placed the great family deeds and records of the West country chieftains and landed proprietors; who constructed the grandest piece of metal work of its age now extant in Europe; whose principal was a Lord Abbot; and who left us the beautiful structure we are now hastening to examine.

To fill up, however, the middle distance, and paint the foreground of the historic picture of Cong after the erection of its abbey and monastery, without stopping to notice the accession or to record the deaths of its dignitaries, we find it the peaceful sanctuary of the last monarch of Ireland during the ruthless times which followed the English invasion, when the O'Conors and O'Donnells, sometimes joining with, and sometimes fighting against, the Anglo-Normans, devastated the country, pillaging and burning the abbeys and churches, and then slaughtering one another;—down through the dark period of Saxon misrule and legalized injustice, when the white-rocheted friars formed their last long-winding procession, as,

* The property of the Abbey of Cong, and especially their great estates in Joyce-Country and Connamara, were, in the reign of Elizabeth, granted to the Provost and Fellows of Trinity College, Dublin.

passing out of their beauteous abbey they wound their way with lingering footsteps over the adjoining bridge, and took their *Iompo-tuaghfil*, or "left-handed turn," ere they cast a final look upon its tall tower and peaked gables, cutting sharp and clear against the western sky.

The Augustinian monks have departed—the bells have tolled their last peal; the altar lights are extinguished; a few valuables, snatched in haste, have been preserved, and Cong is a ruin—whence every sculptured stone that could be removed was built into the hovels around—and which was barely held together by the fostering arms of the luxuriant ivy, until lately cleared of rubbish, and its mullioned windows and decorated doorways carefully restored.

What an eventful period has intervened, during which Cong and its environs were granted to the Kings and Binghams, or were possessed by the O'Donnells and the Brownes—when Macnamara, the freebooter, and Webb, the murderer, left tales for the guides and their gaping auditors to batten upon—when it was attempted to alter and amend religious opinion by persecution and penal enactments—when law, if at all administered without the aid of the cudgel or the horsewhip, was an injustice: and clerical magistrates (not in the days of Cromwell) could command the regular army to remove from public view a stone bearing the name of two venerable, and perhaps pious, ecclesiastics, who flourished here some eight hundred years ago!

Governmental confiscations of property there were in abundance. Debts accumulated as the result of reckless extravagance, contested elections, unsuccessful horse racing, Chancery suits transmitted for generations, bills of cost, interest on loans, and mortgages—the dowers of dowagers, and the jointures of grandmothers and aunts. All these kept the gentry poor; but they were tolerably loyal to the State, which sheltered them in a country where the king's writ did not run. The people were also poor, and likewise ignorant, improvident, and uneducated, although far superior to the same class in the sister country; but they were disloyal—not so much on account of Protestantism, tithes, Catholic disabilities, the want of educational resources, or any other real or sentimental grievance, but because they had never been conquered by either force, justice, or kindness. However, what diplomacy and the sword could not effect for so many centuries, a single night of blight, followed by a few years' failure of the tuber introduced by Raleigh, achieved. It cut off almost in a moment the food of an entire nation. The rent ceased; the mortgagees were unpaid; the agents failed; the poor rates could not be collected. Pestilence followed the famine; the herds diminished; the workhouses buried such of the dead as had not fallen by the wayside; emigration helped off the remaining living; the Incumbered Estates Court sold up the bankrupt landlords, as in a sheriff's sale, and often at half the value of the land; the old properties changed hands; and, although hundreds of thousands were lost both to the owners and creditors, new blood was infused, and new life and energy thrown into the country. And now, the old Abbey of Cong, and the adjoining estates, with many a mile to westward of this famed locality, have been purchased with the produce of ability, honest industry, and successful commercial enterprise.*

The ruins of Cong church and monastery occupy the south-western angle of the island, but have become so mixed up with modern buildings, that it is now difficult to find a point of view from which to give a good representation of the entire. The succeeding illustration, taken upwards of forty years ago by Samuel Lover, R. H. A., from a point somewhat to the north-east of the bridge of the Killeen-breac, so truthfully represents the scene, that with his permission it is introduced upon the following page.†

Among the splendid ecclesiastical remains of Cong, the twelfth century advocates may revel, and defy us to prove an earlier date for their erection than that of the introduction of

* What a great and memorable chronicle it would form, and possibly one beneficial to future generations, could the following be tabulated :—The original name of each territory, and by what tribe or chieftain possessed—into what hands such estates passed, extending over many centuries, which could in most instances be done—who last possessed it; how it was acquired; by what means it was incumbered when put up for auction; and, finally, who purchased it, and how the price of it was created.

† See the "Irish Penny Magazine" for January, 1841, with a memoir on Cong, by the late John D'Alton.

the Augustinian order into Ireland, even if their ornamentation and design did not afford ample data for judging of their age.

These ruins would scarcely have held together to the present day, had not Sir B. L. Guinness restored several of the dilapidations, cleared out much of the rubbish which had ac-

cumulated within and around them, and rendered the burial ground sufficiently decent for the interment of Christian people.* As the following observations, made nearly thirty years

* Among the restorations lately effected may be particularly specified, those of the completion of the arch over the central light of the east window, and the introduction of the missing stones in the decorated doors and windows of the beautiful western *façade*, described at p. 179. All these restorations were carved from the native limestone by Mr. Peter Foy, of Cong, and his work bears careful comparison with that of the original artists.

ago upon this abbey by that keen observer, graphic, witty describer, and patriotic antiquary, Cæsar Otway, faithfully accord with our own early recollections of Cong, we here insert them in order that the contrast may be the more striking:—"Though the Connaught abbeys suffered less waste and demolition from those who originally suppressed them, the busy and fond superstition that turned their interior into places of much-desired sepulture, has defaced and destroyed what the avarice of Henry's courtiers and the curse of Cromwell had spared; and so there is now no one to care for and protect an Irish abbey—it, instead of being allowed to repose in the much-respected solitude of a Tintern, a Bolton, or Fountains, in England, is now anything but beautiful, it is not even decent; the *genius loci*, outraged, we might almost personify as weeping, while all round is disgraced and desecrated." And, after describing the rooting pigs and the rioting boys that he found enjoying themselves among the ruins, he adds, "Whoever enters an Irish abbey, let him be Protestant or Romanist, must sigh for some law appointing conservators* able to restrain the ignorant and reckless hands

* A few years ago, long after the foregoing was written, the author, and other members of The Celtic Society, had considerable trouble in rescuing from destruction the sculptured tombs in the old church of Lusk, and in the Port-Lester chapel attached to St. Audoen's Church, in Dublin, which were about to be sold as "old materials" to contractors by the Irish Ecclesiastical Commissioners, composed of archbishops, bishops, judges, and others "learned in the law," but neither versed in the history of their country, nor anxious to preserve the monuments of the past.

that are, day after day, obliterating the religious monuments of the island. And here let me be allowed another remark respecting the, to me, evident difference that exists between the monastic remains previous and subsequent to the Anglo-Norman conquest. Of the former we find no remains that were not directly devoted to religious worship, churches, oratories, crypts, and shrines (except the round towers, which alone seem to have answered any secular purpose). The old Irish monastic, in his Culdee simplicity, was contented with his little hermitage composed of wattles, his humble cell of perishable materials; living on the milk of a few cows, and the fish that the adjoining river (as at Cong) abundantly supplied; enough for him was the conviction, that at the approach of the barbarous spoiler he could retreat, with his vestments and holy things, by means of a ladder, into the round tower, through its high-placed door; from thence to see his humble cell committed to the flames, there to bear the privations he was so well accustomed to, until the ravagers retreated, and the tyranny was overpast." And, of Cong, he further adds, "I have seldom, indeed, seen a place so dilapidated; I was not only disappointed, but vexed, to see it so overthrown and dismantled."*

We enter the abbey from the village by a very beautiful doorway, which, although it has been often figured, we would

* See the Rev. Cæsar Otway's "Tour in Connaught," 1839.

here present to our readers, but that we know it is of the "composite order," having been made up some years ago of stones taken from another arch in this northern wall. Within it, we find ourselves in the great abbey church, 140 feet long, entirely paved with tombstones;—facing the east window, with its three long, narrow lights, and having in each side wall of the chancel a slender window looking north and south. The chancel walls are perfect, but the northern wall of the nave no longer exists. Underneath the chancel window the guides and village folk maintain that Roderick O'Conor was buried, when, after fifteen years' retirement within this abbey, he died here in 1198. But this we know from history to be incorrect, for the Donegal Annals distinctly state that "Ruodri Ua Concobair, King of Connaught and of all Ireland, both the Irish and English, died among the canons at Cong, after exemplary penance, victorious over the world and the devil. His body was conveyed to Clonmacnois, and interred on the north side of the altar."

But, although Roderick himself was not buried here, others of his name and lineage were. Thus we read that, in 1224, "Maurice the Canon, son of Roderick O'Conor—the most illustrious of the Irish for learning psalm-singing and poetical compositions, died—and was interred at Cong." It is probably his tomb which is pointed out as that of the king. "A. D. 1226, Nuala, daughter of Roderick O'Conor, and Queen of Ulidia, died at Conga Fechin, and was honourably interred in the church of the canons."* And, in 1247, Finola, daughter of King Roderick, died at, and was probably buried at, Cong. But, although the dust of the last monarch is not beneath our feet, that of chieftains, warriors, and prelates remains, and especially that of the abbots, down to the days of James Lynch, whose decorated tomb is dated 1703; and even later, for the Rev. Patrick Prendergast, who was always styled "The Lord Abbot," was interred here in 1829.†

Several of these ecclesiastical tomb flags are decorated with crosses, fleur-de-lis, chalices, and ornate croziers, &c.; and there are a few Latin inscriptions in raised letters, but with one exception no Irish writing can be discerned anywhere within the confines of the abbey. In the south wall there is a recess, with

* "Annals of the Four Masters." Nuala was "the wife of Mac Donslevy, who was at that period styled King of Uladh," or that portion of Ulster "lying eastwards of Glenree, Lough Neagh, and the Lower Bann."—See O'Donovan's note, under A. D. 1226.

† There is a tradition that, when the few remaining Canons were driven forth from this monastery, they were harboured by some of the author's ancestors at Ballymagibbon; and upon one of the farms of that property, now called Abbotstown, Father Prendergast resided till the day of his death, at the round age of eighty-eight. He was a very fine, courteous, white-haired old man—a good specimen of the St. Omers' priest of sixty years ago. He did not nominate a successor, nor was such appointed by any Irish chapter, or by the General Abbot at Rome. Prendergast succeeded Abbot O'Maley. He was the owner of several reliques, which he used to take great pride in showing and explaining to the author, when a boy—the cross of Cong, the shrine of St. Patrick's tooth, and the piece of linen marked with the blood of the martyr, &c.—See pages 188 to 196, &c.

a circular arch, probably the tomb of the founder, or some munificent endower; there are also in his south wall piscinæ, and other minor details of church architecture, unnecessary to describe; and lower down upon the same side is the small chapel-tomb of the Berminghams, once so powerful in Ireland, and who so identified themselves with their adopted country, that they dropped the Norman name, and assumed that of Mac Feoris. They became Lords of Athenry, and acquired great possessions in Connaught.*

During the clearances recently made, a few objects of interest were discovered, and among them a stone, bearing a portion of the incised cross here figured. It is too narrow to have been a monumental flag, the longest arm of the cross being but thirteen inches; it was probably one of the terminal crosses that marked the boundaries of the ancient sacred enclosure.

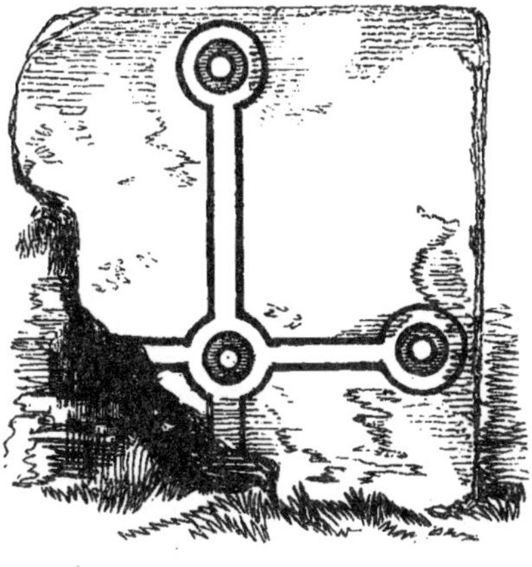

Another stone of still greater interest, discovered in making these restorations, is the quadrangular fragment of the shaft of an ancient cross, which in all probability is a portion of the

* The late Earls of Leitrim and Charlemont married the last two of the female line of the Mayo and Galway Berminghams, who held the Ross-Hill and other large estates westward of Cong.—See p. 189.

village cross referred to at page 185; for not only does it bear the same names as those on the base of the latter, but it accurately fits the mortise in that plinth, being 16 inches by 8. This stone, now about 2 feet high, and the two inscribed faces of which upon opposite sides are here figured, is at present placed in the east window.

The inscription, which is in ancient raised letters, means—A prayer for Niahol and Gillebard O'Dubthaigh, or O'Duffy, who were abbots of Cong; but which inscription is more perfect on the plinth of the market cross, figured and described at page 185.

The O'Duffys were distinguished ecclesiastics in this locality, and the Annals contain many entries concerning them. Thus we read that in "A. D. 1150 Muireadhach Ua Dubhthaigh, Archbishop of Connaught, chief senior of all Ireland in wisdom, in chastity, in the bestowal of jewels and food, died at Conga on the 16th of the month of May, on the festival of St. Brenainn, in the 75th year of his age." His name is inscribed on the great processional "Cross of Cong," made in 1123.—See page 194.

"A. D. 1168. Flannagan Ua Dubhthaigh, bishop and chief doctor of the Irish in literature, history, and poetry, and in every kind of science known to man in his time, died in the bed of Muireadhach Ua Dubhthaigh, at Cunga."—See page 196.

Cadhla or Catholicus O'Duffy, and several of the name, attained to the see of Tuam; in 1136, we read of the death at Clonfert, of Donnell O'Duffy, "Archbishop of Connaught, and successor of Ciaran, head of the wisdom and piety of the province;" and Kele O'Duffy was Bishop of "Mayo of the Saxons" in 1209. But none of these died abbots of Cong, and the only Abbot of the name referred to in the Annals is the one described by the Four Masters in the following quotation, under the year 1223:—

Ꝺuḃṫach ua ꝺuḃṫaıᵹh abb Conᵹa ꝺecc.
"Duffagh O'Duffy, Abbot of Cong, died."

As to who this "Gillibard," or Gilla-Bard, was, we have no clue from an examination of the Annals, and cannot, therefore, state when his death occurred; but it must have been subsequent to that of Duffagh and Niahol; and was probably in the beginning of the thirteenth century.

Before leaving this church and its crosses, let us perform an act of partial expiation, by introd cing to the visitor the following illustration, showing the four decorated sides of a portion of the shaft of a very beautiful sandstone cross, which was abstracted from these ruins many years ago, but is still in existence.* The two end portions of the illustration represent the sides; the left-hand middle is the front, and the right the

back, which latter is countersunk, evidently for the insertion of a metal plate, which was probably inscribed with the name of the person who erected it, or to whose memory it was raised. The top is mortised for the reception of the tenon of the upper portion of the shaft.

The original plan of this abbey is not easily made out at present. Through an arched doorway in the southern wall

* This cross, which is now 23 inches high, is in the pleasure-ground at Moytura, and is by some believed to have been in the possession of the late Father Prendergast. Others say it was rescued from the dilapidations at Cong by the late Mr. Fynn, the author's relative, and at that time proprietor of the Moytura property.

When the broken shaft of O'Duffy's cross, now in the east window, is restored to its position upon the base of the market or street cross, this beautiful piece of mediæval work shall be restored to the abbey.

we pass into a low vaulted apartment, and thence into a large open space containing the principal stairs, which lead up to the second story of the great tower, the upper portion of which, however, no longer exists. The space to the east and south of this, which was formerly occupied by the monastery, is now a graveyard, and the site of the Roman Catholic chapel, and is divided by a high screen wall, the western façade of which forms the present great architectural feature of this splendid pile, and is well shown in the subjoined illustration. It measures 80 feet in length, and contains a doorway and two

windows, with circular arches; and two large and most elaborately ornamented lancet-headed doors, with under-cut chevrons along the deep moulding of the arches, which spring from clustered pillars, the floral capitals of which—all of different patterns—present us with one of the finest specimens of twelfth century stone-work in Ireland.* This cut represents a portion of these highly ornate imposts. Above the string course appear some narrow lights, probably those of the dormitories. To the west of this wall stood the open cloisters, which were probably so low as not to obscure the decorated front represented on the foregoing page. From this point

the ground slopes gradually to the river, where, according to tradition, the friars of old had a fish house—the walls of which are still standing—so constructed that, when the salmon or trout got into the crib below, it touched a wire, that rang a bell, to inform the providore or cook of its arrival.

Standing between the river and the abbey, the picture naturally rises before us of the aged monarch, broken down by the calamities which his country was suffering from a foreign

* Several stones have been recently inserted in these doorways, which now present us with some of the finest and most enduring specimens of carved limestone in either this or any other country.

invasion, which he was no longer able to resist—but still more so by the opposition and ingratitude of his own children and relatives—passing up the river with his retinue, landing here in 1183, and received by the Lord Abbot and his canons and friars; and then taking leave of his faithful adherents at the water's edge, being conducted in procession to the abbey, which, it is said, his munificence had endowed. There, as a recluse untrammelled by the weight of state affairs, and possibly unaffected by the quarrels of his chieftains and kinsfolk, the Last Monarch of Ireland, abdicating his authority because the country no longer supported him, died, a sad, but fitting and prophetic emblem of the land over which he had ruled.

Within the abbey grounds, on the north-west, formerly stood the ruins of Macnamara's house, which Bishop Pococke, writing in the year 1770, says, was the most delightfully-situated residence he had seen in the course of his travels; a fragment of it still remains. More to the west there recently existed the residence of the late proprietor, A. C. Lambert, Esq., constructed of the unhewn, weather-worn, but square stones, collected in the locality. Being no longer required, and not being quite congruous with the scene, it has been removed.

Passing under an arch,* and over a bridge lately con-

* The antiquary may think that the royal head with which the keystone of this arch is decorated should have been crowned with an Irish diadem, and not an English crown.

structed of immense flagstones taken from the river's bed, we pass into Ashford, the demesne of Sir B. L. Guinness, the view of whose residence, taken from near the quay, is figured below. Let another describe it, and its environs. "Whether,"

says Sir Bernard Burke, in alluding to Cong, "you consider its unbounded fertility, the varied beauties of its surface, or the historical events which invest every plain and every mountain with an interest peculiarly its own, it stands forth to the lover of the wild and the beautiful, to the antiquarian and the geologist as unsurpassed by any portion of the British Empire. And we do not hesitate to insist that in this island, so favoured, the ancient town and neighbourhood of Cong are pre-eminent; in each of the particulars above alluded to, this portion of the counties of Galway and Mayo is unrivalled in its peculiarities. It presents a varied surface of contradictory elements—streams of barrenness and fertility, exquisite beauty and wild desolation; green valleys and rocky plains, lakes and rivers, and huge mountains, are so thrown together in wild confusion, that it would almost seem as if nature had wandered here in one of her sportive moods, producing on every side such a marvellous contrast and variety. It is in the loveliest part of this district that the property is situated, of which we have engaged to furnish a few particulars. Ashford, formerly a residence of Lord Oranmore, occupies one of the most striking and beautiful sites in the whole island; and is situated on the right bank of the river, which, flowing past the ruins of the ancient abbey of Cong, is adorned in its short course with all that can constitute the interesting and picturesque. The writer," and the author also, "well remembers this mansion, now comfortable, a dilapidated building, in the midst of a neglected domain—a very picture of poor Ireland herself when stricken by famine and pestilence. It was built by one of the family of Brown, about a century and a half ago, somewhat in the style of the French chateau. The situation was well chosen; and the founder made it an exception to the almost general rule, that Irish mansions are erected near to, but not upon, the most eligible spots. The river, the lake, the deep and solemn woods that environ it, the extreme fertility of the domain—encircled as it were by a framework of bare rocks and interminable waters—constitute a species of oasis in this wild district, at once lovely, striking, and peculiar."*

Within the demesne, and in the immediate vicinity of the handsome tower recently erected here, and shown in the foregoing illustration, there can be seen one of those artificial caves formed by the ancient Firbolgs, or Tuatha de Dananns, to which we shall have occasion to refer hereafter; but, as it is so nigh at hand, the visitor should inspect it now. This cave, called *Lisheenard*, "the small fort of the height," which is sunk within an ancient circular rath, now surrounded with aged hazels, measures 27 feet from its eastern entrance to its turn to the south, which latter portion is 24 long. Its average height is 6½ feet; and it is roofed with immense flags, supported on projecting corbels, as explained in the general description of these troglodyte habitations, at page 203. There is also here a natural grotto, called *Teach Aille*, "the house in the cliff," where the waters of Lough Mask present themselves externally in their transit through the various north-western pools and caverns to Lough Corrib. Let us re-cross the river by *Toin-a-Chaislean*, "the bottom of the castle," or site of the old castle of Cong, which certainly existed in the days of Roderick

* See "A Visitation of the Seats and Arms of the Noblemen and Gentlemen of Great Britain and Ireland," by Sir Bernard Burke, Ulster King of Arms: 1858, pp. 241, 242.

O'Flaherty, but the last fragment of which was removed about twenty years ago, when "the circular road" of Cong was constructing.

Now, that we come prepared with historic knowledge, derived from our visit to the abbey, let us inspect the Street or Market Cross, the dark limestone plinth or base of which, with a carefully engraved *fac simile* of its inscription, is here shown,

the translation being—"A prayer for Niahol [Nicol, or Neal], and for Gillibard [Gilbert] O'Dubthaidh [O'Duffy], who were abbots of Cong."* It is 16 inches high, and measures 36 by 30 inches upon the upper surface, into the step or mortise of which the present shaft in the abbey originally fitted. There is now a plain modern shaft in its place, the cap of which, together with the three steps on which the plinth now rests, was

* This inscription—which is in substance the same as above, but not transcribed from a rubbing—was brought under the notice of the Royal Irish Academy, in 1855, by the Rev. Dr. Todd, and has been printed in the Proceedings of that body, vol. vi., p. 225.

erected by the Elwood family in the famine year of 1822: prior to which the base stood upon a large block of natural rock, which, however, together with the inscribed base, &c., was removed, as it was regarded as an obstruction to the thoroughfare.* This inscription is not in the Irish character, but in the black letter text of the fourteenth century; and as it is, perhaps, the last place in our route where we shall meet with such writing, and as this junction of the counties of Mayo and Galway affords a fitting place for its introduction, a few words upon the present statistical condition of the Irish language may not be inappropriate.

Except the gentry, nearly every person, young or old, in this parish speaks the Irish, and many do not use any other tongue. When Hely Dutton wrote his Statistical (?) Survey of the County of Galway, in 1824, he remarked upon the increase of the English language in the West, and repeated the well-known adage, that "The natives of Ulster have the right phrase, but not the pronunciation; Munster, the pronunciation, but not the phrase; Leinster has neither; Connaught has both." The first Census of the Irish-speaking population was taken in 1851,†

* This is the circumstance alluded to at p. 168. After the inscribed stone had been removed as an "offender" to the barracks, the gentleman who had it taken down placed it a little way to the north of the abbey door; but the popular feeling was so strongly expressed upon the subject, that it was eventually restored to its former site, where it now stands.

† At the instance of the author, then one of the Census Commissioners.

and then it was found that, in a population of 6,574,278, as many as 23·3 per cent. spoke Irish ; but ten years subsequently a decrease of 4·2 per cent. had taken place throughout the country in this respect, as in March, 1861, when the last Census was taken, and the total number of inhabitants was 5,798,967, the entire Irish-speaking population amounted to only 1,105,536, or 19·1 per cent. Of these, 163,275, spoke Irish only, and the remainder professed a vernacular knowledge of both languages. Comparatively few literate persons could either read or write Irish. In 1851 more than half the inhabitants of the province of Connaught could speak their native language; even still the counties of Galway and Mayo afford the greatest number of Irish-speaking people, and in 1861 as many as 73,740 therein were returned as unable to speak English. The spoken Gaelic is hourly dying out; and in twenty years more the oldest language in north-western Europe, if we except that of the Lapps and other extreme northern tribes, will have ceased to be used. Fortunately, however, and thanks to the exertions made by a few patriotic individuals, and to the labours of O'Donovan and O'Curry, the written language has been preserved—for ever.

Had the Irish language been cultivated by the upper classes as was proposed by many eminent scholars and divines, it might, perhaps, have had an influence upon many subjects connected with the interests of this country. The old tale is still repeated, that when Elizabeth, wishing to learn something of the tongue of her Irish dependency, asked for a specimen, this was repeated to her—*Digh dabh dubh uv labh,* "A black ox ate a raw egg"—which certainly, when pronounced rapidly, is not very euphonious, although, perhaps as much so as the reply said to have been given to her of, "Beg-a-big-egg, beg-a-big-egg," as a specimen of *her* native language. At all events, the Irish-speaking people never make a grammatical mistake when conversing in their vernacular, and most usually speak the English language more correctly than the same classes on the other side of the Channel.

To follow out the history or annals of Cong in succession during the fourteenth and subsequent centuries, would be a mere recital of the dissensions of rival chieftains, the feuds of hostile clans, or of the Saxon against the Celt; but, before we leave the shadow of the abbey walls, some memorabilia of this parish and abbey claim a passing reference. These reliques consisted formerly of the *Crois-Cunge,* or great processional cross of Cong; the *Fiachal Phadrig,* or shrine of St. Patrick's tooth; the *Clogh-dubh,* or black bell of St. Patrick; and the *Foil-a-ree,* or King's blood. This last consisted of a bit of discoloured linen, said to have been dipped in the blood of Charles I. at the time of his decapitation at Whitehall, and which was believed to possess the royal or Stewart faculty of curing the king's evil. Hundreds came to be "touched" by Abbot Prendergast; and in all probability this was the latest instance in which this rite was exercised in the British Isles. When last

Bermingham was probably the Lord of Athenry in the thir-
enth or fourteenth century; but certainly the original shrine older than his time.

On the back or reverse side is a raised, but unfigured cross, each side of which are a series of figures—two raised, and o engraved on the silver plate. Two of these are of eccle- astics, holding croziers; and one is that of a female holding harp, which is well worthy of inspection, as it is probably one the oldest representations of that instrument which we now ossess. The shrine is also highly decorated with crystals, ones, and amber, placed in collated studs, like those in the rine of St. Monchan of Leigh. Upon it there are also several ieces of gold and silver filagree work, similar to those around e central crystal of the Cross of Cong It is to be hoped at accurate illustrations of this relique, so interesting for its rtistic details, will ere long be published. Probably this shrine emained in the hands of the Berminghams, who had large ossessions all round Cong. Its modern history is this:—About fty years ago a man named Reilly, said to be a native of Sligo, nade a living by going about this part of the country with it performing cures upon man and beast." Ladies and ewes are aid to have held it in especial repute, and far and near the opulation and the flocks "were the better of the blessed tooth.")ne day the old Abbot met the custodian of the shrine, and sked him to show him the *Fiachal*. "Whose is this?" said the riest, when he had it in his possession. "It belonged," said heard of, this scrofula-curing rag was in the posse family near Ballindine.

The *Fiachal Phadrig* is a handsomely decorated wood, in the form of a horse shoe, satchel, or reticule, high by 9 wide, and somewhat wedge-shaped; and it is ditionally, to have been constructed to hold one of th our Patron Saint. It is, however, believed that there reliques of a similar kind still in the country. It is 1½ in at bottom, and fines off to a thin metal plate at the nar in continuation of the highly decorated rim which o surrounded it, but which, like other portions of th silver, and gilt materials, has been much injured, an the marks of "tinkers' hands" in the mode of solderin the chief or front side is a crucifixion in metal work, w figures on each side; and below it an arcade of trefoil Beneath, there is a row of four (there were five orig raised gilt figures, holding books, shrines, and croziers from an inscription underneath we learn that they rep ed Saints "Benon, Brigida, Patric, Columqille, Brendan between which and the silver plate to which they are at is inserted, either as a relique or for artistic purposes, tion of fine linen.

On the front is an imperfect inscription, the upper l which is in embossed—the lower is in the raised charac the twelfth or fourteenth century:—"*Thomas de Bramic Dñs: de Athen—me fecit ornari pisca parte.*" This Th

Reilly, "to the canons of Cong." "Then," said Father Prendergast, "I am the last of the Augustinian canons of that monastery, and I'll keep it;" and so, to the amazement of the owner, he rode off with it. He afterwards lent it to Mrs. Blake, who preserved it at Blake Hill, near Cong, whence it was removed to Menlough, upon the occasion of the serious illness of one of the family, who afterwards presented it to Dr. Stokes, by whom it was deposited in the Museum of the Royal Irish Academy, where it remained until the present year. According to a tradition in the parish, this shrine came from the county of Sligo, where there are still some recollections of St. Patrick's tooth.

The origin of this shrine is as follows:—In later life St. Patrick began to lose his teeth; and some of these were preserved by his friends and disciples, and gave names to churches commemorative of the circumstance, as in that of Kilfeacle, or "the church of the tooth," near the town of Tipperary, &c. It is stated that, in the Irish Apostle's visitation of northern Connaught, he proceeded along the coasts of Sligo and Mayo, and, crossing the river Moy at Bartragh, he raised a cross there, and afterwards erected the church of Cassel Irra, in Hy-Fiachrach — probably in the present parish of Killaspugbrone. And while there sojourning, bishops Bronius and Macrinee came to him, "and he wrote out the alphabet for them; and he gave a tooth from his mouth to Bishop Bronius, because he was dear to Patrick. There also the holy man laid the foundation of the church of Cassel-Irra, in the court of which is the stone upon which fell the tooth."*

The large processional cross, now preserved in the Museum of the Royal Irish Academy, and known as "The Cross of Cong," is undoubtedly one of the finest specimens of metal work, enamel, niello, and jewellery of its age in the western world. It stands 30 inches high, and the breadth of the arms is 19. The illustration on the next page affords so faithful a representation of it, that it is unnecessary, especially in a work of this nature, to enter into a minute description of its artistic details. It consists of an oaken cross, covered with plates of bronze and silver, washed in many places with a thick layer of gold, and having interspersed golden filagree work of most minute character around its front centre. All the front and back plates are elaborately carved with that intertwined pattern, or strap work, with grotesque animals, which is specially characteristic of Irish ornamentation on stone, metal, vellum, and vitreous composition, and which is seen on so many of our great monumental crosses, and is well represented in the Moytura Cross, figured at page 178. The outer corners of each compartment were originally studded with precious stones, glass, or figured

* See the Tripartite Life of St. Patrick, *Trias-Thaumaturga*, p. 142, &c.; see also the Annotations of Tirechan, in the Book of Armagh; and O'Donovan's Notes to the Annals of the Four Masters, under A. D. 511, in which year "Saint Bronn, bishop of Cuil-Irra, in Connaught, died." See also the "Genealogies and Tribes, &c., of Hy-Fiachrach," published by the Irish Archæological Society.

enamel paste, in white and dark blue colours. Supported upon a raised boss, decorated with niello in the centre, there is a large polished crystal, under which was placed originally the relique sent from Rome to King Turlough O'Conor, in 1123, and thus stated in The Annals of Innisfallen under that year:—"A bit of the true cross came into Ireland, and was enshrined at Roscommon by Turlough O'Conor." And, again, in the Book of Clonmacnoise, under the year 1136, we read, that Roderick O'Conor and Nuada O'Concennan were arrested by Turlough O'Conor; although under the protection of the Cohorbs of St. Jarlath, and of O'Duffy and of the *Bachall Buee*, or "the yellow staff," by which name, as Dr. Petrie, in his learned article upon the subject,* has shown, this shrine was popularly called from its golden appearance. Around its sides there are a series of Latin and Irish inscriptions, both in the Irish character; the letters are punched into the silver plate, apparently by dyes or types, and so deeply that the metal plates beneath are indented with almost equal sharpness; and this enables us to

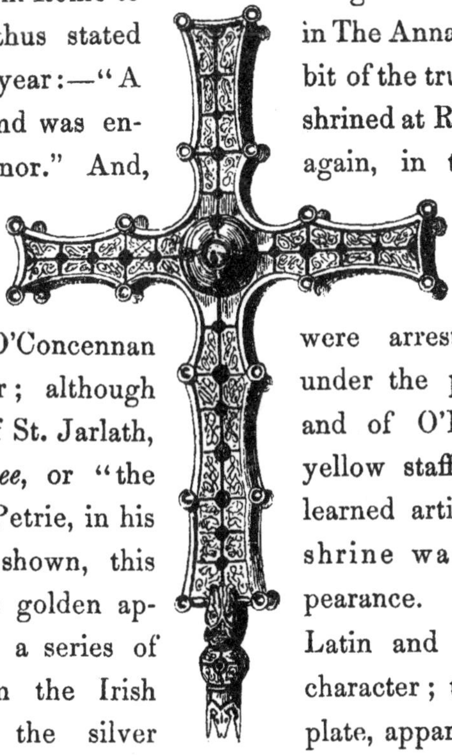

* See Proceedings of the Royal Irish Academy, vol. iv., p. 572;—also Dr. O'Donovan's dissertation on this inscription in the Journal of the Kilkenny Archæological Society, vol. i., new series, p. 37; see also his Irish Grammar.

read uninterruptedly even where the external plate has been injured. The foot of the cross springs from a highly decorated dog's head, which rises out of a globe, the ornamentation of which, in detail, is a marvel of the workmanship of its own or any other period. Beneath that ball is a decorated socket, into which was inserted the staff or pole with which the cross was carried. The inscription affords, unerringly, the history of this magnificent relique, the time and purpose for which it was made, and recounts the names of those in any way concerned in its formation. The following is a *fac simile* engraving, taken from a rubbing, of the Latin inscription, which is in duplicate on both sides of the lower portion of the edges:—

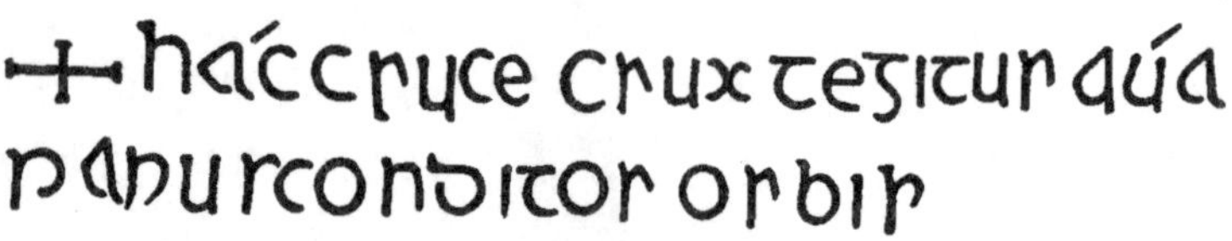

Or, in modern characters—*Hac cruce crux tegitur qua pasus* [*passus*] *conditor orbis.* "In this cross is preserved [or covered] the cross on which the Founder of the world suffered."

Some of the Irish inscriptions are slightly defective, but sufficient remains to furnish us with the following information:—"A prayer for Mureduch U Dubthaig, the Senior of Erin"—the notice of whose death at Cong, in 1150, is given at page 176.

"A prayer for Therrdēl U Choño [Turlough O'Conor]—for the King of Erin; for whom this gressa [or shrine] was made."

Another portion of this inscription refers to the ecclesiastic whose death is recorded at page 177:—" A prayer for Domnull Mac Flannacan U Dubdaig [O'Duffy], bishop of Connacht and Coharb, of [Saints] Chomman and Chiaran, under whose superintendence the shrine was made"—which also lends support to the assertion already made that the work was completed at Ross-Common, where O'Duffy was Abbot of the cebrated monastery of St. Comman, as well as that of St. Keerin at Clonmacnois.

"The fourth, and last compartment," says Dr. Petrie, "of these inscriptions, is not the least valuable, though it only preserves the name of a person of inferior station—that of the artificer who made the shrine, as it proves incontestibly what without it might, and probably would have been deemed doubtful; namely, that the shrine was of native workmanship."

"A prayer for Maelisu Mac Bratdan O'Echan, who made this shrine." This O'h-Echain was comharba of St. Finnen, of Cloncraff, in the county of Roscommon.

Probably the cross was brought to Cong Abbey by the O'Duffys; but as to what became of it for five centuries we have no historic account. There is a tradition in the parish that it was kept in an iron box, with other reliques, about a hundred years ago. The author remembers it during his boyish days, in the possession of Abbot Prendergast, who kept it with the other reliques already mentioned, in a three-cornered cupboard in his little sitting room at Abbotstown.—See page 174. It used, however, be placed upon the altar of Cong chapel at the festivals of Christmas and Easter. After Prendergast's death it was removed to Cong, at which time the central crystal had been removed, and was usually carried by a lady in her pocket. If still in existence, it is not known where the relique for which this cross was made is at present. It must have been a very small fragment, such as can at present be obtained in the Vatican.* The cross was purchased by the late Professor M'Cullagh, and presented, in 1839, to the Royal Irish Academy, where it served to form the nucleus of that great national collection of secular and ecclesiastical antiquities, that for its age and the scanty means at the disposal of those who have created it, is undoubtedly the finest national collection in Europe.†

The fourth and last relique connected with this locality was the Black Bell of St. Patrick, which the author procured many years ago for the Academy, and of which the accompanying is an illustration. It had long been in the possession of the Gerarty family, near Ballinrobe, who brought it every year to the "pattern" held on the top of the Reek or Croagh Patrick,

* Father Prendergast, although a good scholar and worthy man, was, like most of his brethren at the time, utterly ignorant, and totally careless about, the historic memorials of the country. Of the valuable collection of Irish MSS. transmitted to him with the cross and other *in*-valuables, it is said that one day, when he left home, a tailor, who was working in his house, laid hands on the vellum books, and cut several into strips for "measures." Need we wonder at much of this Vandalism still existing, when there is no chair of ecclesiology or archæology at Maynooth, and the chief Protestant schools of Ireland do not teach Irish History?

† See Proceedings of the Royal Irish Academy, vol. i., p. 326.

on "Garland Sunday," and where, in the little oratory there, the pious pilgrim was allowed to kiss it for a penny; and, if he had been affected by "rheumatism pains," he might put it three times round his body for two pence. But times got bad, the pattern thinned, and the *Maor* or keeper of the *Clog-dubh* sold it, to help to pay his passage to America. Certainly, if wear and tear is a sign of age, this antique should claim our highest veneration. It is 11 inches high, and 6 wide, and is formed, like most ancient of our Irish bells, of iron intermixed with other metals. It formerly belonged to the parish of Killower, near Headford, where, in one of the ancient descriptions of the hereditary property of the O'Flahertys and their dependants, it is said that "Mac Beolan, of Killower, is the keeper of the black bell of St. Patrick." It was believed in the locality that this bell was a present from an angel to the saint, and was originally of pure silver, but that it was rendered black and corroded, as at present seen, "by its contact with the demons on Croaghpatrick, when the Apostle of Ireland was expelling them thence." See O'Flaherty's "West Connaught," page 370.

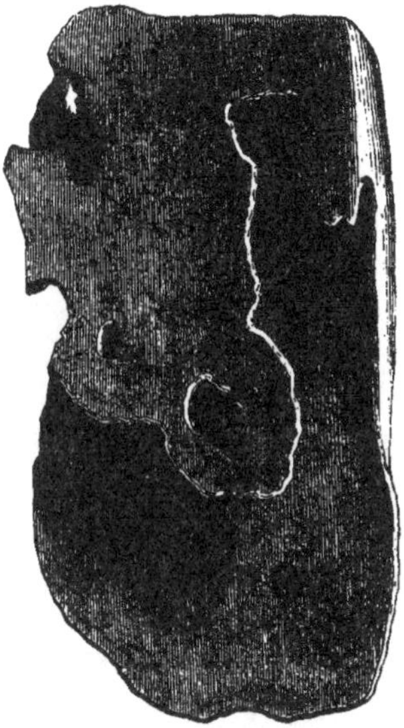

Cong and its environs still claim our attention. The great monumental cairns and stone circles of upwards of two thousand years ago that abound in this neighbourhood seem to have impressed the people—as they appear to have done in the Aran Isles—with a special desire to honour the memory of the dead; and so on all sides we meet with wayside monuments, crosses, pillar-stones, and tumuli erected by those who composed the passing funerals, as they rested at any of these spots on their way to the hallowed precincts of St. Mary's Abbey. And afterwards each relative of the deceased, or the passing friend, or the "good Christian" put up a stone, or cast a pebble

upon one of the little heaps, several of which can even still be identified as belonging to particular families. Upon the eastern road there is the *Cresseens*, a collection of small wooden crosses placed on a wall under an ash tree. And on the west, as we pass into the county Galway over *Togher-na-heithe*, by *Poll-Tuathfill*, and

Poll-Lieben, and by *Poll-achuarteal*, and proceeding westwards towards *Cregaree*, or "Royal Rock," the residence of the Venerable Michael Waldron, the worthy Roman Catholic Dean of this diocese, we pass a great collection of these monuments, some of the principal of which, from Mr. and Mrs. S. C. Hall's very beautiful work on Ireland, are figured on the opposite page.

Along this road we pass several pools, where the waters of Lough Mask appear in their transit to Cong and Lough Corrib; and among the limestone rocks that stretch across the

isthmus stands the tall tower of Aughalard Castle, with its adjoining group of ruins as shown in the accompanying illustration. It is exceedingly well built, and presents several details of considerable beauty and great architectural interest, especially in the loop-holes at the angles, and in the top mouldings of its light, graceful windows.

Among the limestone rocks to the north-west of this castle may be seen two of the caves, for which Cong is celebrated; both are artificial, and one of them can at present be entered.

There are three descriptions of caves in this locality—natural, artificial, and mixed. The first is magnificently represented by the great chasm in the limestone rock, about a mile to the west of Cong, and to the south-west of Aughalard; and which, from the number of pigeons and woodquests that used in former times to flock into it, is popularly known as the Pigeon hole, and in Irish, *Poll na g-columb*, a locality rendered memorable by Lady Morgan; and the legends of which have been so graphically described by Samuel Lover, and where in boyhood we tried to purloin from old Babby, the priestess of the place, "the blessed trout," especially the one with the mark of the gridiron on his side

Call at Mrs. Burke's, tourist, and tell her you want to see the Pigeon hole; leave your car at the stile of one of the green fields that mottle the great limestone crop all round, and walk down a few hundred yards to the east. Hark!—listen!—the ground is hollow; there are sounds issuing from beneath your feet. Draw nearer; stand opposite the little clump of dwarf oak, hazel, and holly, through which these subterranean noises rise to light and air. Look down the flight of steps up which that graceful girl is rising, with a pitcher of water on her head;

descend by a flight of steps into the bowels of the earth, between huge masses of lichen-covered rock, draped with tendrils of ivy, 50 or 60 feet long, depending from the top, and every chink and crevice of which is festooned with ferns and mosses of the greenest hue. Look up; the light of day is obscured by the overhanging branches, and at your feet gushes a rapid translucent river, at which women are beetling clothes, or filling their water vessels. Fill your eyes with the scene—try and penetrate the chilling gloom that broods over the great chasm that spans the mighty rocks that have fallen on your right. Lo! presently on the top of one of these immense blocks stands for a moment a weird female figure, bearing a lighted flambeau, the *genius loci*—the Meg Merrilies of the scene. Away she flits—darkness again, save the reflection of the light on the stalactitic roof above; then, emerging from an unobserved passage, she stands on another and more distant crag, with her long white locks, and pale aged face, personifying the banshee of the ancient Firbolgs. She hurls stones into the deep pools beneath, and utters a loud wail, that reverberates through the cavern, till the repeated echoes fade in the distance, and we watch the lurid light of the expiring *glossogs* she has thrown on the waters, as they float on through these subterranean caverns to the lake, or to rise in the great mill pond of Cong. "That's the Pigeon hole, yer Honour."

In the grounds of Strandhill there are two caves somewhat similar, "The Ladies Buttery" and the "Horse Discovery;"

the latter so called because it was discovered by a horse and plough having fallen into it, owing to a portion of the roof having suddenly given way, many years ago. They both adjoin the road leading from the steamer to the village—see page 159—and through both the waters of Lough Mask pass into Lough Corrib. Still more to the north-east there is "Webb's Hole," and in the townland of Cooslughoga, adjoining the roads leading to Cross and The Neale, a miniature pigeon hole, called *Poll-na-dorragh*, or "the dropping-hole, with steps leading down to it; and several other natural caverns, through which the waters of the upper lake percolate to that of a lower level.

All these the guides will show those interested in such matters; and also relate the atrocities of Captain Webb, and the marauding exploits of "Macnamara the robber," and the prowess of his bay mare; and also point out the hiding place of "Kelly the outlaw;"—most of the legends concerning all which have been graphically related by that most entertaining of all Irish tour writers, Cæsar Otway.

The artificial caves abound all over the plain of Moytura, from Knockma to Benlevi. Probably they were all originally within, or surrounded by, forts or cahers, to which they served as places of protection and security for women and children, and the wounded or defenceless; or to stow away valuables in case of attack. They may also have been used as sleeping apartments, and perhaps as granaries and storehouses, although at the time they were built the chief food of the Irish was animal. The following general description will apply to most of them, and the details and illustrative plans and sketches of a few particular ones will enable the reader to understand the manner of their construction, and the tourist to identify those he may desire to inspect by candle light:—

By fancying a trench sunk in the ground, 10 or 12 feet deep, and from 12 to 14 wide, and about 30 or 40 feet long, either in a straight line, or turning at an angle about midway, probably to avoid an obstruction—the sides lined with walls 2 feet thick, of moderate sized stones, put firmly together without cement, and not in courses; and the roof formed of enormous flags, many of them 8 and 9 feet long, 4 or 5 wide, or upwards, of a foot thick, laid on top—we have a good general idea of a Mayo Firbolg, or Tuatha de Danann cave, of probably two thousand years old. Towards what must be considered the entrance end the cave narrows, and the floor rises; but the general level of the roof is preserved, and the upper side of the flags of the roofing is now about 2 feet under the sod. At the distant end the cave widens often into a large oval chamber, and there is in some caves a small aperture, possibly for air and light, or communicating with those above, or to let out smoke. They were all entered by square apertures in the roof, as whenever the cave is perfect the ends are built up. This trap door may have been covered in case of emergency with a flag.

The Moytura caves present one remarkable peculiarity: they are nearly all divided into two chambers by a contrivance evidently intended, not merely for security, but concealment, as follows:—A few years ago the author discovered a cave at Kildun, "the dark wood," adjoining the road leading from Cross to The Neale, sunk in the centre of the remains of a large caher to the north-east of the "Plain of the Hurlers," and of which the two following diagrams, drawn to a scale of 16 feet to the inch, present the elevation and ground plan. Its direction is from south-west to north-east; but, from the great variety in the line of these *souterrains*, it is manifest their constructors paid no regard to the points of the compass. Descending through an aperture at the low, narrow, southern end, which is now only 3 feet high, we pass into a chamber 22 feet long, but widening and deepening towards the northern extremity. It is 6 feet wide, and 4 feet 9 inches high; and in the lower part of the end wall there is a horizontal passage, about 3 feet square and 6 long, at the end of which a perpendicular shaft or chimney, 18 inches by 30, rises; getting through which, we land on a platform of masonry, 3 feet 4 inches high; beyond which is a another larger chamber, 24 feet long, and averaging 6 feet wide, and 7 high—roofed over, like the southern portion, with immense flags that span the top. In the left corner is a small square recess, like a cupboard; and overhead a small aperture, through which light and air were admitted. This end of the cave approaches the outer circle of the fort, with the wall of which it may have communicated.

The upper diagram shows the section, and the lower the

ground plan of this great cave, which is altogether 54 feet in length. A marks the first hall with its descending entrance; B, the low, narrow, connecting passage; C, the perpendicular shaft; D, the ledge at the southern end of E, the second, or great hall, at the extremity of which is the recess and ventilating aperture.

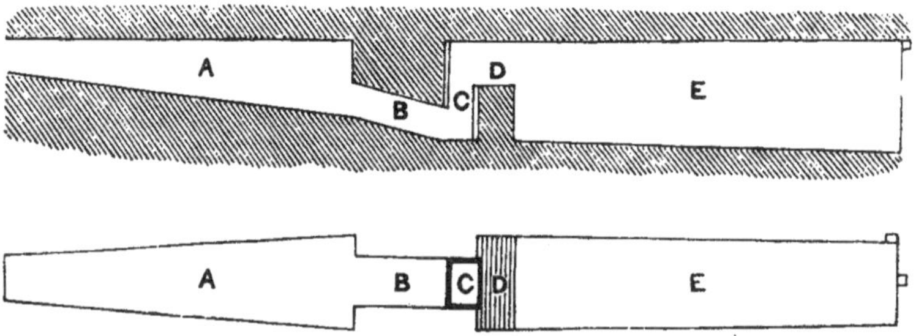

While, however, in modern architecture the general design of a dwelling, church, or fortress, is the same, the details often differ widely; so it was in cave building, for we find a great uniformity of purpose in all. In the townland of "Cave," at the south-west foot of Knockma, one of these straight subterranean habitations may be seen, and from thence to the eastern rise of Benlevi numbers of the same class of underground structures are met with; and as we approach the battle-field they abound in every townland; and, if we refer to the Ordnance Maps, we see the great number of localities in which the word cave is marked. The cave at Attyricard, mentioned at page 155, is of this class, as is also that in the great enclosure of

Caher-Paetar, or "pewter fort," at Ballymagibbyon, although that extensive passage took a somewhat curved direction; and there can be no doubt that the remains of caves are still to be found on the sites of all the great cahers in this locality. That at Lackafinna was only closed within the last twenty years.

Another form is the Angular or Crooked Cave, of which that at Lisheenard, in Ashford, described at page 184, is an example; but one of the most curious of this class is that at *Cooslughoga* or Cusloughe, "the rat's foot," which is placed within the circle of an ancient fort, near Calliaghdoo, about midway between the roads leading to Cross and Ballinrobe. Scrambling down through the narrow dilapidated north-western entrance we get into a chamber, marked A on the following ground plan, 21 feet long, 7 high, and 6 feet 3 inches wide, and running nearly east and west. The roofing flags are of immense size, and supported on corbels that jut inwards for about 9 inches. At the extremity of this hall the walls narrow, and a small door appears, as shown in the left-hand cut at top of the illustration given on the opposite page. Creeping through this very small doorway, we get into the second or larger apartment, marked B, which is 24 feet long, and differs from

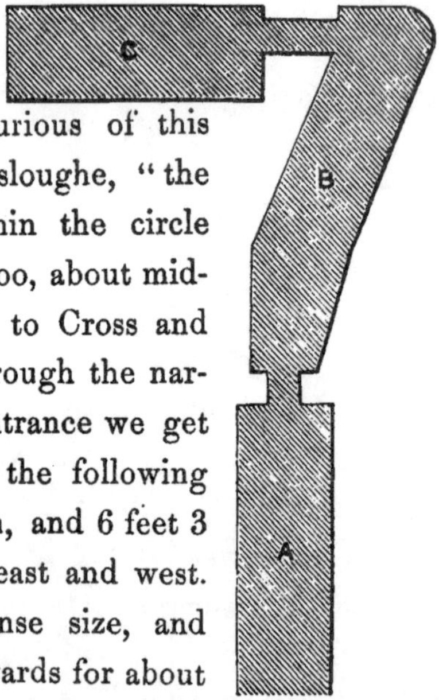

that of most other caves in having the western side wall composed of large upright flagstones, not unlike those that support the roof of the passage into New Grange; and, like those of that remarkable structure, some of these are indented with artificial depressions along their sides and edges, as shown in the lower compartment of the following illustration. We

have not, however, as yet found on any of the Moytura caves those peculiar carvings, spires, lozenges, and volutes, such as characterize the caves of Meath. Either such were not known at the period of the construction of the Mayo caves; or, what is more likely, they were only used in sepulchral caverns, and probably expressed ideas connected with the life of the deceased, or the artist's ideas of futurity.

This second chamber turns somewhat to the north, and is curved round its extreme angle, in the southern side of which we meet the high doorway shown by the second top figure in the foregoing illustration. From that, a narrow passage leads through a very small aperture at its top, over a barrier similar to that in the cave of Kildun, into a third, or northern, chamber, 22 feet long, marked C upon the diagram.*

Not far to the north-east of this place, and upon the boundary of the Plain of the Hurlers, to be described presently, is Caherduff, "the black fort," of which there are still some remains of the outer wall at the mearing of the townland, to which it gives name. Within this enclosure there is a very extensive curved cave, in good preservation, and remarkable for having still perfect the oblong doorway in the roof, by which access was gained to the interior. Having passed for 20 feet in a south-eastern direction, a long narrow passage

* All the caves in this locality were carefully measured, and ground plans and sections of them made for the author, by Mr. James M'Donagh, an intelligent surveyor of the neighbourhood; but the two foregoing diagrams are considered sufficient for explanation. The visitor should supply himself with candles before commencing the investigation of these caves, as the interiors of most of them are in utter darkness.

leads at an acute angle into a chamber 24 feet long, and widening towards its northern extremity.

These details of a few out of the many caves in this locality, and in the neighbouring townland of Creevagh, that may be visited by the antiquarian tourist, will serve to give a general idea of their construction. *Muillean-a-Leprochaun*, or "the fairies' mill," not far from hence—where in former times the people left their *caskeens* of corn at nightfall, and found them full of meal in the morning—is worthy of inspection as a natural cave. Although the grinding stones are still heard, no meal has been ground there since an old woman complained that she had been defrauded by the little miller.

"Kelly's Cave," at Learg-a-Neal, "the path to the Neale," to the left of the road leading from Cong to Nymphsfield, affords a good example of the mixed variety already referred to, in which the natural and artificial were combined; for, while it is evidently a huge cleft formed by nature in the rock, portions of the wall in front and on the sides are undoubtedly artificial. But the best instance of this description of cave will be found in the great cavern to the west of the hill of Carn, near Lough Mask, where the entrance and a long passage, evidently artificial, and roofed over with immense flags, leads into a very large natural cave, from the roof of which depend numerous stalactites. As most of the ostensible overground monuments around Cong are identified with the great battle of Moytura, their description is reserved for the next chapter.

CHAPTER VIII.

THE BATTLE AND BATTLE-FIELD OF MOYTURA.

THE PRIMITIVE IRISHMAN. FOMORIANS. PARTHOLAN. NEMETH. THE FIRBOLGS. TUATHA DE DANANN. THE PLAIN OF MOYTURA. KNOCKMA. CEASAIR. KINGS EOCHY AND NUADH. THE BATTLE-FIELD. THE WARRIORS, DRUIDS, AND PHYSICIANS. EXISTING MONUMENTS; CAIRNS, CAVES, CAHERS, STONE CIRCLES, AND PILLARS. THE FOUR DAYS' FIGHT. THE MEANE UISGE. SEPULCHRAL URN. STANDING STONES AT INISHOWEN. THE DAGDA AND THE FATHACH. NYMPHSFIELD MONUMENTS. CAHER MAC TURC. BELOR OF THE MAGIC EYE. THE NEALE MONUMENTS. THE HILL OF CARN. CAHER ROBERT. HISTORY OF THE MOYTURA MANUSCRIPT.

BEFORE entering upon the topography of the locality, or describing the battle-field of Moytura, a short epitome of the early history and colonization of Ireland may not be out of place. The computed period of man's residence on our globe has undergone much modification of late years; but, with respect to Irish chronology, at least we believe it will be found to approach the truth as near as that of most other countries; and the more we investigate it, and endeavour to synchronize it with that of other lands, the less reason we shall have to find fault with the accounts of our native annalists.

The author has elsewhere stated his belief that man first set foot on Erin in a very rude state, as a nomad hunter and fisher, depending for his food on the chase, or feeding on the uncultivated fruits of the earth, or the produce of the waters; clad in skins, and having no knowledge of metal, but forming his simple weapons, tools, and ornaments out of flint, stone, and shell, &c.* These early or aboriginal people were termed, in later times, Fomorians. A colony under three leaders—Bith, Ladra, and Fintan—and several females (of whom Ceasair, or Cesarea, was the chief), who were supposed to have come across the Spanish Main, arrived on the south coast, and have left their names in different localities in ancient Erin, and among the rest in Knockma, the great hill of the plain, which forms so conspicuous an object in the district; and in the great monumental cairn surmounting which, called Carn-Keasrach, it is said, in The "Ogygia," that Cesarea was interred.

Another large colony, believed to have been of immediate Oriental origin, under a leader named Parthalon, followed, and, also landing on the south coast, defeated the native Fomorians, but were themselves cut off by a plague, or *Thaum*, and were interred at Tallaght (*Tamh-Leacht*, or the "plague stone"), near Dublin, where their urns have been frequently exhumed; but Parthalon himself, it is thought, was buried in the cromleach at Ben Edair, now Howth.† The leaders of that colony also left

* See the Author's Catalogue of the Antiquities in the Museum of the Royal Irish Academy, part i.

† See Mr. Ferguson's poem on Howth.—See also the Author's Table of Pestilences in the "Irish Census Report for 1851," vol. v., page 45.

their names to various places in Erin ; and by these people it is said that several of the plains were cleared of wood, and cultivated. Our histories state, that in these early times many lakes were formed, and several rivers broke out—relations that some years ago would have been regarded as fabulous by many, and miraculous by some; but now that cosmical phenomena are better understood, such accounts will rather afford subjects for calm scientific investigation than for ridicule. After the days of Parthalon another immigration into Erin occurred, under the leadership of Nemedh (from whom the original name of this very plain, to the east of Cong, was derived), with his sons Starn ; Hiarbanel the prophet from whom the Dananns descended ; Fergus Redside, the father of Britannus, who gave his name to "the great island" adjoining; and Ainnin, from whom Logh Ainnin, now Lough Ennell, in Westmeath, is called. They also were clearers of woods, and promoters of civilization; and their chief settlement was in Dalaradia, in the northern portion of the island, where they contended for the mastery with the old Fomorians, and destroyed their great tower of Conang, at Tor-innis, now Tory Island. As in many modern instances, the plague combined with the sword to thin their army ; and, after an occupation of a portion of the island, Nemedh himself, and three thousand of his followers, died of a *Thaum* at Ard-Neimedh, now Barrymore Island, on the Cork coast; and then, More the son of Dala, rallying the Fomorians, attacked the remaining Nemedhs, and caused them to emigrate to Britain.

We now approach more probable, if not more certain history. A Belgic colony, called Firbolgs, under five chieftains—Slainghe, Radruic, Seangan, Genan, and Gan, passing over from Britain, arrived in great numbers, conquered the native Irish of the day, established a kingly form of government, and divided the country into a pentarchy. They also left their names in several places, and erected those stupendous barbaric monuments which may be seen in the Aran Isles to this day.

During all this long period the Fomorians, although conquered, were neither subdued nor extirpated; they frequently espoused different sides with the several invaders (just as the native Irish did after 1172), and by intermarriage became allied to them. Eventually their political power was crushed, and their chiefs retired to Tory Island, on the Donegal coast, where they earned the name of "pirates." They come on the scene at a later period.

The fifth colony, sprung, it is said, from the race of Nemedh, who had emigrated northward, possibly driving the Lapps of Middle Europe before them, prior even to the date of "the March of Odin," and perhaps coeval with the time of the oyster-eaters of Jutland, returned to Ireland as Tuatha de Danann, under the leadership of their king, Nuad, and, advancing into the interior as far as the south margin of Leitrim, demanded a portion of the island from the Belgæ, with whom they had, it is said, a common language. Prior to that date, whatever it may have been, the entries in our annals, transmitted by the Bards, and probably recited at the feasts of chieftains, or at national assemblies—as very likely the poems of Homer were sung, before being committed to writing—are meagre, and consist chiefly of records of pestilences and cosmical phenomena, which latter, however, bear the test of scientific investigation.

Henceforward, Irish history becomes more detailed, if not more certain. Thus we read of colony after colony coming down from the cold regions of the north, passing on from the warm sunny plains of the south, and crowding in even from the distant east; seeking, as the destiny and the impulse of man ever is the land of the setting sun--the most distant point of habitable earth to which he can reach, or whereon he can by any possibility exist; but above all because, from its geographical position, its climate, and its soil, Green Erin afforded these pastoral people then, as it does now, a greater amount of food for herbivorous animals than any equal extent of land in North-western Europe.

The Firbolgs were a small, swarthy, dark race, as were probably their Fomorian precursors. The Teutons or Scandinavian Dananns, on the other hand, were a large, fair, light or sandy-haired people, of superior knowledge and intelligence, which obtained for them the attributes of magical skill and necromancy; they were also musical and poetic. Both races were Druidic in religion; and, so far as can be gleaned from remote history, both possessed a knowledge of metal, and were armed accordingly.

The Belgæ having refused to divide the country with the invaders, the Dananns proceeded westward, and occupied the great plain of Nemedh, or Magh-Ith, which stretches for about 12 miles from the hill of Knockma, in the county of Galway, through the fertile barony of Kilmain, in Mayo, to *Slieve Belgadain*, now called Benlevi, a short distance from the village of Cong, in the barony of Ross, and county of Galway, and forms the eastern barrier to the western highlands. Both eminences, as already stated, may be discovered at a great distance all round. Lough Corrib forms the southern, and the shores of Lough Mask the immediate western, margin of this plain, which, extending for four or five miles in breadth, is bounded on the north-west by the River Robe. How long the Scandinavians occupied that situation, or whether they or the Belgic people formed those numerous forts, raths, cairns, and cahers, that cluster on its western extremity in groups resembling cities, or, whether such were constructed prior to the battle, must remain matters of speculation. Certain it is, that in remote ages an immense population must have occupied that plain; for, notwithstanding the vast lapse of time, the progress of cultivation, and the ruthless hand of the despoiler, almost every field bears evidence of its existence.

Eochy, son of Erc, King of Erin, advanced to the hill of Knockma with all his forces from Tara, in Meath, then the seat of government, to attack the Tuatha de Dananns, whose leader, Nuad, took up his position on Benlevi, with his warriors, sages, Druids, bards, poets, and physicians, &c., whose names have been all recounted, and their prowess sung in story, so that throughout the whole thread of Irish history they remain recorded. By this means the wily Dananns had the fastnesses of Joyce Country and Connamara to fall back on in case of defeat, as it is said they destroyed their fleet on landing.

Knock-Magha, or Knockma, the great "hill of the plain," so conspicuous in the landscape, is about five miles to the west of Tuam, in the barony of Clare and county of Galway; its northern slope is occupied by the woods and cultivated grounds of Castlehacket, the seat of Denis Kirwan, Esq.; and on its summit stands the great cairn within which tradition and ancient history say Ceasair, one of the earliest colonists of Ireland, was interred.* (See page 211). Perhaps we do not err in assigning to this ancient burial place a date anterior to that of

* During the last fifty years an eccentric person residing in the locality made a castellated stone structure to the west of this great cairn; but it in nowise either interferes with or invalidates the old sepulchral monument referred to in the text; and it is not clear that, despite its Brummagem architecture, there is not beneath it a second tumulus, consecrated to the remains of some early Irish notability.

any other identified historical locality in Ireland; and hence tradition, as well as popular superstition, has thrown over it the investiture of fairy legend beyond all other places in the country; for here Finvarra, the Oberon of Irish sylvan mythology, holds his court. From this point may be obtained one of the grandest panoramic views in Ireland;—the great plain stretching beneath and round Knockroe; the beautiful abbey of Knockmoy; the towers and city of the Ford of the Kings; the Tuam of St. Jarlath; the Round Tower of St. Bennan; the ruined keeps of the De Burgos; the ships riding in the Bay of Galway; the Slievebloom and Clare mountains; the blue island-studded waters of Lough Corrib; and, in the far western back ground, the Connamara Alps, with their clear-cut edges, and their sides momentarily varying in tints from the marvellous atmospheric effects of that region stretching round by the Partry range to the lofty peak of Croaghpatrick; and in the extreme north-western distance the bulky form of Nefin, and even some of the Achill mountains skirting Clew Bay.

King Eochy, with his Firbolg host, descended into the plain of Moytura, and, passing westwards, was met by the heralds and ambassadors of Nuad, on that portion of it subsequently called Conmaicne Cuile Toladh, extending from the present village of Cross to the neck of land that divides Loughs Mask and Corrib. They then, as was not uncommon with nations in kindred states of civilization, agreed upon a trial of skill and manly prowess; and twenty-seven youths from each army engaged in a game of hurling, in a valley denominated in the tale "The Plain of the Hurlers." Now, presuming that we are correct in our interpretation of the MS. account of the engagement and the topography, this extends in an eastern direction for three quarters of a mile from the bridge of Garracloon to the rise of Cath-na-Bunnin, south-east of Nymphsfield, and is bordered on the north by Caherduff, and on the south by the rise of Knock, on both of which we find several monuments of the battle that subsequently ensued. In fact, it is the only hurling ground in the district; it was used as such within the memory of the present generation; and it is said the fairies still have their games of "common" there on bright moonlight nights. The northern boundary of this smooth valley is the rocky space, covered with dwarf hazel, which gives the name of *Ceaslean-na-Cuillagh*, "The castle in the wood," to the old haunted ruin shown in the subjoined illustration; and to the west of which is the cave of *Caherdubh*, described at page 208. This castle—so often seen, it is said, "afire" on summer nights, when the fairies, after their game of hurling, hold their banquets there—is, however, a mortared structure of great strength, and probably about five centuries old.

This warlike pastime ended in the defeat and death of the thrice nine youths of the Dananns, over whom was erected the great carn or stone monument figured on the next page, and which would appear to be that called in the MS. *Carn-an-chluithe*, or the "monument of the game;" and the valley of the hurlers, where they were interred, was then denominated *Glen-mo-Aillem.* There it stands to this day, about 50 feet high, and 400 in circumference—an historic memorial as valid

as that which commemorates the spot on the shore of Attica, where the Athenians fell beneath the long spears of the Persians on the field of Marathon.

Next day, supposed to be the 11th of June, in the year of the world 3303, the battle commenced; it lasted four days, and it is said 100,000 men were engaged in it. Each army sank a royal rath or fortress; that of the Belgæ called *Rath Crophorta*, and that of the Dananns, *Rath Fearainn;* both are probably still remaining, but not capable of identification among the many monuments of which vestiges still exist in this locality. Both parties were armed with swords, spears, darts, and shields, but no mention is made of either slings or arrows; so it must have been a hand-to-hand fight. They did not, however, forget the wounded; for each sank a "sanative pool" or medicated bath in the rear of their lines, in which the wounded bathed. That of the Dananns was presided over by Diancheacht, the Machaon of the Irish Iliad; and the circumstance is commemorated in the name of a district bordering the Shannon, called Lus-magh, "the plain of the herbs," from the fact that on it were collected the plants that formed the *materia medica* with which the milk of the bath was endowed with its healing virtues. Forward marched the Firbolgean host, headed by the Fathach, or Druid poet—a character still remembered traditionally by the people as the *Faughac Ruadh*, or red giant, who raised a pillar-stone against which he rested, and sang the exploits of his warriors. The stone has disappeared, but the eminence on which he stood is still pointed out within the demesne of Moytura, on *Knock-ard-na-gook*, or "the knoll on the height of the cuckoo," because, it is said that that visitor is usually first heard there in spring. In the history of the battle this pillar-stone is called *Cairthi Fathaigh*, and is said to have been the first of the kind erected on this plain.

On the other hand, we can well imagine the Dananns marching to battle, incited by the Miriam-like chaunt of Edain, or Edena, the poet-prophetess, whose name often occurs in the history of the engagement. The Dagda More, afterwards a king, and whose monument undoubtedly stands on the banks of the Boyne, near Newgrange, performed deeds of surpassing valour, until withstood by the hero Kerb, the son of Buan of the Firbolgs. Adleo, the son of Allai, another of the Dananians, was slain by Nearchu, grandson of Semeon, and a pillar-stone, called *Cairthi Adleo*, was erected where he fell—probably the *Clogh-Fadha-Cunga*, or "long stone of Cong," which not long since stood on the old road to the east of that village, and a portion of which, 6 feet long, is still in an adjoining wall. The only other pillar-stones in the district are, one on the east shore of Holly Island, in Lough Corrib, and the *Clogh-Fadha Neal*, or "long stone of The Neale," at the junction of the roads passing northwards from Cross and Cong, where it is said by tradition the king stood at one period of the battle.—See page 240.

The Belgians, although not absolutely victorious, had rather the best of the first day's fighing, having driven their enemies back to their encampment, which probably extended from the site of this pillar of Adloe to the western end of the Plain of the Hurlers, along by Nymphsfield to the cross roads leading to Lough Mask, and from thence through Creevagh, in which still stand the remains of cairns. Each Firbolg having carried with him a stone and the head of a Danann to their king, he erected "a great carn" to commemorate the event. Taking into consideration the line of the two armies, this must be the cairn of Ballymagibbon, as shown in the following cut, which stands near the road passing from Cong to Cross. It is 129 yards in circumference, and about 60 feet high; and its original base may still be traced by a number of upright stones. Within it there is a large cave, but it is not at present accessible.

The next morning, before the second day's fight was commenced, the following incident occurred:—King Eochy, unattended, went down into a certain well to perform his ablutions, and while there observed three of the enemy "overhead," about to seek his life. A colloquy ensued, but the Dananns would give no quarter. He was saved, however, by one of his own band, who slew the three, but died immediately from his wounds on an adjoining hillock. The Firbolgs, coming up to look after their king, there and then interred the hero who so bravely defended him ; and, each taking a stone in his hand, erected over him a monumental cairn. The well is not named in the ancient account of the battle ; but the little hill on which the conflict took place is called *Tulach-an-triur*, "The Hill of the Three," and the monument erected thereon *Carn-in-enfhir*, "The Carn of the One Man." Such is the simple narrative of the transaction sent down to us through bards and wandering poets and chieftains' laureates, who perhaps, as already remarked, recited it at feasts and in public assemblies—as the tales of Troy were sung possibly before Homer was born—until the days of letters, when the tradition was transmitted to writing, and the annalist sped it on to the present time. Is it true? Can it be that a trifling incident of this nature, occurring so far back in the night of history, can possibly bear the test of present topographical investigation, while many of our classic histories have been questioned, and in some instances their statements disproved? Yes; there they both remain to the present day—the deep well, now called *Mean* or *Meeneen uisge*, in a chasm of the limestone rock through which the floods of Lough Mask percolate into Lough Corrib—the only drop of water that is to be found in the neighbourhood—and so deep under the surface, that the king must have looked upwards to see his enemies overhead. Immediately adjoining it, on the south-east, stands the hillock referred to in the manuscript, and now crowned with a circle of standing stones, 176 feet in circumference, in the centre of which are the remains of the cairn, shown by the illustration on the following page; and the monument is still called *Carn Meeneen uisge*.

This well of the *Mean-Uisge*, the precise derivation of which is not known, but which signifies either "the small watery plain," or "the celebrated water," answers well the description afforded by the narrative; for it is reached by a flight of

steps like those in the Pigeon Hole and other similar natural caves near Cong. At certain seasons, when the upper floods accumulate, the water rises almost instantaneously in a jet through this aperture, and forms a turlough to the south of it.

After a careful examination of the locality, with a transcript of the ancient manuscript in his hand, the author, feeling convinced of the identity of the stone heap standing within the circle figured above, and by the kind permission of its proprietor, Charles Blake, Esq., made an excavation in the centre, telling the workmen beforehand that they would assuredly find a chamber in it; and if it had not been already rifled, the remains of the hero who so bravely defended the Firbolg king. As much of the top of the heap had been removed for building purposes some years ago, we soon came upon a large smooth, horizontally placed, gritstone flag, on raising which another, somewhat larger in size, was discovered. The latter remains *in situ*, and covers a small square chamber, 28 inches high, and 37 wide, the walls of which are formed of small stones. On removing some of these on the western side, we found imbedded in the soft black powdery earth that had fallen in through the apertures, and probably mixed with charcoal, the urn here figured, and which contained the incinerated remains of human bones. It is now in the Museum of the Academy. This very beautiful object is about 5½ inches high, and 6 inches wide in the mouth, tapering gracefully to the bottom, which is only 2 inches broad. It is also highly decorated all round the lip, and has six fillets beneath the outer edge of the rim; and, what is unique in vessels of this description, four slightly elevated knobs, like handles. The lower plain surface beneath the fillets and handles is covered with herring-bone ornamentation. The surface of the vessel is of a reddish-brown colour, and the interior of its substance black, showing that it was submitted to the process of baking or roasting, either in its original formation, or at the time of the pyre, or when the hot embers of the human remains were placed within it.

Here, no doubt, the body of the loyal Firbolg youth was burned, and his ashes collected and preserved in this urn. Perhaps a more convincing proof of the authenticity of Irish or any other ancient history has never been afforded.*

Immediately over and to the north and west of the site of the foregoing incident the ground rises into the slope of Toneleane, the "trowel-like elevation;" that of Callagh Dubh, the "black woman," probably in reference to the Danann poetess, the daughter of Dianceacht, and from which name in all probability the present townland of Nymphsfield takes its name; and the little hollow called Cath-na-Bunnen—upon all of which the chief battle monuments of the Danann still remain.

O'Donovan, when examining the barony of Kilmain, in 1839, did not visit any of the monuments, which exist in the hollow south-east of Toneleane; but the translation which he has left of the *Cath Magh Tuireadth* has directed the author to the discovery of this and several other structures still existing. He has also had the advantage of collating, with Mr. O'Looney, O'Donovan's translation with O'Curry's transcript of the manuscript now in the Catholic University.

This second day's contest commenced under a new set of commanders, among whom "Aengabha of Norway," Ogma, Midir, Bodhbh-Dearg, and Dianceacht the Physician, were con-

* See the author's communications upon the battle-field of Moytura, laid before the Royal Irish Academy in 1866, and printed in the Proceedings, vol. x., pp. 22-24.

spicuous as Danann leaders; and Mella, Esc, Ferb, and Faebhar, the four sons of Slainge Finn, son of King Eochy, led the Firbolgs. The battle raged with great fury, and, according to the spirited description in the narrative, a Danann chief named Nemhid, son of Badhri, was slain by Slainge, and "his grave was dug, and his pillar-stone was raised; which is from that day to this called *Lia-Nemhidh.*" If this still exists, it is not at present susceptible of identification.

It would now appear that the battle surged northwards; the lines extending towards the western shores of Lough Mask, where Slainge Finn, the king's son, pursuing the two sons of Caelchu and their followers, who had fled from the left wing of the Danann army to the margin of the lake, killed them there, and "seventeen flagstones were stuck in the ground in commemoration of their death."

Here is another most remarkable confirmation of the tale; for by the margin of the lake in the island (or peninsula as it is at present in summer time) of Inish-Eogan, now Inishowen, there stands this remarkable monument to this hour, within an elevated and entrenched fort, as shown in the following illustration, with thirteen of these flat "flagstones" still occupying the edge of the rath, some of them over 6 feet high, by 9 inches wide, and about 4 or 5 inches thick. The site commands a glorious prospect of the lake and the Partry range, as well as Nephin and Ballycroy, mountains, and the deep valley through which the waters of Lough na Foohy communicate with Lough Mask. The fort is oval, and measures 22 paces across; some of the stones are perforated; upon the

west or water side the ditch is remarkably steep, but now much overgrown with bushes. See page 259. There was great slaughter on both sides during this day's fighting, and the Norwegian general was nearly overpowered in a personal conflict by the Red son of Mogharn, one of the Belgæ; but at nightfall the Firbolgs gave way. They carried home, however, into the presence of their king, the heads of the slain Dananns.

The Firbolgs, says the narrator, "rose out early the next morning, and made a beautiful *scell* [sceall, or testudo] of their shields over their heads, and placed their battle spears like trees of equal thickness, and thus marched forward in Turthas [columns or battalions] of battle. The Tuatha de Danann, seeing the Firbolgs marching in this wise from the eastern head of the plain [probably from the places now known by the townland names of Gurtachurra, Ballymagibbon, and

Knock], observed :—'How pompously these Tuirthis of battle march towards us across the plain!' and hence the plain was called *Magh Tuireadh*, or plain of the Tuireadhs." From this circumstance arose the name so often referred to in ancient Irish history.

On this third day of the battle, the Dananns were commanded by the Dagda; for, said he, "I am your Daigh-dia" (god of hope, or confidence, deliverer); and Sreng, the son of Sengan, led the Belgæ. Several personal conflicts between the most renowned warriors are said to have taken place, the details of which, descriptive of the arms and mode of fighting, are related in Homeric language—in which it is said the helmets were crushed, the metal-bound shields were battered, the long-handled spears were shivered, and the "green-edged [bronze] swords were dyed with blood." The Dagda slew Kerb, one of the most famous Firbolg heroes, and the Belgæ were driven back to their camp; but they were still able to carry each a stone and the head of a foe, and also that of Kerb, which they buried within their lines, and placed over it a cairn called *Carn-cin-Kerb*, or the "monument of the head of Kerb." This name is not now known; but, considering the line of the two armies, we are inclined to think it may be the small stone heap a little to the west of the great monument at Ballymagibbon, erected after the first day's battle.—See page 222.

The line of the Belgian or Firbolg camp, or more probably settlement, can still be traced with wonderful accuracy, stretching in a curvature along the lake side to the east of Cong, where, commencing with the caher, or fort, which lately existed at *Lisloughry*, "the lake fort," it extends by the fort and cave of *Lackafinna*, "the white flagstone," over the high ground where stands *Lisduff*, "the black fort," to Caher Gerrode, that commands the whole scene;* and thence by Cuckoo Hill, described at page 220, where the pillar-stone of the Faugha stood, and immediately beneath which, to the east, is *Caher-Speenaun*, "the thorny fort," shown by the sub-

joined illustration, taken from the north-east. The wall of this fort, although not built of large stones, is 10 feet thick, and 6 feet high; its circumference is 393 feet. An outer

* Caher Gerrode, or Garret's Caher, which stands on the hill to the north-west of Moytura House, is manifestly a modern name. The author has lately erected a tower within it; but the antiquity of the outer wall is undoubted.

wall encircled this fort originally; but at present only a few yards of it remain, as shown by the woodcut. The interspace between these walls is 48 feet. Tradition says there is a cave in the interior of this fort. When the outer walls were being removed some years ago, several antiquities were discovered, especially querns and iron hatchets.*

More to the south-east, on the hill of Tongegee, referred to at page 157, and which commands a grand panoramic view of the lake and mountains, are the remains of *Caher-na-gree*, "the pleasant fort," which, with the cluster of minor erections, both military and monumental, around it, must have been a city in itself. Still more to the east are the *Lisheen*, or "little earthen fort," and the great enclosure and caves of *Caher-Phaetre*, "pewter fort," immediately below the cairn of Ballymagibbon, figured at page 201. Still more to the east, there are the forts on Corgorave hill, and others along the road to Cross, and so on to the immense heap of *Caher-Mayo*, or the great "stone fort of Mayo," which tradition says was intended to have been the capital; and to the north of which, at Attyricard, already referred to, there are several similar structures. Then turning northwards, by Kildun and Caherduff, to the village of The Neale, we meet with undoubted evidences of the existence of a numerous population;

* A *tuath*, or narrow iron hatchet, found here is now in the valuable collection of the late Dr. Petrie.

for it must have been the work of thousands to have brought together those huge masses of stone, and sunk those caves.

Within the Tuatha de Danann lines we have several large cahers, caves, and forts, extending along the eastern and northern slopes of Benlevi, to the tower of Ardnageeha, wherever the ground permitted of their erection. But, presuming that we are correct in the topography of the battlefield, the front of the invaders extended from the site of the Long Stone at Cong across to Nymphsfield, where we find a cluster of most remarkable monuments, to be described presently.

The battle was fought in the space between these two lines, and passing off to the north, turned at The Neale again towards the west, and concluded at the shores of Lough Mask.

On this third day of the engagement the Firbolgs were reinforced by the aged Fintan, and an additional Leinster army. Both the kings commanded in person. Nuad, in a fierce encounter with Sreng, one of the Belgian heroes, lost his arm, but was rescued by Aengabha, his Norwegian ally, whose exploits are most graphically described in the manuscript. Dianceacht, his surgeon, dressed the wound, and Credne Cerd, the artificer, afterwards made for him a silver hand; so that from henceforth he was known as *Nuadhat-Airgead-Lamh*, or "Nuad of the silver hand;" and the circumstance has passed down through the whole stream of Irish history. A monument was erected over the king's hand where the blood dropt from it upon *Cro-Ghaile*, "the enclosure of the foreigners," and whieh monument may, for aught we know, still exist.* It is also stated that the Dananns reared up *Cairtheda*, or pillar-stones, to protect their men, and also to prevent their retreat.

Before proceeding with the narrative, we must here conduct our readers to the existing Danann monuments that accumulate in the fields opposite the glebe of Nymphsfield, to a portion of which the locality tradition has assigned the name of *Cath-na-Bunnen*, "the battle of the butts;" because it is said that here, when the combatants were nearly exhausted, and had blunted, broken, or lost their swords and spears, they fought with the butts, or handles, as the Faugaballaghs did in the Peninsula. But perhaps this term may be only a corruption or mispronunciation of *Cath-na-Danann*, "the battle of the Dananns." There are here five very remarkable stone circles

* Many years ago the late Rev. Dr. Walsh, father of the present Master of the Rolls, presented to the Academy an urn containing the bones of a human thumb which had been found in a kistvane, or stone chamber, at Kilbride, in the County Wicklow.—See Proceedings, vol. i., p. 296. And in the church at Waterloo we can still see the monument commemorative of the Marquis of Anglesea's leg.

In his note to the foregoing circumstances, as related in the Annals of the Four Masters, under A. M. 3303, O'Donovan writes as follows:—"It is stated in the Leabhar-Gabhala of the O'Clerys, that Diancecht and Credne formed the hand with motion in every finger and joint, and that Miach, the son of Diancecht, to excel his father, took off this hand, and infused feeling and motion into every joint and vein of it, as if it were a natural hand.—See O'Flaherty's Ogygia, Part iii., c. 10. In Cormac's Glossary, the name of Diacecht is explained, 'Deus Salatis'—ı. ꝺıa na h-ıce —'The God of Curing.'

still remaining within the compass of a quarter of a square mile, and there are traces of others. The following examples are highly illustrative of these remarkable monuments. That figured below consists of nineteen flat flagstones placed in a circle, each inclining outwards, perfectly smooth on the outside, but grooved and hollowed on their internal faces, which were evidently those originally exposed to the action of air or water.

A considerable portion of this circle has been removed; and its interior, which is now planted, is 54 feet in diameter. Some of these stones are 5 feet over ground, and are 4 feet wide, and 8 or 10 inches thick.

Is this—and are the other circles adjoining—military, religious, commemorative, or monumental? The experience and general belief of antiquarians is, that all these large circles are Druidical, and either monumental or religious. Sometimes they undoubtedly mark the confines of a cairn or tumulus, which latter having been removed centuries ago, the circle has remained—as would be the case, had we continued our excavations, and cleared away the interior of the circle of the "One Man's Cairn," figured and described at page 224. Some stone circles of only a few feet or yards in diameter are, no doubt, the remains of the upright supports of dome-roofed sepulchres; but the experienced eye is sure to detect such use, and it would not have been possible to roof over the spaces that are included within the Moytura circles. Of their Druidical or religious purposes we know nothing, nor are we ever likely to know more. Some of them may mark the outer walls of cahers, where all the other stones, possibly of smaller size, have been removed in the course of centuries; or they may have been originally (in lieu of timber) raised up as defensive stockades where, taking the warfare of the time into account, their interiors would be places of considerable security. Compare one of these circles with an ancient wall in Aran, or that of the fort on Inishmain, figured and described at page 250. Our ancient histories make no mention of these stone circles; legend, tradition, and even popular superstition, are remarkably silent with respect to them; and we therefore hail with thankfulness any inkling which this as yet unpublished tale of the Moytura Battle can afford us as to their use. As already stated the Tuatha de Dananns, it is said, "fixed pillar-stones in the ground to prevent their people fleeing, until these stones should take to flight," and at the same time protect them from the enemy; and certainly a circle of this description, formed of smooth sloping flags, with the interstices filled up so as to form a wall 7 or 8 feet high, within which 200 men could easily stand, would answer all the purposes of an entrenched camp.

Now, among the most renowned personages of that age whose names and exploits have descended to our own time was Belor, the great Fomorian giant, who is said to have had a third eye in the centre of his forehead, with the basilisk power of which, when uncovered, he could, even at a great distance, kill or petrify his enemies.* There is a vivid tradition among the people that such a personage was at the Cath-Magh-Tuireadh-Cunga, and that the persons who erected these forts and circles, dreading his power over their soldiers, painted the figures of warriors on the outer surfaces of these flat stones; so that, as an old man once told me on the spot, "when the Fomorian necromancer, standing on the fort of Lackafinna about half a mile off, or at Ardnagook, and turning his magical eye on them, perceived that he had not tumbled any of them—for he used to *melt* people with his eyes, he went away in disgust." The name of this hero is not known traditionally in this neighbourhood, and there is no mention made of him in the manuscript account of the first

* Could it be possible that at that period Belor had an optical instrument by which he might see at a distance?

battle of Moytura; but we know, that "Belor of the mighty blows" was killed at the second or northern battle of Moytura, subsequently fought in the county Sligo. It is with the Faugha Ruadh, or great red giant, already referred to, that local tradition associates this circumstance.

At the south-west corner of the same field, opposite the glebe of the Rev. E. L. Moore, the present rector of this parish, there is another circle, of which the subjoined is a graphic

representation. It consists of a series of standing stones, and is 152 feet in diameter. Within and around this and the adjoining fields, to the south and east, several perfect circles still exist, and the sites of others can still be traced within the confines of Cath-na-Bunnen; so that here was evidently the stronghold of one of the contending armies.

Where the glebe now stands there existed, about forty years ago, the great Danann stronghold called *Caher-Mac-Turc*, "the caher of the son of the wild boar," and by some called *Caher-more* and *Caher-Biel*, the stones of which were used in erecting the parsonage; and the slope in front of the latter yet marks a portion of its site. Half a century ago, before the same knowledge existed, or the same interest was felt in the preservation of national or historic monuments as at present, but little attention was paid to the preservation of such structures. Thanks to George Crampton, Esq., son of the late Rector of Cong, we have been furnished with a map and description of this great caher, which was perhaps one of the largest in Ireland, and resembled Dun-Aengus or Dun-Conor, and others in Aran. It was circular, and enclosed a space of about half an acre. The inner wall was about 7 or 8 feet high, and 10 or 12 thick, and sloped from without inwards, with an opening or doorway 12 feet wide. In the central space was a small circular building, which in modern times was called by the people "the gaol," the wall of which was 3 feet thick. In removing the caher, several ancient iron weapons, and the stones of some querns or hand-mills, were discovered.

After the Danann king was wounded, Breas, his grandson, charged the Firbolgs with great fury, but was cut down by the hand of Eochy. That, however, Breas, the son of Ealathan, was not killed, is manifest from the context of the MS., as well as the general tenor of history, for he subsequently reigned during the period that Nuad was disabled from his wound. Then the Dagda, Ogma, Allad, and Delway (evidently Scandinavian names), rushed on King Eochy, but were repulsed for a while by his four grandsons, the sons of Slainge, all of whom, however, fell in the engagement; and "the place where they were interred is called *Leaca-Mhac-Slainge*, 'the flags of the sons of Slainge.'"

On the other side, the four sons of Gann charged down the Danann lines, but they also were killed by Gobnen, the smith; Lucry, the carpenter; Dianceacht, the surgeon, and Aengabha; and their monument was called *Dumha-Mac-Gainn*, "the mound of the sons of Gann." Then the three sons of Orddan, the Firbolg Druid, next essayed to break the Danann columns, but were slain by the sons of Cainte; and "the place where they were buried is called *Dumha-na-n-Druadh*," or "the Druid's mound." Afterwards, the cohorts of the invaders, along with Inchar and Incharba, advanced, and charged the Belgæ, but were withstood by Carbre, the son of Den and the sons of Buan, whom however they slew; and, says the MS., "the leachts at which they were interred are called *Leaca-Mac-Buain*, and the grave of Cairbre lies outside their leachts or monuments." Could we but identify them, there are all round this spot sufficient monuments to choose from for these erections, notwithstanding centuries of cultivation, and, alas! years of ruthless destruction.

The Belgian columns were evidently driven back, and the

battle passed, as on the occasion of the second day's fighting, to the north-east. The sons of the two kings, Looe the strong, son of Nuad, and Slainge the fair, son of Eochy, after a fierce encounter slew each other. The grave where the Danann hero was buried is called *Lia-Looee*, and is in all likelihood the "long stone of The Neale" already referred to, and here figured. It is a very notable object at the fork of the road, to the south of the village, and is now 4½ feet over ground.—See page 221. There are many traditions about Looe-lamh-fada, the long-handed son of King Nuad, still in the mouths of the people in this district.

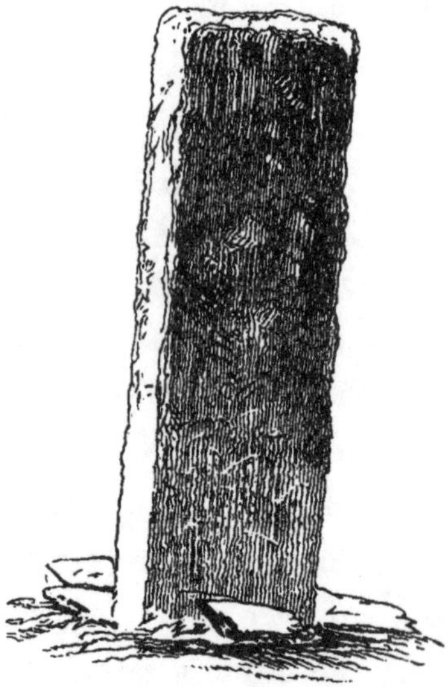

Following the track of the Danann during this third day's engagement, we approach the Parish of KILMOLARA, commonly called The Neale, but the parish church of which happens to be situated in the parish of Cong. Adjoining the village is The Neale House, the residence of Lord Baron Kilmaine, and within the demesne there are several monuments of much interest, although not noticed by writers. A large stone heap, now faced with steps, and crowned by a weathercock, contains, we believe, in its interior the nucleus of a cairn, and may probably be that erected over Slainge himself. In the grounds adjoining a comparatively modern structure has been erected over some sculptured figures of considerable antiquity, although not referrible to the days of Moytura. They are placed in front of an ancient cave, and are popularly known as "The Gods of The Neale." That, however, which is of undoubted antiquity, and well worthy the serious attention of philologists and antiquaries, is a flat mass of gritstone placed in the orchard wall, and now nearly obscured with ivy, and of which, with the permission of the noble proprietor, we have been permitted to publish an account. It measure snearly 15 inches each way, and bears the inscription, in sunken letters, faithfully represented by the accompanying illustration, taken from a carefully made rubbing. These characters are perhaps the oldest letters that have yet been discovered in Ireland, and are evidently of greater antiquity than those upon the Inchangoill monument. Mr. J. O'B. Crowe reads this denotative inscription thus:—

Lon Fecnan, *Ecclesia Fecnan*, the *lon*, *laun*, place, or church, of Fecna (genitive Fecnan), perhaps the Fecnan of Adamnan or some Fechna of Mayo of the Saxons.—See Colgan's "Trias Thaum." page 378. Other philologists to whom it was submitted have not as yet thrown more light upon its interpretation. Of the antiquity of this inscribed monument there can be no doubt. It is said to have been brought here from the old church of Brefy, below Castlebar.* The mode in which the letters were picked out, possibly with a flint or hard sharp stone, is well shown in the illustration.

The fourth day's battle drew to a close; the flower of the Firbolg army was cut off; and its king, greatly fatigued, and far removed from the well of the Mean-uisge, and there being then—as there is literally now—no water in the place, was sorely oppressed with thirst; so he committed the command to Sreng, and fled with a chosen band across the plain, from near The Neale in a north-western direction towards Lough Mask. The MS., which rather inclines to the native or Firbolg side of the question, relates that the Dananian Druids, hearing of the extremity in which Eochy was placed, magically concealed all the wells, rivers, and fountains—probably a mist surrounded them.

The king and his attendants were pursued by the three sons of Nemed Mac-Badhrai, and 150 followers; and after a fierce conflict on the lake shore, which is described with great spirit,

* On a stone built into the wall, beneath this monument, can be read the following inscription:—"The above stone was found at Brefy, in the Co. of Mayo, A. D. 1732, in a coffin, inscribed in Irish characters, the coffin of Genan, which contained a skeleton, 12½ feet long. Genan was King of Ireland, A. M. 3352, P. D. 7024, A. C. 1681; and this monument is erected to show the antiquity of the Irish character and the size of mankind in those early ages. A. D. 1756." The foregoing speaks for itself.

and in which the king slew his three youthful assailants, he himself expired. "Thus fell," says the MS., "the mighty Eochy! A lofty carn was raised over his body, which is to this day to be seen at Traigh Eothuile, and called *Carn Eathach* from his name; and at the western extremity of that strand still exist the monuments of his slayers, called *Leaca Mac-Nemidh*, 'the flags of the sons of Nemidh.'"

On the great grassy hill of Killower, or Carn, from which the townland takes its name—overlooking Lough Mask, from which it is about a mile distant, and commanding a view of the entire country, stands to this hour the most extensive and remarkable cairn in the West of Ireland—that figured below,

and which, we entertain but little doubt, was erected to commemorate the fate of Eochy Mac Erc, the last of the Firbolg Kings of Erin.

Crowning the summit of the eminence is a ditch and rampart, the top of which is 2500 paces in circumference, and on it are still some standing stones, especially near the entrance on the W. N. W. side. A space twenty yards wide intervenes between the top of this rampart and the outer margin of the cairn. The tumulus undoubtedly contains central chambers, and a remarkable and partially open passage encircles its base. The view from the top is very grand; on the extreme west we have Benlevi and the Partry range of mountains rising from the lake, with the Reek of St. Patrick peeping over them; more to the north is Nephin, the hill of Cultamaugh, Balla, and the country about Claremorris, and so all round the distant eastern end of the plain to Knockma, whence the eye again turns westwards to the shores of Lough Corrib.

Between this point and The Neale, on the east, and stretching round to Nymphsfield, on the south, the ground over which King Eochy fled exhibits no trace of water, and scarcely any vestige of early occupation. As yet the flagstones of the sons of Nemid have not been identified, although a ruined cromleach, somewhat to the south-west of our position, on the sloping ground above Caher Robert, evidently mark the site of an ancient monument. Above these are the remains of two caves; and about half a mile to the south-east of the "Carn" stands the remarkable square dry-stone enclosure, forty-four paces in width, and containing a well-built cave in the centre, which is called *Caher Ribert*, or "Robert's Fort." Its walls are 6 feet high, and 2½ thick; and the western square-topped doorway, with its massive lintel and sloping sides, would appear to be the type of the early Christian edifices to which reference has been so frequently made. It is 4 feet 10 inches high, 3 feet 2 inches wide at the bottom, and 2 feet 10 inches at top. This form of caher, although represented in Aran, is rather scarce, and is evidently of later date than the circular ones. A square fort or enclosure may still be traced among the rocks, about half a mile to the north of Aughalard Castle.* Immediately at the western foot of this hill is the great natural and artificial cave mentioned at page 209; and nearly in the same line we see several other raths and cahers—Lough Mask Castle, Ballinchalla church, the ruins of Inishmain Abbey, and the fort and standing stones over the water's edge at Inishowen, already figured and described at page 227; while more to the north rises the last great battle monument,

* In order to visit this portion of our route, the tourist, passing along the road from Cong by the Glebe and the cross roads to The Neale, reaches a site once known as Cross-Davy, where an ancient sculptured cross formerly stood, until removed about fifty years ago by religious fanaticism, backed by legal injustice. Then, taking the northern road through Creevagh—Caher-Robert, Eochy's Carn, and the antiquities to be described in the next chapter, can be visited. The lower road from Lough Mask Castle into Cong will take the tourist to Aughalard, and on by the Pigeon Hole, to his hotel; or carry him by the lake margin to Maam.—See the map.

called Caher Bowen, and also the well of Dermod and Graine: and the forts in the demesne of Cushlough.

Our accouut of the battle and battle-field of Moytura here closes; both parties withdrew after the fourth day's fighting—the dispirited Firbolgs to their camp along Corrib shore, and the Dananians to their mountain fortress. Both parties interred their dead; and it is said the former "raised *Dumhas* [or tumuli] over their nobles; raised *Leaca* [or flagstones] over their heroes; *Ferthas* [graves] over the soldiers; and *Knocs* [or hillocks] over the champions." Sreng and the other remaining descendants of Gann held a war council; and, having but 3000 men remaining, they discussed the question of leaving the country in the possession of the invaders, dividing the kingdom, or risking another battle; and, as they were inferior in numbers, they demanded single combat, and challenged the Dananns to fight man to man. This was refused; but a peace was ratified, by which Sreng and the Firbolgs, or Belgæ, retained the province of Connaught, to which those of that nation then resorted from all quarters, and where there is no doubt some remnant of that race still remains. A portion of the Belgæ, possibly the warriors and soldiers, fled across Lough Corrib to the Islands of Aran; where, perhaps dreading another invasion, they raised those stupendous barbaric monuments that still exist there, the wonder and admiration of antiquaries and historians, as they are undoubtedly the most extensive, as well as the oldest, structures of their kind in Europe.*

The Tuatha de Dananns elected Breas, son of Elaethan, to reign during the period of Nuada's convalescence, which it is said occupied seven years. Under A. M. 3310 we read—"This was the seventh year of Breas over Ireland, when he resigned the kingdom to Nuadhat, after the cure of his hand by Diancecht, assisted by Creidne the artificer, for they put a silver hand upon him;" and in 3330, "at the end of the twentieth year of the reign of Nuadhat of the Silver Hand, he fell in the battle of Magh-Tuireadh na bh-Fomorach, by Balor of the mighty blows, one of the Fomorians." From this we learn that, according to the computed chronology, twenty-seven years elapsed between the first or southern and the second or northern battle of Moytura, which was fought in the parish of Kilmactranny, barony of Tirerrill and county of Sligo. By many writers, ancient and modern, these two battles and battle-fields have been mixed up; but we trust the foregoing narrative and topographical description will prevent further mistakes of this nature.

The bare historic fact, with but few details of the great battle of Moytura, has been mentioned in all our annals, and is told in most of our ancient Irish MSS. of authority; from which,

* See Mr. Haverty's graphic account of the visit of the Ethnological section of the British Association to the Islands of Aran in 1857, which the author had the honour of conducting.

however, it was here unnecessary to quote, as they do not enter into details, and no effort has heretofore been made to identify the locality. The unpublished manuscript from which the foregoing account has been extracted is preserved in the Library of Trinity College, H, 2. 17, commencing at page 291; it was transcribed at Moy-Enne, near Ballyshannon, by Cormac O'Cuirnin, probably in the fifteenth century; but the tale itself is referred to by Cormac Mac Cullinan, King and Bishop of Cashel, the most learned man of his age, when he wrote his celebrated Glossary, in the ninth century. The translation which the author had access to was that made for the Ordnance Survey by the late Dr. John O'Donovan, and which is preserved in one of the manuscript books of the Ordnance Survey for the county of Mayo, to which we have so frequently referred.* It would have exceeded the limits of this book to have described the battle more at length; but an alphabetical list of the names of those who fought upon both sides, and the significant meanings of which so much resemble those of North American Indians, would, we think, be of some interest to the philologists of the present day.—See Appendix.

* There are also other copies of the *Cath-Magh-Tuireadh* nearly paraphrastic of the foregoing, and also giving descriptions of the engagement at Ballisadare, or Kilmactranny, preserved in the British Museum; and a copy of which, made by a son of the late Eugene O'Curry, is now in the Library of the Catholic University.—See O'Curry's Lectures upon "The Manuscript Materials of Ancient Irish History," pp. 241, 250, &c. The British Museum manuscript was transcribed by Gilla-Riabhach-O'Cleary about the year 1460.

CHAPTER IX.

LOUGH MASK.

PARISH OF BALLINCHALLA. LOUGH MASK CASTLE. EDMOND DE BURGO. INISHMAIN. EOGAN-BEIL AND ST. CORMAC. INISHMAIN ABBEY. ANCIENT FORT. THE PENITENTIARY. INISHOWEN. THE HAG'S CASTLE. ROSS HILL. ST. PATRICK'S CHURCH. UPPER LOUGH CORRIB. DOON AND CASTLE KIRK. ST. FECHEN'S AND ST. ENNA'S WELLS. CAISLEAN NA KIRKA. MAAM.

THE battle of southern Moytura, which we traced in a curved direction from the vicinity of Cong, ended, as already stated, on the borders of Lough Mask, and in the parish now popularly called BALLACHALLA, where we are at present supposed to stand. In the hagiologies this parish is called Cala-Locha-Measga; and in the Irish, *Baile-an-Chala*, "the bally or town of the *Caladh*, or 'Port of Lough Mask;'" for, although the term "callow" is applied, in the counties of Roscommon and Galway, to the holm, flat, or inch, generally subject to inundation on the borders of a lake or river, it is here applied to a landing-place for boats.— See O'Donovan's letters in the "Ordnance Survey Book" for Mayo, page 80.

This parish extends along the eastern border of Lough Mask from the parish of Cong to that of Ballinrobe, having

Kilmolara on the east. Within it are the great tumuli of Carn Bowen and Killower, and also Caher-Robert, already described; but we have now only to visit its lake margin. To the left of the road leading down to the water stand the ruins of the

little church of Ballachalla, of no great antiquity, but still much used as a burial place. Continuing our route to the water's edge over a road formed of the natural limestone rock, which here rises to the surface in enormous flags—and which path is called *Ballin-Coirp*, "the road of the corpses," on their way to the cemetery, in the adjoining abbey of Inishmain, —we pass under the picturesque ruin of Lough Mask Castle, standing on a high scarped rock, and commanding a glorious prospect of the scenery to the west.

This ancient fortified dwelling of the De Burgos, faithfully pictured by the foregoing illustration, is known in the annals by the name of the townland of Baile-Locha-Measga, in which it is placed. Upon a massive decorated chimney-breast adjoining one of the mullioned windows is the following inscription:—**Thomas Bobrke · IHS · 1618 · Elles Bbtler,**— who, no doubt, occupied, and probably restored, this structure. It is said to have been built by one of the "English barons" in 1238; and we know that in 1338, when Edmond De Burgo, the ill-fated son of the Earl of Ulster, was abducted from the Friars' House at Ballinrobe on Low Sunday, the 19th of April, "he was that night carried to Lough Mask Castle,"* which then probably belonged to Sir William Burke, of the Eighter or Mayo branch of that great family.

The next night he spent in Ballindeonagh Castle, near Petersburgh, at the southern or lower end of the lake; and on the third he was murdered at an island in that arm of the lake, since known as "The Earl's Island."—See page 98. His sister

* See O'Flaherty's "West Connaught," p. 47. Lough Measg, Measca, or Mask, is so called from its mingling, *meascadh*, with the waters of Loughs Carra and Corrib. Sir Thomas Bourke re-edified this castle after the battle of Kinsale, in 1602.

and heir married Lionel, Duke of Clarence. In 1412 Brian O'Conor destroyed the castle of Baile-Locha-Measca by fire; and in 1416, when another Edmond Burke plundered the territory of Mac-Feoris, round the southern end of the lake, he took Bermingham himself prisoner, and confined him in this castle.

Passing over the little stream that now divides Inishmain (no longer an island, but a peninsula) from the mainland, we approach a charming group of ruins, standing by the water's edge, surrounded by well-grown timber, and consisting of the outer castellated gateway of an abbey, and beyond it one of the most beautiful churches in Ireland.* Before, however, we enter the sacred precincts, or proceed to examine the ruins of Christian times, let us look back upon the early history of this locality. Across this and the neighbouring island to the west, both of which were probably always accessible in summer time, the Firbolgs pursued the Tuatha de Dananns, and slew the sons of Cailchu upon the lake shore, where their stone circle still remains, as already shown at page 227. It is said Eogan-Beil, King of Connaught, had a "palace" here in the sixth century, from which circumstance the western island is to this day called *Inish-Eoghain*, or Inishowen. O'Donovan, labouring under the impression that this stone circle, which is evidently

* Lough Mask Castle is the property of the Earl of Erne; the islands of Inishmain and Inishowen, that of Lord Baron Kilmaine; and the great carn of Killower belongs to Captain Cooper.

monumental, might have been the habitation of the old king, says in one of his letters, written in 1838, "The remains of this palace puzzles me very much, though it is not very unlike *Dun-an-Sciath* at Lough Annuinn, now Ennell, in Westmeath." There can, however, be no doubt that it is one of the Moytura monuments. It is equally certain that the foundations of the ancient caher, or stone fort, of King Beil, stood upon the site of the abbey, and a considerable portion of its circle may yet be traced beyond its western end.

From the Book of Lecan Colgan gives a translation of the following saintly legend, which possibly refers to the end of the fifth century:—"St. Cormac came first to the palace of Eugenius, surnamed Bell, son of Kellach, King of Connaught, who at that time dwelt in a certain fort, called afterwards from his name Dun-Eogan, lying in a certain lake in West Connaught, which is commonly called Loch Measca. But the servant of God was not received with that honour due to him, nor with the offices of humanity. Wherefore, the saint, with a menacing and true prophecy, foretold what he had foreseen by inspiration would happen to that residence. For he predicted that that fort would not be hereafter the seat of kings, but that a domicile of the servants of Christ, and of monks, was to be erected in its place. The truth of this prophecy has been proved by the event; for on that island, commonly called Inis-Moedoin, in which the vestiges of that fort, afterwards level with the ground, are seen, a monastery was erected, which from that time remained the habitation of devoted servants of Christ."

The next notice of *Inis Moedoin*, Inishmain, or the middle island, which we find is in the Annals of the Four Masters under A. D. 1223, "Maelisa, the son of Turlough O'Conor, prior of Inishmain, died." This ecclesiastic was the eldest of the three legitimate sons of the great Turlough More; and it appears that he embraced a religious life in his youth, and left his younger brothers to contend with each other for the sovereignty of Connaught and the crown of Ireland.

When, by whom, or for what order this abbey was erected, neither history nor tradition gives the slightest clue; but it was probably built between the twelfth and fourteenth centuries, and it very likely occupies the site of the original church of St. Cormac, and the small square-headed doorway of which is in all probability that by which the nave of the church was entered from the northern side, although it may have been carried there from its original locality in the west gable of the saint's *Daimlaght*. This door-

way, here figured, is quite incongruous in either period or architecture, with the noble, highly-decorated structure in which it is placed. There is no arch above it. Whoever built Inishmain exhibited great taste, as well as skill, and, possibly in pious remembrance of the prophecy of St. Cormac, preserved this portion of his church, which was very likely all that remained of it when the more modern building was commenced. The entire length of this great church is 62 feet, the breadth of the nave is 21½ feet, the chancel is 20 feet by 15. Its arch no longer exists; but, the grand cluster of pillars that still remain upon the southern side, show that it must have been of great beauty and vast size, as may be seen by this illustration.

Fortunately that great Irish church preserver, the *Hedera Hibernica*, has long since thrown its arms around this beauteous ruin, or a single stone of Inishmain Abbey would no longer stand upon another. The capitals of these pillars are decorated with floral embellishments such as that here exhibited, which somewhat resembles those of Cong and Athenry, with which it was probably coeval. Upon each side of the narrowed chancel there is a square structure, 16 feet by 12½, apparently more for domestic than ecclesiastical uses. The east window consists of two narrow circular-headed

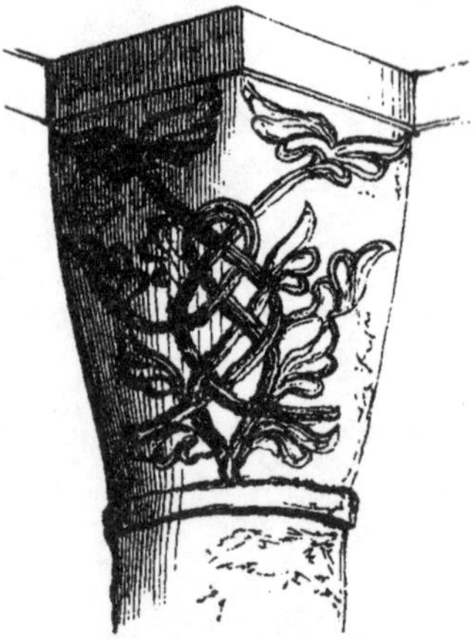

lights, the outer mouldings both upon the inside and the outside of which terminate in well-carved grotesque figures; the square doorway on the northern side; and a breach into one of the side structures, previously alluded to, are well shown in the foregoing illustration. If this was indeed an abbey, it probably belonged to the Augustinians, and was dependent on that of Cong.

Among the rocks, a little to the west of the ecclesiastical enclosure, there still exist the remains of an ancient circular fort, the walls of which, although frequently repaired, as it is used occasionally for a sheep pen, are so characteristic of the ancient mode of building, and so like those seen in similar structures in Aran, that the following sketch is inserted. It was probably one of the outworks of King Biel's fortress. If the intermediate masonry were removed, these long upright stones would present what is termed a Druidical circle

Passing westwards from Inishmain church by the stone enclosure figured above, the author last year discovered, among the limestone rocks that slope towards the lake, a very curious structure, of which the illustration on the following page is a graphic representation. It is a square unmortared building, 12½ feet high, and 15 feet wide, with a set-off 7½ feet from the ground; and, with the exception of the crypts on the west face, as shown in the cut, is perfectly solid, and formed of undressed stone.

These crypts are certainly the most remarkable and inexplicable structures that have yet been discovered in Ireland. At top they are formed somewhat like the roof of a high-pitched Gothic church, with long stone ribs or rafters abutting upon a low side wall, and meeting each other at top, as shown in the accompanying engravings. The intervals between these

sloping stones, some of which are 4 feet long, are filled up with layers of stone laid horizontally. The illustration upon the opposite page, taken from the inside of the northern crypt, gives a fair representation of this roofing, above and around which the entire structure seems to be a solid mass of stone work. The flooring is also composed of narrow stone joists placed a few inches apart, so that air can come up between them, and the partition between the crypts is so thin, that, although not pervious to light, conversation can be kept up between them. Each is on an average 5 feet high throughout, and about 3 wide; there are five stone ribs or rafters in the roof of the south, and seven in that of the north crypt; both outer jambs are slightly revealed, and the division between them does not measure quite 2 feet. The masonry of the outer wall strongly resembles that of some of our most ancient churches.

There is no history and there are no legends attaching to this building, and no person in the neighbourhood ever heard of its existence until last year, neither has any analogous structure been described in either this or any of the neighbouring countries.* Possibly it may have been a prison, or penitentiary, in which some of the refractory brethren of the neighbouring abbey were confined. Of its antiquity there can be no doubt.

* Presuming it to be modern, the only structure which this building in any way resembles, is that of a lime kiln; but, being solid, it would be quite inapplicable to that purpose, neither could fuel be carried to it with facility, or the lime removed. Subsequent to its discovery by the author and his son Oscar, in August, 1866, and after Mr. Wakeman had taken drawings of it, the Earl of Dunraven had a very perfect photograph made of the western face of this structure. The author is also indebted to J. E. Rogers, Esq., for some very accurate measurements and highly illustrative coloured drawings of the interior.

Still proceeding westward, and skipping with considerable labour and fatigue from rock to rock, over the huge limestone masses that intervene between the two islands, and which are perfectly dry in summer, we pass over into the island of Eogan, the son of Beil, now called Inishowen, to visit the great fort and flagstone circle of the sons of Caelchu (of which the drawing and description have been given at page 227), and again to rest, while enjoying the lovely prospect of Lough Mask and the Partry range, from where the river of Lough na Foohy enters at the foot of Kilbride wood upon the south, along by the slopes of Tourmakeedy round to its Lough Carra end, where the view brings within our ken the last object which shall engage our attention at this end of Lough Mask—the small, and partially artificial island, almost entirely occupied with *Caislean-na-Cailliighe*, or "the Hag's Castle." This ancient stone fortress may certainly be regarded as the earliest castle in Ireland; for there is historical notice of its existence anterior to the Anglo-Norman Conquest, and it truly resembles, as O'Donovan stated many years ago, a "Cyclopean caher with cement." The island itself is, partially at least, artificial; and this great circular enclosure, which is 90 feet in diameter, and nearly 30 feet high, occupies almost the entire of it, as shown by the accompanying illustration from a drawing by Master Wilde. The walls are upwards of 8 feet thick at top, and slope outwards towards the bottom. There is no doorway at present existing, but it probably occupied the eastern face, opposite Creagh, which portion is now quite dilapidated. It is quite impossible that this outer structure could ever have been roofed; but within there is a small beehive-like edifice, which, no doubt, served somewhat

the same purpose as that in the enclosure of Aughnanure Castle on Lough Corrib, described at page 288. It is about 10½ feet in diameter and 12 feet high, and has several joist holes about 5½ feet from the ground, and also two large loopholes near the top.

In 1195 Cathal Mac Dermot O'Conor, advancing into Connaught, and plundering as he went, brought the spoil to Caislean-na-Cailllighe, whence he proceeded to commit great ravages on all sides. Again, in 1586, Sir Richard Bingham, Governor of Connaught, attacked this Castle, which, say the Annalists, "was the strongest fortress in Connaught." It is still well worthy of careful investigation.

Opposite Inishowen is Devenish Island, upon which there are some ancient remains. In various directions along the Lough Mask road, and through the surrounding fields, may be seen numerous excavations, like old sand quarries, which resemble modern rifle pits, and may be as old as the days of the Firbolgs and Tuatha de Dananns.

Passing round by the lower margin of Lough Mask, and along the south of the natural wood of Ballykine, in which there are the remains of another castle by the water's side, we re-enter Galway county by the barony and parish of Ross, and reach the beautiful demesne of Ross Hill, formerly the property of the Berminghams, and then of the Clemences, but now of Sir B. L. Guinness. Near the lake's edge stands the ruin of the very ancient church of Teampull Brendan, a portion of which may be coeval with that at Inchangoill. There is a square-headed doorway, with remarkably sloping jambs in its western gable, and a few feet within the church is a dividing wall similar to that at Killursa, described at page 104. This little church, which is styled on the Ordnance map an abbey, is now 69 feet long by 21 wide outside; but a portion of its eastern end, as well as its western bell turret, is comparatively modern. A scarcely legible, and not very ancient inscription, can be traced upon the sill of the sacristy window.

We are now in the district called Joyce Country, which includes the entire parish of Ross, that part of the parish of Cong which lies in the county of Galway, and those portions of Ballinchalla and Ballovey to the west of Lough Mask, and extends from this point through the valley of Maam to the Killeries. O'Flaherty thus writes of it:—"The half barony of Rosse, commonly called Joyce Countrey, from a Welch family of Yoes, Joas, or Shoyes, which held that land from the O'Flaherties (formerly part of *Partry-an-tslevy*, which extended from St. Patrick's Hill in the Owles to Lough Orbsen), hath the barony of Balynahinsy, Koelshaly Roe [The Killeries—see page 22], and the Owles on the west of it; and by a high ridge of mountaines called Formna-mor, is divided on the north from the same Owles. From that mountain, Bruin River falling into Lough Measg, separates Partry mountains, in the barony of Kera, from Kilbridy townland, the north side of Lough Measg [where there] is a chappell and well dedicated to St. Bridget. There is on the south of it an arm of Lough Measg, which shoots into the country westward about four miles to Glenntresky [Glantrague]. On the west of Kilbridy townland is Lough-na-fohy Lake, out of which the river of Gairge comes into that arme of Lough Measg,"* within which is the Earl's Island, already referred to at page 251.

These Shoeys, or Joyces, were a Welch colony, who settled

* See Hardiman's Edition of O'Flaherty's "West Connaught," page 44, where much information may be obtained respecting *Partrigia de Monte*, the Joyces, and the various localities noticed in the foregoing extract. See also the Annals of the Four Masters; and O'Donovan's Ordnance Letters upon the barony of Ross, from whence most of the information contained in Hardiman's notes was obtained; and also the Hy-Fiachrach.

here under the O'Flahertys in the thirteenth century; but, although the name is still common, the tribe has nearly died out. They were men of large stature, and generally of fair complexion—the last memorable man of the name in this region was *Shaun-na-Baunia*, "John of the Jacket," or big white Jack Joyce, who formerly lived at Imaire-an-Linain, "the ridge of Leenane," and was well known to tourists thirty years ago. Westwards of Ross Hill, on the lake shore, is the ruin of Ballyndeonagh Castle, beside Petersburg, the residence of the Joyce Country Lynches.*

Along the slopes of Benlevi, from the fort of Cahergal, over the ridge of Fairhill, now called Clonbur, down by the tower of Ardnageeha, "the windy height," to Corrib shore we meet with several ancient remains; but, having been so long on land we must again betake us to the water, either by boat from Cong, or on board the Eglinton in one of its excursion trips from Galway.

* Before leaving this portion of our route, we beg to express our obligations to the Rev. Mr. O'Callaghan, of Ross, and the Rev. Abraham Jagoe, of Castlekirk, and to the various clergy and gentry around Lough Corrib, who have been good enough to reply to our queries respecting measurements, local histories, and other matters connected with this work, which has enabled us to render it more accurate in local details than most others of its class. What a contrast this presents to the complaint made by Dutton, in the preface to his "Survey of the County of Galway," in 1824, where he mourns over the "indolence" of the clergy and gentry, who would not even reply to his questions!

Taking leave of the battle field of Moytura and its monuments, we offer, in conclusion, the accompanying illustration of Dun Aengus in Aranmore, the last great stronghold of the Firbolg race, as it presented in 1847, and which will serve to

explain the character and structure of those Moytura cahers and duns, of which only the vestiges now remain.*

Again taking our western course up the lake from the point midway between the open of Cong river and Inchangoill, where we deviated from the steamer's usual track to visit the latter locality, as stated at page 133, we find ourselves within view of some of the best scenery in our route. On our right is

* This illustration was made for the author by C. Cheyne, Esq., during their visit to Aran, twenty years ago, and was published by Professor Babington in the "Archæologia Cambrensis" for January, 1858, and afterwards in Mr. Haverty's "Report on the Excursion to the Aran Isles," Dublin, 1859.

Ashford, the tower of Ardnageeha, the heights of Ardane, and farther westwards the plantations of Toomnenaune, the seat of W. B. De Montmorency, Esq., creeping up the bold sides of Benlevi—here rising to a height of 1370 feet—flecked with grey and brown from the mixture of rock, bog, and heather, but having its sombre hue turned into azure as the mists are lifted from its face, and reveal the great cairn on its summit. From thence, it is said,—as has been related of a hundred other places,—that a hag or caillagh—for we suppose there were no calleens in these days—pelted another witch, who occupied the top of Carn-Seefin on our left, where a similar stone heap, at a height of 1009 feet over the sea level, on the southern shore of the lough, raises its bulky form in the parish of Kilcummin. This great tumulus, which is about 24 feet high, and 324 feet in circumference, and evidently monumental, can be seen from a great distance all round.

The long line of cormorants that sentinel the great shoal to the north-west of Inchangoill dip their tails in the water at our approach, and clouds of wild ducks, curlews, and gulls, rise on the wing. The peninsulas jut out from the land, the islands and rocks accumulate, and the lake narrows, as we pass into the strait between Doorus and Cannavar; and the Joyce Country and Connemara mountains, on either hand, rise up from the water's edge. On our left is the chapel of Glann, in the district called *Cappa-na-laura-baun*, and still nearer the lake margin is Corrarevagh, the seat of H. Hodgson, Esq., the planting upon which is beginning to give a civilized look to the brown bogs along the water's edge.

We are now passing between the parishes of Cong and Kilcummin; and in the latter, opposite this point, the Dooghta river enters the lake to the east of the peninsula of Doorus, and in the valley through which it flows may be seen St. Mary's, and beside it "St. Fechin's well," or *Tober Fechin,* where his celebrated altar-stone was preserved until it was removed to Claggan. See page 269.

Passing Lannaun Island, we are again in an inland sea, but not landlocked, as those who sail upon it have frequently experienced; for, while it is calm as a fishpond one moment, in another it is lashed into wave and foam, as a squall, which had accumulated upon the upper lake, rushes out suddenly through the gap of Doon, and expends its fury upon the eastern sheet of water.*

Steering through the narrow intricate passage under the wooded promontory of Doon, we literally leave Lough Corrib and the scenery of Mayo behind us, and pass into another region, grander, wilder, and more romantic; the mountains which

* In the summer of 1839, as the Hon. Augustus Browne, with two men, in a sailing boat, were making a tack across the upper end of this part of the lake, the boat was suddenly struck with a squall, and, the main sheet being belayed, she was laid on her beam ends, and went down with all three. The author, having assisted in raising the boat, spent several days in the locality, and became perfectly familiar with the scene which he has now attempted to describe.

we had been admiring from a distance now rise up almost perpendicularly around us; the green slopes and sienna-tinted hills change into grey abrupt bare rocks, glowing with ever-varying hues of purple and opal, as the light flickers on the bold sides of Lackavrea, that stands up in an inaccessible pile 1307 feet high on our left, or brightens up both sides of the great wall of hills that margin the calm lonely valley of Maam, which stretches into the western distance with the Twelve Pins on its southern aspect. But immediately around us the adage is reversed; for contiguity "lends enchantment to the view," and an entirely new condition of nature surrounds us—a placid lake, untenanted by islands, save one lone rock near its northern shore, on which stands in bold relief the picturesque Castle of the Hen—*Caislean-na-Circe*—justly considered to be the oldest fortress of its kind in Ireland, as it is undoubtedly one of the best built.

On our right is the missionary settlement of "Castle Kirk," with its pretty church, glebe, schoolhouse, and mansion; and in the distance, where the great waters of the Maam valley are "mingled in peace," is seen the hotel, where a true-hearted English nobleman, representing Her Most Gracious Majesty, was once upon a time refused that hospitable reception which the tourist may now fully expect to meet.

Behind the rock that shelters the church and glebe from the north, St. Fechin's, sometimes called St. Enna's Well, pours its limpid spring into a rock basin, set in greenest moss, draped with ferns, festooned with ivy, and overhung with red-berried rowan tree, gnarled oak, and dark-leaved holly—the remains of the great mountain woods that once overspread all this region. A curious superstitious practice once attached to this lone retreat: sheltered from the rude blasts of the outer world lay an oval-shaped flagstone called the *Leac-na-Fechin*, "St. Fechin's stone," probably brought from his well at Dooghta, and which was the "touchstone" and the terror to all evildoers for miles around; for whoever was accused or suspected of a crime was either "dared to the Leac-Fecheen," or voluntarily underwent the ordeal of turning the flag, with certain rites and incantations not now necessary to describe.* As usual in such cases, there was a *maor* guardian of the stone, who instructed the pilgrim in the mysteries of the procedure, and drank the profits of the instruction in potteen. A few years ago there was in Connamara a well-known personage called *Phaudrig-na-Mullaun*, or "Paddy of the bullocks," who thought it necessary to "clear his character" by reference to the test of this stone, and in the subsequent orgies, the guardian, while endeavouring to swallow half a pint of raw whiskey at a draught, fell dead; since then the stone has disappeared. Many other tests of truth existed in former days in Ireland:

* See the author's tale on the subject, as well as the legends of the Hen's Castle, published in 1839, in "Otway's Tour in Connaught," page 232, as the "picturesque description of a young friend who is intimately acquainted with the country."

similar stones, crystals, the shrine of the *Domnach-Airgid*—the basis of one of Carleton's legends—and the *Gahr-Barragh*, or short crozier of St. Barry, were used for like purposes; but the influence of the Roman Catholic priesthood, general enlightenment, ridicule, the decrease of population, and the National Schools, have all combined to do away with these popular superstitions.*

Along the valley on the northern shore, in the townland of Drumsnauv, the ridge or "back of the snow," there is a fort and artificial cave similar to those upon the plain of Moytura, which persons interested in such matters should visit.

Before us to the south-west, on a rock not quite half an acre in extent, with the bold outline of Lackavrea in the background, stands the picturesque ruin here figured, from a sketch made by Mr. Wakeman in 1839. This ancient castle, which occupies almost the entire island, originally consisted of a quadrangular keep, 40 feet by 38 internally, placed in the direction of the cardinal points, and having square towers at the corners; and upon the south, or entrance face, an oblong additional tower, containing several apartments. It is all built of limestone; the intermediate walls between the towers are of rubble masonry, composed of undressed stones, not ar-

* See also Mr. Hennessy's paper "On the Forms of Ordeal anciently practised in Ireland," in The Proceedings of the Royal Irish Academy, vol. x., p. 34.

ranged in courses, but grouted with fine white mortar; while the towers are constructed with great regularity, and their *sawn* quoins average 15 inches long and 6 square. Unhap-

pily, before this noble historic ruin became the property of Sir B. L. Guinness, a few years ago, vandalism reigned in the district, and hundreds of these beautiful quoin stones were removed to erect residences in the neighbourhood. The original entrance appears to have been on the south side, between the middle and south-west towers, the slopes or "battering" sides of which present architectural peculiarities well worth the attention of artists. Scrambling up into this aperture, a small guard-room in the eastern tower, 6 feet 10 inches long, by 5 feet 10 inches wide, and 7 feet high, with a stone arched roof, called O'Conor's chamber, may be entered through a circular-arched doorway, 26 inches wide. On the inner face of this tower, at the south-west angle, there is a deeply splayed pointed-arched window, 7 feet 5 inches in span internally; and a circular-arched light exists in the northern tower, the external angle of which overhangs the bare rock, and is supported with an uncemented arch and corbelled work, as may be seen in the illustration. There are long narrow lights in the north and west walls of the keep; and in the northern wall, which is 45 feet 8 inches long externally, the garderobe aperture may be seen.

The interior of the keep is now a mass of stones and weeds; but about 10 feet from the present floor a series of joist holes show that it was floored, and must have been roofed in whole or in part. Each tower has a winding staircase leading to the top, and also opening into horizontal galleries which lead through the thickness of the wall. All these towers batter at their bases, which are solid; and that at the north-east is 13 feet wide. The south-west tower has a remarkable deep recess, but its base slopes more than any of the others, and runs out in an angle towards the lake, where there are the remains of ancient foundations—probably of the landing place. The view which we have given of this castle was taken from the water on the north-east side, and gives the best general idea of the building; but the southern aspect, especially the peculiarity of the entrance through these towers, is well worth illustration and architectural description.

The south-east tower is much dilapidated; but it evidently had an entrance to the small green platform on the eastern side of the castle, which led by a staircase to the middle tower, that was evidently the chief domestic portion of the building; while probably the keep and northern towers were appropriated to the soldiery and dependents. There is a square apartment in this middle tower with pointed-arched doors; and here we also find one of those speaking holes built through the substance of the wall, like that already described in Annadown Castle, at page 75. The intervening wall between the eastern towers measures 29 feet on the outside.

If well provisioned, and defended with any degree of bravery, this castle must have been impregnable at the time of its erection; and, as the rocks slope abruptly into the water on all sides, it is only accessible in a few places. At the north-east angle its height over the rock is now 35 feet. Viewed from any side—from the level water surface, as we pass round the point of Doon; or as glimpses of it are caught as we approach it from the Killery road; or when it first bursts upon our view, as we commence the descent of the mountain road leading from Curnamona to Maam: or as we look down upon it from "the yellow pass" upon the Galway road—it presents, with all its mountain surroundings and water settings, the most picturesque ruin in the country.

The legends respecting its name, origin, and history, are as numerous as they are fabulous—how it was built in a night by a cock and a hen—how it was defended by the Lady O'Flaherty after *O'Flaherty-na-Coileach*, or the Cock, had been slain, whence the heroine derived the soubriquet of the Hen, or *na-Cearc*—again, how it was built by a chieftain named Darka—and how the celebrated *Graina-Uaille*, after she had abducted the heir of Howth, carried him thither, &c. &c.; some of which fables the guides and boatmen will no doubt relate to the tourist. Antiquaries have, however, always regarded it as one of the oldest mortared castles in Ireland. From the notices of it given in the Annals of the Four Masters, it would appear to have been erected by the sons of Roderick O'Conor, assisted by the son of William Fitz-Adlem, the original De Burgo; and the tradition among the oldest inhabitants to this day is, that it was built by "O'Conchubhair, King of Connaught." As already stated at page 89, the Lord Justice, in 1225, caused Odo O'Flaherty to deliver up Kirk Island, and the boats of Lough Corrib, to Odo O'Conor, King of Connaught; and in 1233, "Felim, son of Cathal Crovderg, assumed the government of Connaught, and demolished the castles which had been erected by the power of the sons of Roderick O'Conor, and the son of William Burke, namely, the Castle of Bungalvy, Castle Kirk," and that on the Hag's Island, already described.

In 1256, Walter De Burgo, first Earl of Ulster, marched against Roderick O'Flaherty, plundered the territories of Gnomore and Gnobeg, and took possession of the lake, its islands, and castles. "These he fortified, and by that means considerably increased the power of the English in Connaught;" so that, although it might have been built by Irish chieftains, it would appear to have been within the power of the English settlers in the thirteenth century. Roderick O'Flaherty, writing in 1684, says, "Kirke Isle, or the Hen's Island, lyes in that part of Lough Orbsen which is within Ross half barony, and had a castell till broken in Cromwell's time." It is in the parish of Cong, which divides the lake in this place from that of Ross, which latter turns round by the bridge of Maam, and occupies the western shore of the lake, to a point exactly opposite the Hen's Castle.

We now pass up to Bunbannon, where the confluence of the Failmore and Beal-na-brac rivers, already described, enters the lake; and, as we row by the sedgy margin of the latter stream, we have before us the hotel and bridge of Maam, both erected by Alexander Nimmo—a man whose memory should be revered in the West; as, with the assistance of Dick Martin, he was the first to open up Connamara; and whose well engineered and admirably constructed roads, and valuable reports upon the capabilities and resources of this great district can never be sufficiently appreciated. The Maam Hotel—where good accommodation and conveyances can always be obtained, and which in the days of Rourke, its original proprietor, became attractive, not merely as a summer residence, but on account of its good cheer—is the property of the Earl of Leitrim, who possesses a great extent of country in this neighbourhood and throughout the valley of Maam. A very handsome limestone arch spanned the river at this point, but a slight settlement having taken place, some of the top stones were never put in their places. It remained, however, without any further injury, until a few years ago, when an immense flood coming down suddenly, and filling the valley on either side, rose above the arch, and immediately the whole fabric was swept away. Possibly side arches might have prevented this catastrophe. An iron bridge now occupies its place.*

The hotel was built by Nimmo as a residence and pay office, at the time of the erection of the bridge, and, if well managed, would be a most attractive resting-place for tourists, as, independent of the beauty of the scenery, and the interest attaching to the neighbourhood, and its admirable trout and pike fishing, it is within four miles of the main road between Galway and Clifden, upon which several conveyances ply daily.

* Upon the morning preceding the night on which the bridge of Maam fell, the author passed over it, and stated to his companion, Mr. G. F. O'Fflahertie, that it would surely fall during the next flood, for he perceived that the old settlement presented a fresh appearance—in fact the bridge had moved nearly two inches during the previous flood, but it was only when the water rose to the battlement that the whole gave way.

Passing up the road by the bridge and waterfall of Tiernakill ; winding over The Yellow Pass, with its bold mountain ridges on either hand, and proceeding down along the wooded lakes, we leave Joyce Country and the parish of Ross, and approach Connamara proper, or the barony of Bally-nahinch ; but again, turning eastward at the cross roads, we once more enter upon the district of Iar-Connaught by the extensive parish of KILCUMMIN, which, stretching across from this point for many miles both east and west, occupies the space between Killannin parish and that of Moyrus, and extends from Lough Corrib to the sea. To the east is the post-office of Bunnakyle ; and as we approach Oughterard, Inishanboe, on the lake, already referred to at page 129, is on our left hand.*

* "Dermot of the Lakes"—a chieftain of the O'Flahertys, not much known to history, but well to tradition—in one of those forays that ensued upon the passing of his tribe from the east to the western side of the lake, found himself with his followers at sundown one evening at the foot of the fairy hill of Knockma, and, mindful of the occupancy of that venerated spot, treated "the gentry" or "good people" with every possible respect; and in return was visited during his sleep by an emissary from Finvarra, who assured him of his master's friendship and assistance. Next day the O'Flahertys fled across the lake; but Dermot left his wife and child with other helpless persons at this island, and passed on to give battle to the Joyces, or probably the O'Cadlas, on the western shore. Dire was the distress of those left on the island, and especially the chieftain's heir, until a milk-white cow was discovered on its western shore, which supplied him with nourishment, and hence the name of *Inis-shan-boe*, or "the island of the old cow," has been ever since applied to it: the legend is invested with an air of romance well worthy the attention of the novelist.

CHAPTER X.

MAAM TO GALWAY.

PARISH OF KILCUMMIN. OUGHTERARD. LEMONFIELD. GNOMORE AND GNOBEG. KILLEROON CHURCH. AUGHNANURE CASTLE. KILLANNIN PARISH. LOUGH NANEEVIN. KILBRECAN. ROSS LAKE, CASTLE AND CHURCHES. TEAMPULL-BEG-NA-NEAVE. THE YEW WOOD. MOYCULLEN PARISH AND ITS CHURCHES. DANESFIELD. THE BATTLE STONE. BALLYCUIRKE LAKE. CLONIFF CHURCH. RAHOON PARISH.

LIKE the novelist who, having dwelt over-long on the early descriptions and salient points of his tale, or the special peculiarities of his favourite characters, and finding himself near the end of the third volume, has to hasten to an abrupt conclusion; or, like the great dramatist, who it is said had to kill Mercutio in the third act lest Mercutio should kill him in the fourth, so we must now bring our book to a close. Still, there is comparatively little of interest on the southern shores of the upper and middle lake, except wild mountain scenery, and no object worth stopping for, from Maam to Oughterard. Brown bogs, bare mountains, a succession of small lakes, some turf clamps, and a few cottages, are all that are here presented to the tourist, of the great Martin estate, which it was hoped would have been turned into a garden, by the vast wealth, good management, business habits, thrift, honesty, and energy of that great London Company, from whose mild rule such brilliant expectations were entertained twenty years ago. Looking around now, and not seeing any effort at their fulfilment—with no drainage, no reclamation, and scarcely any planting—those who remember the baronies of Ballinahinch and Moycullen, and the ancient territory of Gnomore in former days, are reminded of the lunatic in Judea, out of whom the devil was cast, and of whom it was said, that having taken with him seven other devils more wicked than himself, "the last state of that man was worse than his first."

A cold, wet day—and such is not uncommon in this district—with the mist drifting along the mountains, renders the drive, from Ballinahinch to the village of Oughterard, not over-pleasant to the tourist who occupies the windy side of an outside car, of either long or short dimensions. As we approach Oughterard through other properties, the *débris* of mining operations show that capital, energy, and enterprise, are still required for a line of country, along whose magnificent road we well remember, in our early fishing days, to have seen a goodly sprinkling of snug cottages, potato fields, and cabbage gardens,—where now the bog has again grown up, and the purple heather, and yellow asphodel, and other wild flowers of nature, are hourly turning back to its original state what the spade and the strong arm had rendered subservient to the service of man.*

The Connamara bogs are of comparatively recent formation, and are growing with great rapidity, and must continue to do so until proper engineering and an extensive system of arterial drainage shall have afforded the proprietors of that region an opportunity of effectively turning the surface water off the hills by sheep drains; when, even if a failure of pasturage

* Of the various heaths and ferns in Connamara we have not now time or space to speak; but there is one plant that has given such a tone to the landscape, that we cannot refrain from a passing notice of it—the *Narthicium*, or Bog Asphodel, that abounds everywhere throughout Connamara, and forms the chief plant upon the surface of our great mosses, and the long white roots of which compose the principal portion of the upper layer of turf. It grows up everywhere; and the moment man's efforts at cultivation cease, it reasserts its rights, and spreads with immense rapidity. In spring, its slender, bent-like leaves of bluish-green freshen the surface; in summer its yellow blossoms give a rich warm tint to the landscape; and in autumn, when it bears a brownish-red seed, and the tops of its leaves turn crimson, it presents us with another colour, equally rich and impressive; while it also feeds hundreds of black cattle. It was the tints chiefly derived from this plant, heightened by the wonderful atmospheric peculiarities of the region, with the ever-varying blue of the mountains, and the white fleeciness of its clouds rendering the scenery independent of trees, that Petrie knew so well how to display in water colours; but which persons unacquainted with our western highlands were unable fully to appreciate or understand.

With respect to the London "Law Life Insurance Company's" agents and managers in Connamara, we have nothing to state but what is to their credit for justice and kindness; but what we do complain of is that, with the great wealth of that society, so little has been done to improve the condition of either the land or the people during the last twenty years.

should result, it will enable heath to grow, and grouse to hatch; and thus provide, if not mutton for the Liverpool and Manchester markets, at least sport for the rich manufacturer, and game for the London table.

As we approach Oughterard, some evidences of civilization appear. Claremont, formerly called "Dick Martin's Gatehouse," is on our right; and beside it the pretty fall of the Faugh, or Owen Riff, "the sulphur river," carries down the surplus waters of the great catchment basin to the east of the summit level of the road into Connamara. We pass along its picturesque margin, studded with trees, and overhung by ledges of the natural rock, by the pretty residence of the Roman Catholic clergyman, formerly occupied by Dean Kirwan, and by the usual public buildings of a small provincial town, into Oughterard, or "the upper height," a pretty little town of 155 houses, and 896 inhabitants, in the parish of Kilcummin. There is a very comfortable hotel at Oughterard; and from this point, as well as from Cong, on the opposite shore, several of the most interesting localities on Lough Corrib can be visited with facility. There is also admirable fishing in the neighbourhood.*

At its eastern extremity is Lemonfield, shown in the follow-

* Mr. Henry Coulter, in his useful work on "The West of Ireland," published in 1862, tells us, "that a railway has been projected from Galway to Oughterard The Law Life Insurance Company has been asked to subscribe to the undertaking, because the line would pass through and benefit their property; but the directors have refused to encourage the project, believing that it could not pay under any circumstances."—Page 131.

ing illustration, the seat of G. F. O'Fflahertie, Esq., whose ancestors occupied so much of this territory, and performed so notable a part in the history of West Connaught for many centuries. The house stands in a spacious lawn, reaching down to the

lake, and is surrounded by well-grown timber, and highly cultivated gardens and pleasure grounds; while in the immediate vicinity there are several objects worthy of inspection, but which want of space will not now permit us to describe in detail. Among these objects of interest may be enumerated a series of remarkable subterranean chambers in the townland of Cregg, for plans of which we are indebted to Mr. Kinahan; also a natural bridge over the Owen Riff, at Oughterard, in which stream may still be found fresh water pearl-bearing mussels, and lampreys;—the traces of the old Castle of Faugh, near the military barracks;—the curious old church of Kilcummin, the burial place of the O'Flahertys in later days, a little to the east of the demesne of Lemonfield,—and also the church of Portacarron, near the edge of the lake.

We would willingly linger a little longer about Oughterard if space permitted, and gossip with our hospitable friend respecting his ancestors, whose original territory on the eastern shore of the lake we have already described under the name of *Hy-Briuin Seola*, which, with *Muinter Murchadha*, was the ancient tribe name of the O'Flahertys ; or, as the name is written in one of the old patents, O'fflahertie. We should like to trace the fortunes of that very ancient Irish family, descended from a line of Connaught kings, through the times when they fought with the O'Conors and De Burgos, and became lords of Iar-Connaught, down through the days when a chieftain of that race, fleeing from his enemies, was awoke from sleep by a lizard, the emblem of which subsequently became the family crest; through the times of *Murrough-na-Tuath*, or of the "battle axes," who was knighted by Queen Elizabeth; and of *Morough-na-Maor*, or "the steward;" and *Moragh-na-Mart*, or the chieftain of "the beeves;" and of *Emuin-Laidir*, or "Edmond the strong;" down to the days of Sir John, who was buried in the adjoining mortuary chapel of Kilcummin;—but have not they and their genealogies and exploits been all recited by Hardiman, in his Annotations to Roderick O'Flaherty's "Chorographical Description of West Connaught," so frequently referred to in this work?

From the Faugh river at Oughterard to Ballycuirke Lake, near Moycullen, the antiquarian tourist may again with great profit resume his explorations either along shore, or by making detours to the north of the Galway road. The south-western shore of the middle and lower lakes, comprising the ancient territories of Gnomore and Gnobeg, in the barony of Moycullen, and including the parishes of Kilcummin (part of) Killannin, Moycullen, and Rahoon, stretching between Oughterard and Galway, is a very remarkable region, and one with which, as seen from a distance at least, the tourist passing from Galway into Connamara is not altogether unacquainted. It possesses some special characters, and abounds with objects of interest, both natural and artificial. Its southern and western boundary is the range of hills that stretch from Galway towards Connamara through the extensive district of Iar-Connaught, along which the road runs, and its eastern and northern margin is the lake shore. The hills are brown with bog, and dappled with the grey bare rocks that rise towards their summits, or margin the streams that course down their rugged sides, and in autumn are purple with occasional stripes of heather, which the continuous waterflow along their sides has permitted to enjoy a partial inflorescence. In the boundary line, popularly termed "between hair and hoof," along which the main road runs, patches of culture—small lakes catching the downfall from the hills—wooded glades, a few villages, and some gentlemen's seats present themselves, and beyond these to the lake margin all is stony and sterile ; and, but that there are still Irish hearts beating upon it, and vestiges of early Christianity existing thereon, it might be styled one of the most inhospitable regions of the globe. Along the lake shore there are entire townlands of grey limestone rock, here stratified, and forming tables of continuous and partially level acres of surface—there disruptured, and appearing like the scattered *débris* of some ruined building, with stunted hazel bushes interspersed.

This great stone crop is here and there intersected with scraps of "sad-coloured bog;" and, in the neighbourhood of the villages, a few acres of oats and potatoes. When we see the miserable sheep that eke out an existence among these rocks, and the old Irish "crumpledy-horned cow" that picks a few blades of bent or grass on the road side, we cannot help asking ourselves how the light-haired, blue-eyed inhabitants,—especially on a Sunday or holiday, when cleaned up for Mass,—present such an amount of health and happiness, or why they remain in such a region. These, however, are questions in political economy, which are without the scope of this little work.

Taking up our itinerary again from Oughterard by the main road to Galway, we pass the site of the holy well of St. Cummin, who gave his name to this parish ; and a little farther on we pass his church, already referred to, and then by the remains of the picturesque ruin of Killeroon Church, near the natural bridge over the Drimneen river, that runs down from Buffy Lough, and along by the circle of standing stones on the townland of Laghtgannon towards Ross, in the Parish of Killannin, which here indents that of Kilcummin.* From this portion of the road we obtain a view of the tall massive tower of Aughnanure Castle, which stands to the north by the water's edge, and is by far the finest fortified dwelling upon any part of the shores of Lough Corrib. Turning to the left, north of the main road, and nearer Oughterard than Killeroon, we approach this noble ruin from the west, where there are the remains of extensive outworks; and where probably a drawbridge and portcullis originally existed. The scene here is very picturesque—the Drimneen river passing in several places underground, like its larger brother at Cong, and then forming deep, clear pools among the crags and along the foundations of the castle walls, and, after playing hide and seek with itself, turns from the west by the north face of the castle, where it laves the waterport, and then winds in slow and easy pace to a deep indentation of Lough Corrib.†

* The little church by the roadside is styled on the Ordnance Map Killeroon; but that may be an error, for in a parchment Quit-rent receipt of 1816, for which we are indebted to Mr. O'Fflahertie, it is styled Kilnonan. The six-inch Ordnance Map for this portion of our route has not been altered since the road was changed from the north to the south of this church, through the townland of Laghtgannon—*Leacht-Gannon*, "the stones of Gan" or Gannon. The small one-inch map recently published and the map attached to this work are, however, quite correct, and may be followed at this point.

† In this bay was lately discovered a long single-piece oaken canoe, of

Along this western face of the ruins, the sketcher will find many points among the broken bushy foreground from which to take away a remembrance of the great stronghold of the once powerful sept of the O'Flahertys, the chieftains of the West.

Aughnanure—*Achad-na-n-Inubhar*, "the field of the yews," is so called from the number of these trees that of old grew all round this spot, and that probably extended for a long distance eastward; so that there is a tradition still alive that the wild cats and tree martins—nay, that man himself could have walked on their tops from here to Tullokyan without putting foot to ground! To a portion of the remains of this yew wood in an almost fossilized condition, eastwards of this spot, we shall presently conduct our readers.—See page 299. Near the western entrance of this extensive fortress the last living specimen —probably five hundred years old—of this ancient forest still flourishes.

The ground plan of Aughnanure is nearly square, with an offset at the north-western corner, where the river assists to form a natural defence. There were circular flanking towers at the eastern corners of the great enclosure, the entire of which latter measures 150 feet along the interior of the connecting wall, and 178 feet by the southern. At the north-

great antiquity, which Dr. R. Willis, of Oughterard, has presented to the Museum of the Royal Irish Academy.

west corner of the quadrangle stands the great keep, or square tower, of six stories, over 60 feet high, and measuring 40 on the northern, and 28 feet wide on the southern face—which, with all its architectural details; the adjoining Round-House; a portion of the walls of the banqueting hall to the left of the view, and part of one of the gateways to the right, is most faithfully re-

presented in the accompanying drawing, recently taken from the south-east by Mr. Wakeman. This tower is admirably built, and is likely to last for centuries yet to come. Within the enclosure, and a short distance from the south-east angle of the tower, stands the round house, with a cupola at top, which is reached by a flight of steps, the roofings of which afford most remarkable examples of the perfection of that style of beehive doming by overlapping stones, of which we have so many very early specimens in Pagan structures throughout Ireland, the finest example being that of Newgrange. This curious structure may have been intended for a magazine; but, being loopholed in some places, it was also probably used for a citadel. Nearly parallel with the great tower, and in connexion with the western angle of this round house, there existed some years ago the remains of another building, 23½ feet wide, but this has been for some time removed; and its site is at present occupied by a modern structure.*

For seventy-six feet along the western face of this enclosure, and to the south of the keep, stand the remains of the great banqueting hall, the mullioned windows of which, looking eastward, and gorgeously sculptured on the round soffits of their interiors, afford us, undoubtedly, the finest specimens of floral decorative stone carving of their period in Ireland; and perhaps, if we said in the British Isles, our boast might not be susceptible of verified contradiction. Two of these windows are well worthy of minute examination; and the top of

* Captain O'Hara is the owner in fee of Aughnanure Castle; his tenant, Mr. Edmond Flaherty, a descendant of the Moycullen branch of the great Iar-Connaught family, is at present utilizing the manor and castle as a dairy farm.

one of them here displayed gives but a faint idea of the richness, variety, and delicacy of carving by which these beauteous arches were characterized. Our only wonder is, that in these days, in which architects have endeavoured to reintroduce forms and appliances in art quite inapplicable to the present period, colouring unsuited to our climate, and, with a blind

subservience to the necessities of times, countries, habits, and tastes long gone by, have been labouring to reproduce mediævalism in stone, brick, plaster, and woodwork, as well as in opinion and thought,—they have never copied the graceful decorations of the banqueting hall of Aughnanure.*

* Dr. Willis, already referred to at p. 286, has presented a series of rubbings on muslin of all these soffits to the Royal Irish Academy.

The east wall alone of this grand revelling chamber is standing. Under it flowed the Drimneen, covered by a natural arch, which having given way, all the western side was precipitated into the abyss below; where, no doubt, if excavations were made, many of its sculptured stones would be discovered.

The De Burgos claim the erection or re-edification of this castle; but, besides all other probabilities as to its being originally built by, as it was undoubtedly occupied by, the O'Flahertys in the sixteenth century—when in all likelihood the bulk of the present structure was erected—we learn from various sources that the latter occupied this district uninterruptedly from the eleventh century till almost the present time. In the records relating to this family will be found the best account, as well as the last remnant, of the feudal or clan system in Ireland; when The O'Flaherty, besides the various petty chieftains dependent on him, had his allotted body guard, comorbs, physicians, equerries, and brehons, as well as his standard bearer, guardian of reliques, poet, historian, genealogist, master of the revels, steward, keeper of the bees, and collector of revenues, &c.; whose names, and the townlands allotted for their services, were enumerated in the twelfth century.* One of the last notices of this fortress is that given under

* See the Annals of the Four Masters; but particularly Hardiman's notes to O'Flaherty's "History of West Connaught," already frequently referred to; also, Petrie in the "Irish Penny Journal" for 4th July, 1840.

the year 1572, in which Sir Edward Phiton [Fitton], President of Connaught, "after having half destroyed the castle, took complete possession of it, and left such part of it as remained undestroyed to Murrough-na-Dtuagh O'Flaherty."

Part of Kilcummin parish stretches still further eastwards along the lake shore, which it separates from the parish of Kilnin, until the latter divides it from Moycullen, near the ferry of Knock, already described at page 86. Retracing our steps, and regaining the Galway road, we again proceed eastward by Killeroon church, near which there is a granite boulder with a *bullaun* excavated in it; and then by the standing stones* of Lact-

* Mr. and Mrs. S. C. Hall, in their "Ireland, its Scenery, Character, &c.," say that, when within a few miles of Oughterard, "our astonishment was excited by perceiving a prodigious collection of *Cromleachs*, of the existence of which we believe no traveller has taken note, but which certainly demand extensive and minute attention. These huge *circles* of stone were so numerous, that at first we imagined them to be merely accidental occurrences in the rocky soil; but repeated examinations convinced us, that they were as much artificial erections as any of the monuments of which we have encountered so many in various parts of the country." They also fix the site of "this great city of the Druids" as being near the old road at this point, and say, "It occupies the whole of an extended plain on the height of a steep hill, and in the valley beneath is seen the old Castle of Aughnanure," of which latter magnificent fortress they take no further notice, except by a short extract in a note from the "Irish [not the Dublin] Penny Journal." The authors go on to say, "The space literally covered by these Druidic stones, of all shapes and sizes, extends for above two miles, and we imagine it would not be difficult to count a *thousand* of them. The circles were of varied sizes, some very

gannon, already referred to, into the parish of KILLANNIN, which derives its name from Saint Annin, V., whose well and church stand by the northern margin of Ross Lake, below the main road. Upon the right of the highway is the small sheet of water called Lough Naneevin, the little wooded island upon which is believed to have been artificially enlarged, and fortified into a crannoge.* The next object of note occurring in succession

small, in others so large as apparently to be half a mile in circumference; and although in most instances the props which supported the huge rock had crumbled under its weight, sufficient proofs of their former existence were left in nearly every case."—See vol. iii., p. 466. It would be great injustice to Ireland, and to the tourist or reader who has accompanied us thus far round the shores of Lough Corrib, if we omitted to direct attention to, and, if it existed, to describe this wonderful place; but we fear our distinguished friends either saw it in the gloaming, or were imposed upon by some *pseudo*-antiquary; and indeed their concluding words lead us to believe that they did not pay sufficient attention to this locality; for they say, "Our leisure did not permit us to make a very minute scrutiny of this truly wonderful place; but our brief note of it may, and no doubt will, induce such an examination of it as it undoubtedly demands." There are no cromleachs, and the only remains of stone circles in this district are those at Laghtgannon, referred to at p. 286. In one of these there are still seven standing stones, and the site of ten others is visible in the vicinity. There was also one formerly on the glebe, but an agricultural incumbent had it removed. All these forts are marked on the 6-inch Ordnance Map.

* See Mr. Kinahan's paper on this subject in the Proceedings of the Royal Irish Academy, vol. x., p. 25. We have not availed ourselves of the author's illustration; for, although we were the first to describe these lacustrine habitations in Ireland, so early as 1842, and have since examined and described a great number of them, we have not yet seen any grounds for believing in the "ideal sketch" just published by our friend. The only

along the main road is the extensive, well-wooded, and picturesque demesne of Ross, the property of James Martin, Esq., on the northern or left hand side, with the pretty lake anciently called Lough Lonan, in an island of which there are still some vestiges of the old castle of Ohery.

A short distance from Lough Naneevin, and upon our right, nearly opposite the gate of Ross, embosomed in a thick foliage of trees, stands *Teampull-Brecan*, the small very early missionary "church of St. Brecan," which had, no doubt, originally a square-headed Cyclopean doorway in the western gable, and is especially remarkable for its small circular-headed window in the eastern gable, 42 inches high, and 21 wide, with the arch formed of a single stone, like that at Killarsagh, and which affords evidence of its great antiquity. This gable is 17 feet wide. About 40 yards westwards of this church lies a double *bullaun*, or ancient stone font, such as those described at pages 148, 164, 296, and 303, &c. From this by the main road to Galway, as we pass into the parish of Moycullen, for some distance, there is no object of antiquarian interest, until we reach the little ruined church of Kilcallan, in the demesne of Knockbane, the property and handsome residence of the late Anthony O'Flaherty, Esq., formerly M. P. for Galway town. This church, which stands within the enclosure of an ancient

well-established crannoge in the neighbourhood of Lough Corrib is that upon Lough Kimbe, near the high road between Shrule and Tuam.—See the author's Catalogue of Antiquities in Royal Irish Academy, part i., p. 230.

fort, is 34 feet long, and 18 broad, but possesses no feature of interest worthy the attention of the tourist.

The parish of Killannin, still under our consideration, is, as already stated, of a most irregular form, having appertaining to it the island of Inchmicatreer, ten miles distant, upon Lough Corrib. It lies between Moycullen on the east, and Kilcummin on the west, and has a narrow stripe of that parish, and a portion of the lake shore on its northern margin, while its south-western extremity extends to the sea. The ancient territory of Gnobeg stretching eastward along Lough Corrib from the north-western end of Ross Lake, through this parish, and including those of Moycullen and Rahoon, to the town of Galway, presents several objects of great interest to the north of the main road.

Passing down along a by-road between Lough Naneevin and St. Brecan's church, behind Ross demesne, to the Roman Catholic chapel of Killannin, which occupies a conspicuous position on a bluff esker, running nearly east and west, we reach a group of ruins well worthy of inspection. Upon a knoll in a green field upon our right, and surrounded by thorn bushes, is the very ancient cell, or miniature church, of *Teampull-beg-na-Neave*, "the little church of the saint," probably St. Annin, whose memory is still venerated here; and whose well, which remains by the shore of Lough Lonan, is resorted to on her festival day, the 18th of January. This diminutive building measures on the outside 20 feet 4 inches by 16 feet

4 inches. The eastern gable has fallen below the level of any window which may have existed there, and the side walls are also much dilapidated; but its western gable is still preserved, and marks the style and age of this structure.

The accompanying graphic and accurate illustration, from a drawing by Dr. R. Willis, shows every stone in the western face of this gable, with its square-headed doorway, which latter is 5 feet 6 inches high, and measures 24 inches wide at bottom, and 21½ at top—so as to give the usual incline to the

jambs. These are 2 feet 3 inches thick, and the stones forming their inner sides are the only ones in the church which show any signs of dressing,—and they were probably *rubbed* flat. In a clump of bushes a little to the south-east of this church may be seen a very perfect *bullaun*, "bason stone," or rude font, similar to those already described in several other localities, and referred to at page 294.

Still more to the south-east, and romantically situated among massive rocks and boulders, in the midst of an ancient and well-filled graveyard, stands the ruined, but comparatively modern church of Killannin (or, as it is sometimes spelled, Killannin); but, with the exception of the pointed-arched doorway in the southern wall, the small eastern light, and the fact that it is not placed due east and west like its earlier sister just described, but runs W. N. W by E. S. E., it possesses no interest for the antiquary. It is 48 feet 4 inches long, and 24½ feet broad from out to out; and, with the exception of the door and window, is altogether constructed of large undressed stones. Adjoining the southern side is the mortuary chapel of the Martins, of a later date, and more carefully built than the church; it contains the massive vault of some of the members of this once powerful family. This tomb is now open to the winds, and occasionally a receptacle for some of the neighbouring stock; and, although not a whited sepulchre without, it is perfectly congruous with the scriptural simile within. The present time, in which we are labouring to revive the architecture as well as the opinions of our ancestors, is specially characterized by a want of reverence for the remains of the dead. From an inscription over this mausoleum we learn that it was erected for Anthony Martin, Fitz Richard, of Dangan, in 1748. Much of the surrounding district—over which this tribe reigned supreme, and against whose misgovernment so many eloquent appeals were made in Parliament, and such withering philippics were hurled by newspaper commissioners—remains, as already stated at page 279, in the same, if not a worse condition than when the last of the Martin line fled an outcast from her country, and died in poverty.* We have no desire to digress for the purpose of again inquiring into the condition of the "Law Life Estates," which here, as in other portions of our route, surround us; but we would, for the sake of the country, suggest to those who profess an interest in "tenant right," and such like matters, to take up the reports of Nimmo and Killally, written nearly fifty years ago, at the instance of Richard and Thomas Martin, of Ballinahinch, and with these, and the Reports of the Commissioners, and the leading articles upon the subject, in the days of O'Connell, in their hands, to make an examination of the present condition of this vast property, when, perhaps, they may find, that—although it was bought exceedingly cheap, at a time when Irish property was pressed into the market at a third less than its value—no portion of Ireland of the same extent has made less progress than the Ballinahinch estates during the last twenty years.

Passing over the esker by the chapel, we obtain a view of an extensive limestone ridge that slopes to the lake, grey, bare, and almost verdureless, except where the stunted nut

* See Sir Bernard Burke's "Princess of Connamara," in his "Vicissitudes of Families," page 65.

trees rise out of clefts in the rocks; but which, there is every reason to believe, was once covered with a portion of the great yew forest already alluded to at page 287, and from which the not far distant Castle of Aughnanure, "the field of the yews," derived its name. The neighbouring townland of Kylemore, "the great wood," naturally calls attention to the spot; but we have something more than topographical nomenclature or tradition to guide us in searching for the remains of this ancient forest; for around us may still be seen the withered stumps or roots of no less than twelve of the ancient yews of Gnomore and Gnobeg;—and two of these, about half a mile to the

north of the chapel, claim special attention. Passing down the road towards Lough Corrib, through this barren, grey-coloured rocky region, without a house, or beast, or living thing to claim attention, the eye falls on a lone, grey, tall, spectre-like object, standing in the midst of a large field of limestone; and on approaching it we find it to be the bare knobby stump of an ancient yew tree, here figured from a drawing by Mr. Kinahan, to whom we are indebted for having first directed our attention to this most interesting vestige of the oldest forest in Ireland now over ground. It is 10 feet high, and 9 feet 9 inches in girth; and its snake-like roots spreading far and wide on all sides, crawl into the smallest crevices of the crags, where,

> "Moor'd in the rifted rock,
> Proof to the tempest's shock,"

it broadly grew, and gaily bourgeoned, when the world was many centuries younger than it is now. Standing with our back to the mountains, and viewing this lone withered tree upon that inhospitable tract, a scene of greater desolation can scarcely be imagined. Hundreds of years must have elapsed since this sylvan monarch spread its green arms abroad; and, although not absolutely fossilized, it is at present so hard that it is almost impossible to make an impression upon it with an edged tool, and it is with great difficulty that any portion of it can be hammered off. The outer surface of the lower portion of this tree is covered with sharp, prickly projections, apparently the remains of a late superficial vegetation, after the top had withered, and which contrasts forcibly with the beautiful smooth honest bark that has so long rendered the Irish Palm an object of sacred interest, and caused it to be used in the manufacture of our ancient croziers, shrines, and relics. The yew is not only one of the most beautiful, but longest-lived, of the indigenous trees of Ireland; and, as in life, so in death, it aims at immortality—shading with its wide-spreading green arms the grave of the young and innocent in the lone churchyard;—raising its tall stem in the centre of the ancient cloister; commemorating (owing to the similarity of its pinnate leaves with those of the Oriental palm) the day when Jerusalem's walls beheld the procession from the Mount of Olives; for all which, and for the reasons already specified, the Irish yew possesses special attractions for our people.* A specimen of about the same size, but hollow near the bottom, stands in the adjacent mearing wall to the west of this field; and the remnants of ten others lie scattered throughout the townlands of Corraneilstrum and Kylemore—while, no doubt, others may yet be discovered.

Continuing our route along this lower road by the north and east of Lough Lonan, we re-enter MOYCULLEN parish; and, obtaining a view of the picturesque wooded island, upon which some remains may still be observed of Ohery, the old castle

* Upon the age to which the yew will grow under favourable circumstances it is almost impossible to speculate. The great yew tree still living at Clontarf is believed to be as old as the battle fought there in 1013. Hundreds of massive trunks of yews lie buried beneath our bogs; and the late James Mackay, Curator of the Botanic Garden, T. C. D., at the Meeting of the British Association held in Dublin, in 1835, produced a section of one, from the concentric rings of which he showed that it must have lived at least a thousand years.—See also the author's description of the Dragon Tree of Oratava, and other aged trees, in his "Narrative of a Voyage to Madeira and Teneriffe," &c., 2nd Edition, p. 109.

of the O'Hallorans, who were driven out in 1587, we again reach the main road to Galway, near Deerfield, at present occupied by the Rev. Francis Kenny, the Parish Priest of Moycullen. Thence, with Drimcong and Loughs Hemusmaconry, Arrobaun, Pollahy, and Down, on our left, we proceed through the shaded road of Danesfield, the beautifully-situated residence of George Burke, Esq.; and so on to the little village of Moycullen, which, together with a large district of the adjacent country, originally part of the Barna estate, is now the property of Lord Campbell.

At this celebrated locality, *Magh-Uillin*, the plain on which was slain the warrior Uillin, as already described at page 20, from whence has been derived the name of this extensive barony and parish—and which, besides its ancient history, is memorable for having been the residence of Roderick O'Flaherty, the historian of "West Connaught," and in later times as the scene of Lady Morgan's clever novel of "The O'Briens and O'Flahertys"—we must rest, and make a few *detours* to the right and left of the village. The cross roads here lead, on the south, to Spiddle, and, on the north, to the ferry of Knock, already described at page 85. Passing up the former, two objects of note claim our attention: the first of these, nearly due south of Moycullen, and about a mile east of this road, upon the hill of Killagoola, is the ruin of *Teampull-Eany*, the "church of St. Eany," which is 24 feet long by 12 broad, having a remarkable projecting stone at the south-west angle, like that referred to at Inchangoill, and in the church of Cloniff; there are some remains of a chancel arch, and the doorway was in the western gable. About 30 yards to the west of this church is a double *bullaun*, cut in a rock, and called the kneeling stone, or *Gluine Phadrig*, "St. Patrick's knees," from a belief that our early missionary prayed here, and left these impressions upon the stone. It is held in great veneration, and stations are still performed there; and, as these bason-like indentations are believed never to be devoid of water, it is considered an infallible cure for sore eyes. There is also here a holy well, walled, and draped with ivy, which is also held in veneration. Still further to the south, at Pollnaclogha, about three miles from Moycullen, there are some rocks worthy of examination, as it is supposed that there are characters engraved upon them; but these, it is possible, may be only veins of quartz. There are also traditions attached to this locality worthy of investigation.

Upon the northern "cast," between the main road and the lake, as we proceed downwards towards Tullokian, figured and described at page 62, and Knock Ferry, by the west of Ballinquirk Lake, we have the little church of Moycullen upon our right, of which the side walls and gable still remain; but, except the pointed-arched doorway on the northern side, and one small narrow light in the eastern gable, it possesses no features of either antiquarian or architectural interest. Of this parochial church says O'Flaherty, in 1684, "its chief feast of late is the Immaculate Conception of our Blessed Lady, on the 8th of December, as patroness. What ancient patron it had is unknown."

"Here Uillinn, grandchild of Nuad Silverhand, King of Ireland, 1200 years before Christ's birth, overthrew in battle, and had the killing of, Orbsen Mac Alloid, commonly called Mananan Mac Lir, Mananan the Mankish man, Mac Lir, son of the sea, for his skill in seafaring. From Ullin, Moycullen is named; to wit, Magh-Ullin, the field of Ullin; and from Orbsen, Lough Orbsen, or the Lake of Orbsen. Six miles from a *great stone* in that field (erected perhaps in memory of the same battle) to the town of Galway."* Continuing our route towards Ballydotia, "the burned village," we enter the townland of Leagaun; and in a furze field to our right, not far from the old road between Oughterard and Galway, from which latter this spot is about "six miles" distant, may still be seen what there is every reason to believe is the stone that marks

* "West Connaught," p. 55.—See also O'Flaherty's "Ogygia." In Cormac's very ancient Glossary we read thus of the navigator "Manann-an Mac Lir, a famous merchant, who was in the Isle of Mann. He was the best navigator in the west of the world. He used to discover by observation of the heavens when there would be good or bad weather, and when either would change by the moon. Hence the Scoti and Britons used to call him the God of the Sea, and they said that he was the son of the sea. From him the Isle of Manann is named."—See O'Donovan's translation in the "Ordnance Letters from Galway, 1839," vol. iii., p. 159.—See also an article on the subject of Mananan Mac Lir, by Mr. Brash, in the "Archæologia Cambrensis" for April, 1866.

the precise locality where Orbsen M'Alloid was slain by Uillin; although Hardiman, in his notes to the "Iar-Connaught," stated that it had not been identified, and that "no person in the district ever heard of such a monument." This large limestone flag, which was prostrated by the storm of 1839, and which measures 12½ feet long by 7½ wide, and is 13 inches thick, is undoubtedly that referred to by O'Flaherty. It is called *Clough-more Legaun*, "the great stone of Legaun," by the peasantry, who regard it as a "Fairy monument," under which the warriors of the olden time were buried. The vast and beautiful view commanded from this spot is, perhaps, the finest prospect of the flat country eastward of Lough Orbsen, comprising the distant hills of Clare, a large extent of the lake, and the district from Clare-Galway to Knockma—while, to the west, the mountain scenery possesses an unusual diversity of outline.

Skirting the northern and eastern margins of Ballyquirk Lake,* which is to the left of the Galway road, and passing by Patrick's Well, we alight upon the ruins of *Teampull-beg*, the "little church," in the townland of Clooniff, which is the last ruin that claims our attention. It partakes of the early *daimlaig* form—is 24 feet long by 12½ broad, and has a small chancel at the western end. The walls are now about

* A canal carries off the surplus waters of Ballyquirk, and the small lakes to the west of it; but those of Ross Lake filter under ground, and do not, as stated at page 24, pass through that Canal.

12 feet high, and at the south-western angle a long stone projects from the gable, like those at Inchangoill and Teampull Eany. A little distance to the north of it there is a *bullaun* stone, also called *Gluine Phadrig.*

Once more getting upon the main road, we proceed through the parish of Rahoon to Galway, and here we make our bow, and take our leave. Our task is done. We have endeavoured to direct the attention of the reader and the tourist to all that is historic, picturesque, and beautiful in this grand Lough Corrib region, with its sacred islands, its ancient battle grounds, raths, and tumuli; its splendid ruins of castle and abbey, contrasted with the results of modern civilization; its magnificent scenery of mountain and lake, with the ever-changing lights on the purple hills, and the glorious sunsets peculiar to the West—scenes so full of interest for the antiquary, the historian, the poet and the painter, the politician and social economist—for all who love nature and truth, and like to study national life through its various phases. We have also tried to direct attention to those vast sources of wealth which still lie unutilized in the West; and if, while interesting the tourist, we have also stimulated the work of national progress, the chief objects shall have been accomplished for which this book was undertaken—to illustrate the past, and to benefit the present.

THE END.